MW01004790

INTEGRATED TECHNICAL ANALYSIS

Wiley Trading Advantage Series

INTEGRATED TECHNICAL ANALYSIS

Ian Copsey

John Wiley & Sons (Asia) Pte Ltd
Singapore • New York • Chichester • Brisbane • Toronto • Weinheim

Other Wiley Editorial Offices

John Wiley & Sons, Inc., 605 Third Avenue, New York, NY 10158-0012, USA
John Wiley & Sons Ltd, Baffins Lane, Chichester, West Sussex PO19 1UD, England
John Wiley & Sons (Canada) Ltd, 22 Worcester Road, Rexdale, Ontario M9W 1L1,
Canada
Jacaranda Wiley Ltd, 33 Park Road (PO Box 1226), Milton, Queensland 4064, Australia
Wiley-VCH, Pappelallee 3, 69469 Weinheim, Germany

Library of Congress Cataloging-in-Publication Data

Copsey, Ian.
    Integrated technical analysis / Ian Copsey.
    p. cm. — (Wiley trading advantage)
    ISBN 0-471-82539-5 (alk. paper)
    1. Speculation. 2. Stocks—Charts, diagrams, etc. 3. Investment analysis.
    4. Stock price forecasting. I. Title. II. Series.
    HG6041 .C66 1999
    332.63'228—dc21
                                                            99-19108
                                                            CIP

ISBN 0-471-82539-5

Typeset in 11/13 points, Century Schoolbook by Linographic Services Pte Ltd
Printed in Singapore by Craft Print Pte Ltd
10 9 8 7 6 5 4 3 2 1

CONTENTS

Preface

PREFACE

I have been involved with markets for over 15 years now, my first experience coming from within the Head Office Foreign Exchange trading room of a major UK Clearing Bank as an advisor to the bank's corporate client base. With an educational background in economics, I eagerly attempted to apply what I had learned to forecasting foreign exchange movements but quickly discovered that such projections were often at the mercy of larger flows of funds, which apparently opposed conventional analysis. I persisted with fundamental analysis for a long while, but I have to admit that I was never a resounding success.

My first knowledge of technical analysis came from reading numerous news pages on common data and news networks. Phrases such as "technical levels" and "the market traded technically today" were common and my enquiries to senior colleagues provided little explanation, and even then mostly scornful comments dismissing the efficacy of such techniques.

Indeed, while the acceptance of technical analysis has become more commonplace, comments such as "it's self fulfilling" and "wave bye-bye to Elliott Wave" are all too frequent. The same punsters also chide us with the comment, "Put five Elliott Wave practitioners in a locked room with one chart and they'll come up with twenty different wave counts." This last comment could indeed be true, but it actually refutes the fact that technical analysis is self fulfilling. Well, at any one time at least one of the Elliotticians will be right. The fact is, just as with attempts at economic forecasts, it is the skill of the analyst which differentiates the consistently good forecasts from the consistently bad.

An economist was heard to say recently, "Technical analysis is OK, but at least when an economist gets the forecast wrong, he gets it wrong for the right reason!"

During the five years spent with Dow Jones in Japan as a specialist in technical analysis, instructing and encouraging market participants to acquire and improve their knowledge of the subject, I have observed how partial knowledge can produce poor results and consequently cast technical analysis in bad light. Similarly, the common mistake of failing to integrate several forms of analysis causes analysts to abandon the use of various techniques and instead, to use other methods haphazardly, without the logical understanding of when such indicators should be used. Many traders construct the same path for different indicators believing that one day they will find a single answer to all their prayers.

This lack of or incorrect knowledge together with the experience of having trodden the same path during my own development has prompted me to write this book to explain some of the basic concepts of technical analysis and highlight the need for integration of the various techniques. I have attempted to describe these concepts in simple terms for ease of understanding This book is not intended as a complete guide to technical analysis, indeed the number of differing techniques appears to be expanding continually, but as a description of how a combination of complementary analyses has proven powerful for me. Every analyst has his or her favored tools that he or she understands and uses to obtain good results. The reader therefore has to decide which tool is acceptable, then integrate the results. From the contents of this book, it will be clear that I favor a combination of Elliott Wave, cycles, and momentum analysis.

An introduction on manipulating commonly used indicators is included in the book. Many of these basic indicators, though well-known, are used in a rather uninformed manner that in many cases, they do not yield the results they are supposed to. Remember that basic indicators were introduced before widespread use of desktop computers, so calculations were much simpler. With modern desktop processing power, it is now possible to construct more statistically informative indicators on a real-time basis.

In addition to new approaches to indicators, examples of how to develop indicators for use in individual markets are included. These examples are not particularly sophisticated but will prompt readers to analyze their market and price behavior, thereby placing readers one step ahead of the market.

However I have to stress that technical analysis involves hard work and does not provide an easy answer, otherwise the results would not be as profitable. Do not expect to read this book and be able to apply the techniques immediately and multiply your profits overnight. It is a skill, like any other, that is honed with experience and the ability to recognize and adapt to different situations. Diligence and sound application will eventually allow you to assess market conditions and profit opportunities, while limiting risk from a new and more powerful perspective.

Ian Copsey
January 1999

CHAPTER 1

Chart Construction and Basic Price Behavior

There are several methods of presenting price movement in a chart format within the basic principles of price behavior. These range from the simple line chart to point and figure, and candlestick charts. I rely on two basic charts for my analyses—the line and the bar—as these display sufficient information for effective analyses that use the methods described in the book.

This chapter presents these two charts in a manner slightly different from other books. But the topics of chart construction, and support and resistance are presented more comprehensively in other books. The advanced analyst who is familiar with these topics may move ahead to Chapter 2 without missing out any information vital to the main theme of the book.

THE LINE CHART

The line chart is the simplest form of chart. Line charts usually display a security's closing price. The price of most stocks, commodities, bonds, or currency fluctuates within each trading day. The line chart screens out this volatility or 'noise' to display the security's uncluttered price trend. By plotting on a chart each day's closing price (which represents the cumulative result of demand and supply for the underlying security), and then drawing a line to join each value, we get a line chart with the security's daily closing prices. This type of graph is normally used in most financial newspapers to display market movements. Besides daily closing price, line charts also display intraday (hourly, 15-minute interval, etc.), weekly, or monthly market movements. Each chart displays an uncluttered, easy to understand view of a security's price during the desired time frame.

Figure 1.1 shows the weekly close chart of the Japanese Government Bond Futures market. It shows the progression of price on a weekly basis, by a line drawn between each weekly

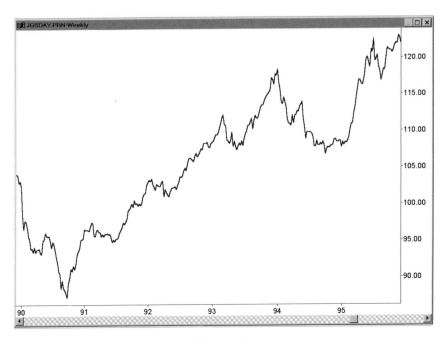

Figure 1.1
Line chart recording the weekly close of the Japanese Government
Bond Futures market.

close. Line charts are good for showing long-term movements and underlying price behavior as seen in Figure 1.1.

THE BAR CHART

Bar charts can be presented in two different forms—HLC (High, Low, Close) and OHLC (Open, High, Low, Close). The OHLC is the most commonly used form as it shows the significant relationship between the open and the close, and also the previous close against the current open. The bar chart displays the total movement from open to high and low of the period, ending at the close. For the following example we will consider the range of movement seen within a day.

The opening price (or open) is the price of the first trade of the day. The open provides a price from where demand and supply will record higher or lower prices. The high is the highest price at which the security traded during the day while the low is the lowest price. The closing price (or close) is the price of the last trade of the day. On an OHLC chart, a vertical

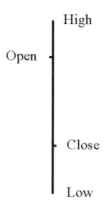

Figure 1.2
Construction of a bar chart.

line is drawn from the highest price to the lowest forming the spine of the bar. The open is drawn as a small "tic" on the left of the bar while the close is a small "tic" on the right of the bar. This is illustrated in Figure 1.2.

The HLC bar is similar to the OHLC but excludes the open tic on the left of the bar.

In contrast to the line chart, the bar chart includes all the "emotion" of a period's trading—the extremes of the bullish and bearish positions. When considering the price range of an underlying instrument, what we witness in the high and low price of a bar are the extremes in price where buyers and sellers believe they are receiving fair value. This is one of the basic functions of a market place—to provide a meeting place for potential buyers and sellers to exchange money for 'goods' at a mutually agreed price. In this manner the market will always find an equilibrium price.

Figure 1.3 shows the bar chart corresponding to same trading period for the Japanese Government Bond Futures market seen in Figure 1.1. Each bar represents the extremes of trading within the trading week.

BAR CHART VERSUS LINE CHART

How do you determine which chart to use? Many analysts use one or the other. Although both are valid, it is important to understand the market you are analysing and what you are

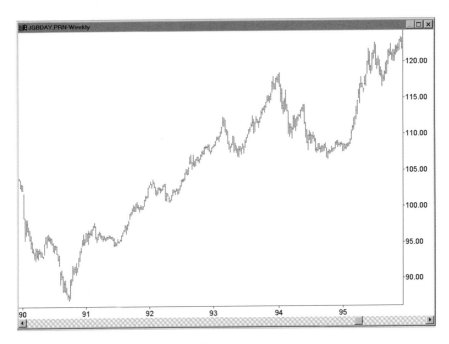

Figure 1.3
A bar chart recording the weekly Japanese Government
Bond Futures market.

measuring. Line charts are useful in eliminating many of the spikes caused by emotional trading while keeping the analyst focused on the underlying direction, or lack of direction, of price. Line charts are also useful when deciphering trends, standard price patterns such as Head and Shoulders or Double Tops, and basic trendlines. In some volatile markets, such as cross foreign exchange markets, it would be useful to look at such analysis on a close basis. While intra-period trading often causes a great deal of confusion on a bar chart, the line chart presents an entirely different picture.

Against this, the bar chart provides more information. Technical analysis deals mostly with the representation of supply and demand, and the support or resistance levels generated. When considering the basic principles of support and resistance, and Elliott Wave (which will be discussed in Chapter 5), it is important to know the price extremes of a given movement in order to calculate potential retracements or target levels of future movements. In any case, it is important to remember the desired result of the underlying analysis and use the most appropriate method of chart construction.

TIME PERIODS FOR BAR CHARTS

When discussing bar charts, a period of one day or a week is considered in this book. The week and the day are obvious periods to choose for a bar because each has a clearly defined opening separated by a break from the close of the previous trading session. In other words, there is a psychological gap between periods during which participants will be assessing their strategies.

What period should traders look at for intraday charts? Although this subject is not generally considered, many traders insist that four-hour charts are more revealing than hourly ones, or that 10-minute periods are better than 15- or 30-minute periods. While traders may have found these periods profitable, there should be some logic to the choice. If these traders merely stumbled across this fact for the market they are trading, we cannot be sure that it will be the same in another market. So, what time frame should we use?

It is possible that the answer lies within the question itself. Why are we so concerned with which *time frame* to use? The key word here is *time*. The suggestion is that time has some relevance to trading. Though cycles are not discussed until Chapter 7, a brief reference here would be useful. Many people believe that time plays an important role in trading. You may hear market commentators refer to a two- or five-day cycle. This basically suggests that the market tends to see similar trading patterns within the time frame of two or five days. If an intraday period is chosen for our bar chart, it could be argued that we should use a bar that is a fraction of the underlying two- or five-day cycle.

Invariably there will be no cycle *exactly* 2 days long, but perhaps 42 hours long. Since the basic concept of cycles is that the shorter cycles will converge with the longer cycles, we could use 10 minutes as the shortest period. (If you divide 42 hours by 2 eight times you will reach a value equivalent to about 9.8 minutes). For the longer bar chart you may choose 4 times that figure—40 minutes and then double it to make 80 minutes.

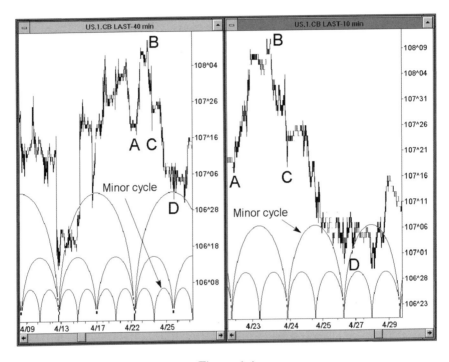

Figure 1.4
US T-Bond Futures. On the left is a 40-minute bar chart and on the right
is a 10-minute bar chart. Note how the minor cycle is shown on each chart
and how price lows tend to match the cycles in both time periods.

Detailed reference to the subject of cycles will be made in Chapter 7. For now, an example of this is shown in Figure 1.4 with basic cycles attached to two charts of the US T-Bond Futures market. The chart on the left has a 40-minute period while the one on the right has a 10-minute period. Both charts have points A, B, C, and D labeled. Note how the smallest cycle on the 40-minute chart (marked as a minor cycle) reaches a trough at point A together with the larger cycles, thus defining price movement. Price then rises to point B, which provides a peak, and subsequently declines to a minor low at point C. This is followed by a minor corrective rally and a further decline to point D. The minor cycle drawn on the left (40-minute) chart is also marked on the 10-minute chart on the right. But in the smaller time frame, the minor cycle is represented by the larger cycle. This chart is also marked with points A, B, C, and D for reference.

By using the concept of cycles, greater attention can be given to choosing bar charts of a time period that is a divisor of the underlying cycle length.

BASIC PRICE BEHAVIOR

This section describes some of the basic elements of price behavior. Although this subject is covered in other books, some areas need to be highlighted as I have seen mistakes being made repeatedly. Some experienced traders make simple errors even with basic trendlines. This section is thus intended to be a review of the subject rather than an introduction to it.

Support and Resistance

As support and resistance is a basic concept of price behavior, an understanding of how it develops is useful.

I had never considered *why* support and resistance develop until a short discussion with a trader in the bank where I ran the technical analysis desk. When he asked for my opinion of the day's trading, I replied that I felt we would find a particular level hard to overcome. "Plenty of resistance there," I told him. Despite being non-technical in his approach to markets, the trader agreed with me.

At this point, fiercely protective of technical analysis in a trading room full of non-technical traders, I asked him how he arrived at the same resistance level. He replied that he remembered taking a long position at around this price some months ago since it had spent some time bouncing off this level before it broke lower. He lost money on this occasion. He therefore concluded that since it had been a hard level to breach on the way down, it would provide resistance on the way up.

It struck me then that this was one possible explanation of support and resistance. Support and resistance are the collective thoughts and opinions of market participants held in their memories—often in terms of profits made or losses incurred.

As basic premise, once a resistance level has developed, it will continue to provide resistance. Similarly, once support has been established, it will continue to provide support. Another point—probably more important to understand for identifying profit opportunities—is that once these levels are breached, *their roles are reversed.* In other words, once resistance is breached, it will subsequently provide support; once support is breached, it will provide resistance. Figure 1.5 illustrates this theory. Figure 1.6 shows a practical example in the hourly US dollar–Japanese yen currency market in May 1996. Notice how frequently supports and resistances repeat their role and then reverse. In Chapter 5 we will discuss how the Elliott Wave Principle can assist us in suggesting which supports and resistances are likely to hold.

The effect of support and resistance can be seen in all time frames, with the longer-term (weekly) charts showing more solid support or resistance than the shorter-term charts. Likewise, breaches of weekly support and resistance provide stronger indication of potential trends. Figure 1.7 illustrates this phenomenon in the weekly Brent Crude Oil cash market. Note how the rallies of 1994 to 1996 found resistance at previous peaks, and how corrections developed clear levels of support within a clear channel.

Support and Resistance in Trends

Support and resistance levels are recurring events in price charts as seen in Figures 1.6 and 1.7, which show horizontal

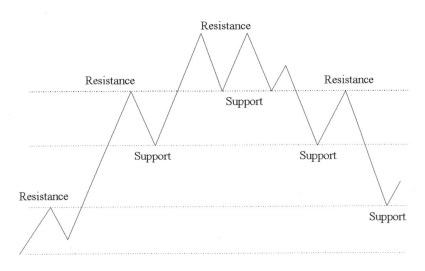

Figure 1.5
Basic theory of support and resistance.

Figure 1.6
Hourly USDJPY currency market in May 1996.

Figure 1.7
Weekly Brent Crude Oil market displaying repeated attempts of support
and resistance levels.

support and resistance lines. Markets move in trends, and rules similar to those governing support and resistance levels can be applied to these trends. Support and resistance in trends are normally referred to as trendlines. Although this is a simple concept—most traders will have drawn a line on a chart—it is surprising how many incorrect trendlines are drawn. During the course of my work, I have visited many different trading rooms, and occasionally I am asked for my opinion of a particular trendline. All too frequently the line has not even been drawn on a trend!

In addition to the fact that a trend is a sustained movement of price in one direction, it is important to note the following.

An uptrend is formed when each successive price low is *higher* than the previous low.

A downtrend is formed when each successive price high is *lower* than the previous high.

Figure 1.8 illustrates this. In an ideal uptrend, a rising support line can be drawn between the corrective troughs. When price fails to hit a higher peak, the uptrend is broken to signal a reversal in price direction. The concept of support and resistance is then revisited and one of the previous support levels will provide support once again. The lower half of Figure 1.8 shows a similar approach for an ideal downtrend with a falling resistance line drawn between the corrective peaks.

We saw earlier that when support and resistance levels are breached, their roles are reversed—support becomes resistance and vice-versa. The same concept can be applied to trendlines. Once a support line is broken it provides resistance. Once a resistance line is broken it provides support.

Figure 1.9 of the US dollar–German Deutschmark currency market shows clearly the trendlines and how each break in the trendline signaled a complete reversal in price direction. In many instances the trendlines reversed their role, and upon retest a support line became a resistance line and vice versa.

To be effective, trendlines and their construction as price moves, should be scrutinised. Often, traders construct trendlines using a hit-and-hope process—the trader draws as many trendlines as possible in the hope that one of them will

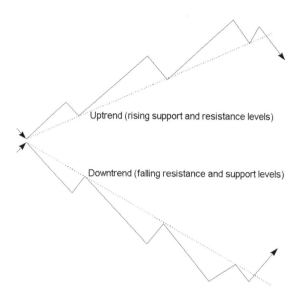

Figure 1.8
Trends: the sustained movement of price in one direction, with successive
rising highs and lows or declining highs and lows.

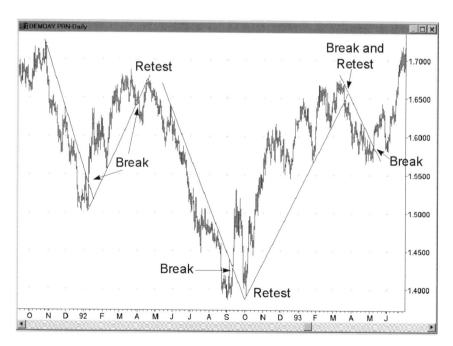

Figure 1.9
Daily USDDEM currency market displaying a strong trending nature.

provide a good signal. By the time numerous trendlines are drawn, so many have failed that the trader has completely confused himself and fails to trade on the profitable trendline. In such instances, the trader is not drawing trendlines but joining two points with a line that does not form any trend.

What needs to be done is to determine *when* a trendline is valid and thus, on a break constitutes a reversal. Using a part of the price action in Figure 1.9, we shall examine the possible pitfalls faced by a trader and when a trendline is valid to be used. The relevant portion of Figure 1.9 is reproduced in Figure 1.10.

Figure 1.10 shows the trendline of the US dollar–German Deutschmark currency market for the period starting October 1992 to sometime in March 1993. Clearly this line cannot be drawn until the first low at point A in late January 1993.

We could also have drawn an earlier trendline D–E seen in Figure 1.11, and this would have proven to be a good trendline for reasons to be discussed shortly. We may also have

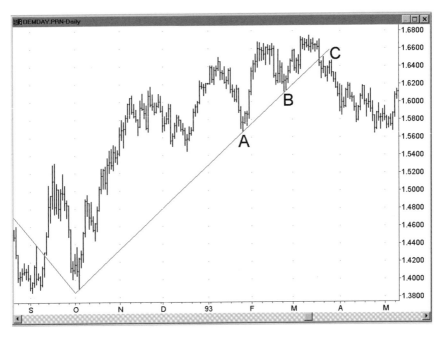

Figure 1.10
USDDEM currency market displaying a trendline from October 1992
to March 1993.

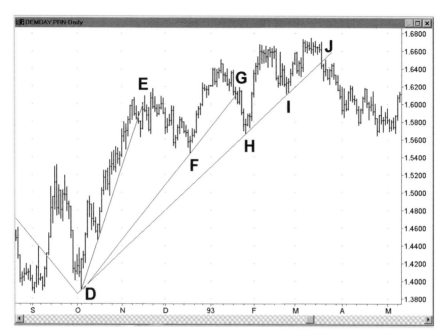

Figure 1.11
The same price action as in Figure 1.10 but with additional potential
(and incorrect) trendlines added.

been tempted to draw another line, D–F. Should we have changed our view with the penetration at point G? The answer is no. Why?

The answer lies in the number of times price touches the trendline. In most markets, it is very easy to draw a line between two lows or two highs. But in the majority of cases, these two touches do not constitute a trend. When drawing a trendline, I usually look for price to touch the line at least three times, including at the point from which the line originates. Hence, we cannot assume from the trendline D–F in Figure 1.11 that there was a reversal since there were only two price–trendline touches and this reduces its impact.

The line D–H is valid because price touches it at point I and bounces off.

Could we have anticipated the bounce off point I? From what has been covered so far, there is little indication that this would have happened. In general, I do not give much weight to trendlines at points such as I since there is no certainty that price will bounce off at that point. (There may be other supporting factors such as an Elliott wave count and momentum divergence, but these will be covered later in this book.)

Thus, in general, it is best to trade on a trendline only *after* three touches with price, whether this is to anticipate the line holding, or buying/selling on the break of the trendline. In the case of the USDDEM market in Figure 1.11, we could have sold on the break and again on the retest at point I. This would have resulted in a very profitable trade. We will show in later chapters how we can anticipate a move to its eventual target.

Now, as another exercise, we shall look at the same period in time for the USDCHF currency market. Figure 1.12 shows the same bullish run for the US dollar.

The initial trendline A–B works well with a retest of the line after break. Then we could have drawn A–C but would have waited to see if there was a bounce off the line on the next attempt. As there was not—we saw a bounce off point D instead—we would have ignored A–C and drawn A–D. We

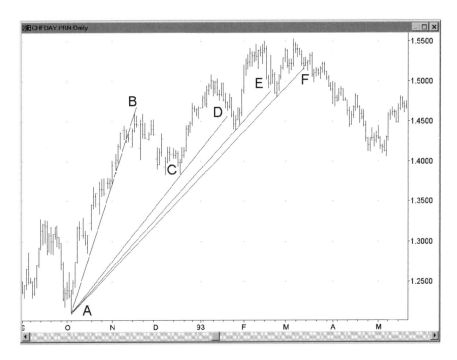

Figure 1.12
Potential trendlines applied to the USDCHF currency market.

would then have waited to see if another bounce came off on the next attempt. We again saw penetration and the subsequent bounce off point E. We would then have drawn a new trendline A–E and seen what would happen. We saw penetration at point F, but price then passed through the line and back down in a larger bearish correction.

The argument used successfully in the USDDEM market of Figure 1.11 does not appear to have worked in the USDCHF market. We have to use a little more thought here. It is a common but mistaken practice to always draw a trendline from the extreme of the very first move (in this case at point A). In some instances this may work, as it did in the USDDEM market in Figure 1.11. For every situation that works, there are probably two that do not. Once again, the answer lies in my opinion that since most of the market is looking at the same incorrect trendline, it has less chance of being effective.

However, do not despair! There is a technique that will help you draw the correct trendline. Figure 1.13 shows the correct trendlines for the USDCHF market of Figure 1.12. It is common to find a trendline drawn along an *intermediate* trend. In Figure 1.13, the intermediate trend began at point C through points D and E, eventually seeing penetration *and* retest at point F.

Observe that this intermediate trendline satisfies the requirement of three touches by price action, and on breach, we see no re-penetration, but retest and bounce off. This would have offered greater profit potential.

The two lessons here are: first, do not always draw trendlines from the lowest or highest start points of the trend, and second, it is advisable to wait for three touches of the trendline by price action before assessing the trendline as stable and tradable.

TRENDLINES ON VOLATILE MARKETS

In volatile markets, it is common to find that the two guidelines (for drawing trendlines), can break down. Figure 1.14 illustrates this.

Figure 1.14 shows the DEMCHF currency market. Following penetration at point A, price reversed upwards and penetrated the trendline that may have been expected to hold. This suggests that the original break of trend support had been

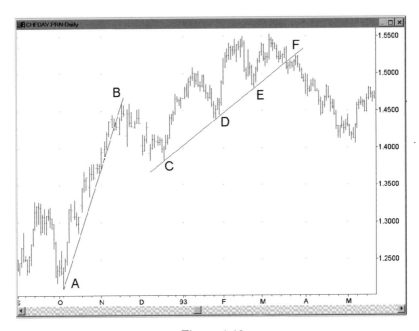

Figure 1.13
A trendline applied to an intermediate trendline in the
USDCHF currency market.

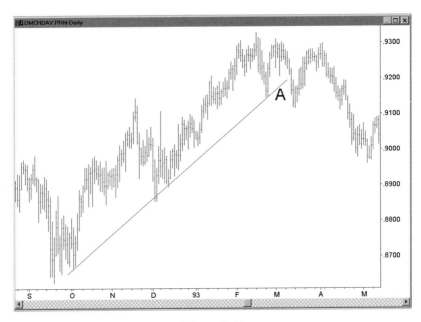

Figure 1.14
A trendline drawn on the volatile DEMCHF currency market.

Figure 1.15
A line chart of the price action of Figure 1.14.

false. However, price then reversed downwards to confirm a subsequent decline.

With volatile markets, it is better to draw trendlines on line charts of closing price. While this infers obtaining a breach of the closing price through the trendline, and though this may cause some false breaks if just looking at extremes, it is a safer way to assume reversal. Figure 1.15 has been plotted as a line chart of closing price seen in Figure 1.14.

Notice how Figure 1.15 displays a cleaner trendline touches by price, and after breach at point C on a close basis, we see a good movement lower. This would have avoided the potential loss incurred if we had used the trendline in Figure 1.14.

Figure 1.16 provides another example, this time of a trendline drawn on both a line chart and a bar chart of the daily British pound – Japanese yen currency market. Note how the bar chart on the left cannot be used satisfactorily to draw a trendline from the low around 220 and how after the breach, the trendline would have been penetrated on the subsequent

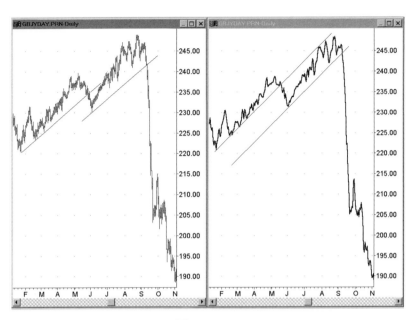

Figure 1.16
A comparison of the bar chart and line chart of the daily GBPJPY currency market displays the advantages of displaying trendlines on a line chart.

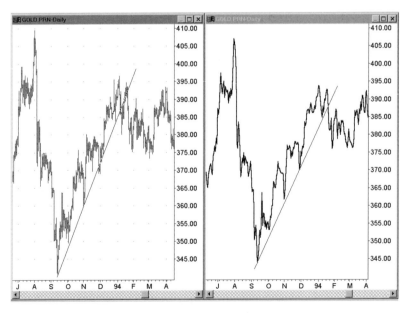

Figure 1.17
A comparison of a bar chart and a line chart on the volatile gold market.

rally. On the other hand, the line chart of closing price of the same market seen on the right in Figure 1.16, shows a clear uptrend line, which after breach, was tested once again on the subsequent rally. Furthermore, if a second parallel line was to be drawn from the first corrective decline after the first line had been breached, this second line would have closely supported price and upon breach, would have signaled a stronger decline.

A further example showing how trendlines on daily line charts give better signals is seen in Figure 1.17. This figure shows the comparison of the daily gold market drawn on a bar chart on the left against a daily line chart on the right. The gold market is a particularly volatile one, and a trendline displays few opportunities for trading on the bar chart but gives stronger signals on the line chart.

CHAPTER 2

Moving Averages

The moving average is a common tool in technical analysis because of the simple concept behind both its calculation and usage. This section will cover the basics and introduce some less common applications of moving averages.

SIMPLE MOVING AVERAGE

The simple moving average (SMA) is the most common form of moving average. It is as its name implies, a simple addition of the closing prices for a number of periods (e.g. 10 days) and then dividing the total by the number of periods. This will return the average price of the security over the time period.

$$\text{Hence, SMA}_{10} = \frac{C_1 + C_2 + C_3 + C_4 + C_5 + C_6 + C_7 + C_8 + C_9 + C_{10}}{10}$$

This gives today's simple moving average of the closing price for the last 10 days.

Similarly, yesterday's simple moving average gives the average closing price for the previous 10 days, and so on. This results in a moving series of values which, when plotted on a graph and connected by a line, forms a 10-day simple moving average chart.

Figure 2.1 shows three simple moving averages for the periods of 10, 30, and 60 days. A fundamental point to note here is that a moving average calculated over a shorter period is more sensitive to short-term price changes as it tends to "hug" price action more closely. It therefore follows that price action will tend to touch and cross the shorter-term simple moving average more frequently than the longer-term simple moving average. Note in Figure 2.1 how the 10-day simple moving average rarely moves far away from price, while the 60-day simple moving average rarely touches price.

Observe the slight lag of the 10-day simple moving

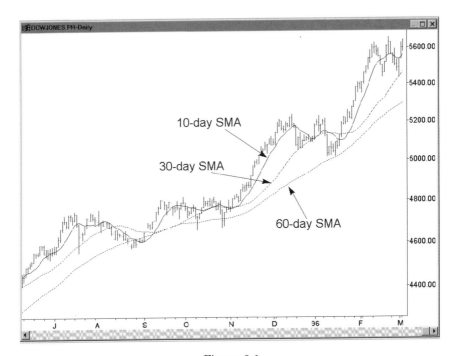

Figure 2.1
A daily bar chart of the Dow Jones Index with three simple moving averages applied.

average behind price action—the turn in the moving average occurs several days after price has moved. Basically, the 10-day simple moving average mimics price action with a slight lag and eliminates the volatility that price tends to display.

Similarly, the 30-day simple moving average follows price but at a slower pace. This longer-term simple moving average includes closing prices from the previous 30 days, and these closing prices can be substantially different from the prevailing price. Although the 30-day simple moving average tends to mimic price action, it reacts less to changes in direction. Its lag behind price change is therefore greater than that of the 10-day simple moving average.

Finally, the 60-day simple moving average displays a similar fact but because it represents data for the previous 60 days, it reacts even more slowly than the 30-day simple moving average. In addition, it lags more slowly behind price action.

Essentially, the simple moving average displays the underlying trend of price movement as it is calculated using the closing price. This therefore strips it of the excessive swings of daily price—high and low—which are associated with the extremes of the bar. Owing to its lagging nature, the simple moving average shows changes in trend quite late.

If the longer-term simple moving average is late in signaling changes in price direction, then why not choose a shorter-term simple moving average to detect price change more quickly? Well, on the face of it this seems a reasonable argument. But remember that as the shorter-term simple moving average hugs price more closely, it will tend to provide whipsaws (rapid movement of price in both directions) in much the same way as price.

This may not be bad when the market displays a trending nature, but statistics show that price tends to trend for only 20–30% of the time, the balance being consolidation. Figure 2.2 shows the Dow Jones Industrial Average, the same market as in Figure 2.1. During consolidation, notice how at points A, B, and C we would have suffered losses with the change in price direction.

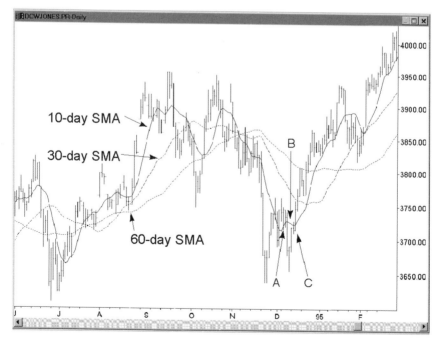

Figure 2.2
Daily Dow Jones Index with 10-, 30-, and 60-day moving average applied during a consolidating market.

In a later section, the various methods of using moving averages to generate trading signals will be discussed.

WEIGHTED MOVING AVERAGE

In the previous section, we discovered that the simple moving average is a *lagging* indicator. To overcome this, some analysts prefer to use the weighted moving average.

The main argument behind the weighted moving average (WMA) is current price action is more important than price action of the past. The simple moving average gives equal weighting to each value in the series while the weighted moving average gives more importance (weight) to recent price and less to that of the past. Therefore the weighted moving average changes direction more quickly than the simple moving average.

A five-day weighted moving average is calculated as follows:

$$WMA_5 = \frac{C_5 \times 1 + C_4 \times 2 + C_3 \times 3 + C_2 \times 4 + C_1 \times 5}{1 + 2 + 3 + 4 + 5}$$

From the calculation above, we see that today's price (C1) is given the most importance by multiplying it by a weight of 5, yesterday's price (C2) is multiplied by 4, and so on. This gives five times more weight to today's price than the price of five days ago. Once we have added these values together, we divide it by the total of the weights we have used, which, in this case, is 15.

Figure 2.3 shows a comparison of a 10-day simple moving average against a 10-day weighted moving average. Clearly, the weighted moving average is closer to price action and generally turns more quickly than the simple moving average. Just as with different time periods of simple moving average, the longer-term weighted moving average will display a smoother line that lags price action by a larger margin than the shorter-term weighted moving average.

While this appears to be beneficial, we should be reminded that if weighted moving averages shows changes in direction more quickly, then they will also be subject to whipsaws during swift moves that see sharp corrections and resumption of the trend.

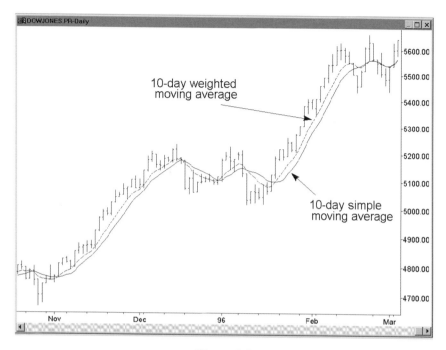

Figure 2.3
Comparison of simple and weighted moving averages.

EXPONENTIAL MOVING AVERAGE

The exponential moving average (EMA) is slightly different from the simple and weighted moving averages. While the weighted moving average is designed to be more responsive to price action by suggesting that recent price action is more important than past price action, exponential moving average makes the assumption that *all* price action is important, even that of a year ago or more, in some very small way. The formula for an exponential average takes this into account.

$$EMA_{10} = EMA_{10}[1] + \{SF \times (Price - EMA_{10}[1])\}$$

or

$$EMA_{10} = SF \times Price + (1 - SF) \times EMA_{10}[1]$$

where: the smoothing Factor, $SF = 2 / (1 + 10)$
[1] represents the previous period
$EMA_{10}[1]$ represents the 10-day EMA of the previous period

Essentially, by retaining in the calculation the value of the previous period's exponential moving average, the exponential moving average maintains reference to price from the beginning of the data series.

Figure 2.4 shows a comparison between the simple, weighted, and exponential moving averages. Note how the exponential moving average tends to fall between the simple and weighted moving averages when in a trend, but as price action sees a correction (circled area), the exponential moving average tends to fall back more quickly than both simple and weighted moving averages. This can be quite useful in picking out trends where price makes a correction that often penetrates the simple or weighted moving average, thus causing a possible reversal in position, while the exponential moving average may not be breached.

SMOOTHED OR RUNNING MOVING AVERAGE

The smoothed or running moving average (SmMA) is seldom used. J. Welles Wilder, Jr. relied heavily on the smoothed moving average in many of his indicators including the RSI and ADX. Wilder intended the smoothed moving average to provide additional lag by ensuring that drop out of a large movement n periods ago is smoothed. This is effected by including the value of the average from the previous period.

The smoothed moving average can be calculated as follows:

$$SmMA_{10} = \frac{(SmMA_{10}[1] \times (10 - 1) + Price)}{10}$$

where: SmMA $\quad$ = smoothed or running moving average
SmMA[1] = SmMA of one period ago

Figure 2.5 shows a comparison between smoothed and exponential moving averages. Note how the smoothed moving average tends to lag behind the exponential moving average in an uptrend, but during the pull back at the end, the exponential moving average falls behind the smoothed moving average. This reflects the different manner in which the two formulae treat price change.

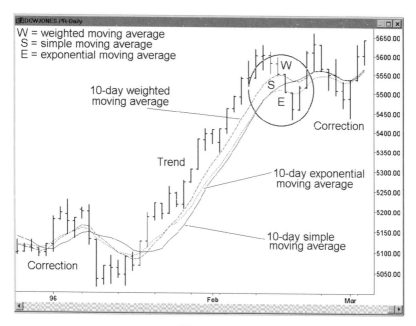

Figure 2.4
*Comparison of a 10-day simple, weighted, and exponential
moving averages.*

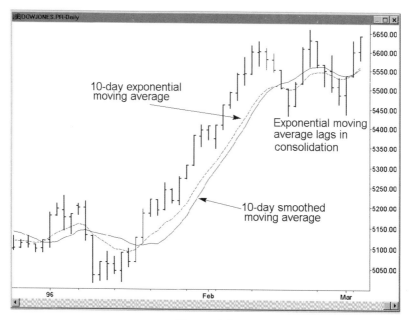

Figure 2.5
Comparison of exponential and smoothed moving averages.

DOUBLE SMOOTHED MOVING AVERAGE

The double smoothed moving average (DSMA) is not commonly used. It was created in an attempt to correct the general lagging nature of moving averages. It is generally accepted that the lag is *half the period of the base moving average.* In other words, a 10-day simple moving average lags price action by 5 days ($10 \div 2$).

The formula for calculating the double smoothed moving average is as follows:

$$DSMA_{10} = 2 \times SMA_{10} - (SMA_{10} \text{ of } SMA_{10})$$

Figure 2.6 shows a 10-day double smoothed moving average and compares it against a 10-day simple moving average. Note how the double smoothed moving average clings to price action very closely, even in an uptrend, while the simple moving average lags behind. At the end of a trend, the double smoothed moving average swings more than the simple moving average and reverses quite promptly.

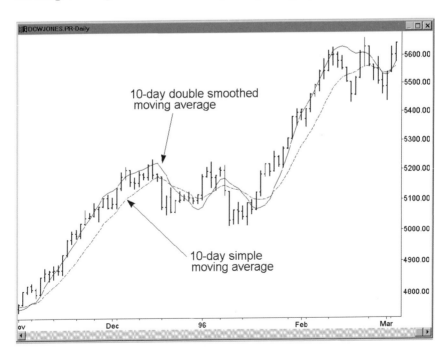

Figure 2.6
Comparison of simple and double smoothed moving averages.

As the double smoothed moving average hugs price action closely, it is unsuitable for strategies that require price to cross a moving average. They can, however, be useful in strategies involving other types of moving averages. This will be explained the section Moving Average Strategies.

DISPLACED MOVING AVERAGE

The displaced moving average is another moving average that is rarely used by traders, but it has its benefits. It is basically any of the moving averages already described shifted in a horizontal direction, either a period of bars backwards or forwards.

Figure 2.7 shows both backward and forward displaced moving averages as well as the underlying simple moving average. Note that all three moving averages have exactly the same shape but are drawn at different points. The central bold line is a 10-day simple moving average. To the left is the same average but displaced backwards by five bars. (While not a rule, the five-bar displacement is a reflection of the simple moving average lagging price by approximately half the average time period length). The third line to the right is the same average displaced five bars into the future.

By displacing any moving average backwards, it is possible to see the divergence between price and the base moving average. This, however, can only be seen five days after price action. Notice that the backward displaced moving average displays no value for the final five trading days. This is because the current day's simple moving average is displaced five bars into the past. Despite this, the displaced moving average can be used in conjunction with other trading signals.

The forward displaced moving average is pushed horizontally to the right. One of the problems with the simple moving average is the shorter its period, the more it hugs price action and consequently, the more frequently it crosses price action. By displacing the simple moving average forward, it stops price from touching the moving average line, thus preventing false signals. The downside of this strategy is price may correct later, thus giving potential profits before it crosses the moving average.

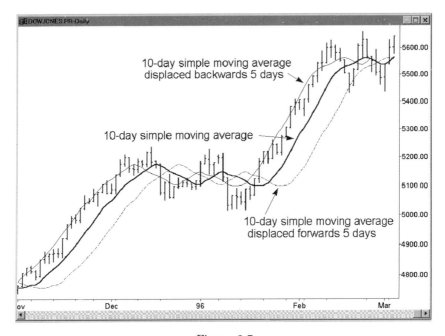

Figure 2.7
A 10-day simple moving average displaced forwards (to the right) and backwards (to the left).

MOVING AVERAGE STRATEGIES

Single Moving Average

Let us recall what we have discovered about moving averages. The predominant feature of the moving average is its tendency to follow trends. As it is intrinsically a lagging indicator, it will follow price, displaying an average of recent price action, and in a trend, it usually remains just behind price action. The obvious question then is, if the moving average shows a trend and if price action reverses through the moving average, does it imply that the trend has changed? We can thus initiate a long position when price turns up through the moving average, and reverse the position when price falls back below the moving average. At this point, we need to establish a methodology for trading with a single moving average. There will be instances when price will break through the moving average within the trading day, possibly crossing through the moving average, then back again. There will also be instances where by the end of the trading day, the closing price may not have crossed through the moving average. Generally, most traders or analysts wish to see the closing price cross the moving average rather than a high/low extreme before establishing a counter-directional trade.

Figure 2.8 shows a 1993 daily gold chart with a single moving average. We would have been delighted with the results of the trades established when the *close* crossed the moving average. However, if we consider the price action that followed, the profits gained would have been lost with the number of times price reversed through the average, as seen in Figure 2.9.

What has happened? In 1993, gold prices trended well; even when price reversed, the trendlines reversed with price. During the following months, gold price stopped trending and went into a long period of consolidation sideways, thus causing numerous whipsaws as price often reversed through the moving average daily.

There is another disadvantage. When creating the chart in Figure 2.8, a longer-term moving average which touched price

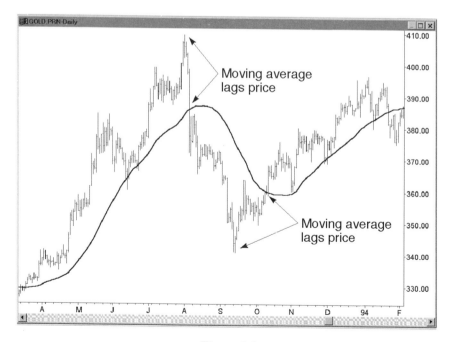

Figure 2.8
Using price crossing over a single moving average as an indicator
of trend reversal.

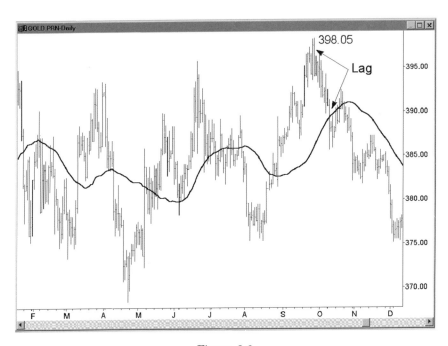

Figure 2.9
The same length moving average that was used in Figure 2.8 is shown but
plotted on subsequent data. Note how the sideways movement in price
causes late reversal signals.

as few times as possible was deliberately chosen. The use of a longer-term moving average also creates problems. The first thing we learnt about moving averages is the longer the period of the moving average, the more bars used in the calculation, and thus the greater the lag of the moving average behind price. When gold prices peaked at $398.05, the moving average lagged so far behind price that price was able to reverse a long way before it eventually crossed below the moving average to signal a reversal. Similarly, after traveling down the trough at around $340, price was able to reverse to nearly $360 before moving back above the moving average to signal the reversal.

As can be seen, this is the second major problem of moving averages—they are slow to signal reversal, thus allowing for a large degree of profit "give back" at reversals.

By shortening the length of the time period of the moving average, the moving average will stay closer to price. But price will also reverse through the shorter-term moving average more frequently, thus causing the type of whipsaw that occurs during periods of consolidation. This suggests that price is too volatile for this type of strategy.

Dual Moving Averages

On some occasions price can be too volatile to make the single moving average strategy profitable. We can therefore introduce a second moving average to smoothen price action. Instead of using price breaking through a moving average, a second moving average can be used to represent price. Figure 2.10 shows the same gold chart as in Figure 2.8, using two shorter-term moving averages with the original moving average shown as a bold line.

From the bottom left-hand corner of the chart we see that the two shorter-term moving averages would have entered into a long position slightly ahead of the longer-term moving average. (Remember we are referring to the closing price crossing the moving average). Both the single and dual moving

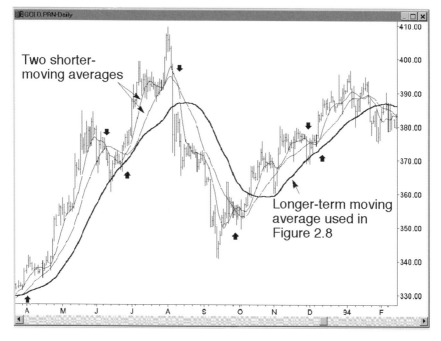

Figure 2.10
Comparison of a single moving average (as seen in Figure 2.8) with dual moving averages to imply trend reversal. Arrows show crossover of the two shorter-term moving averages.

average systems would have stayed long but the dual moving average would have seen a reversal to a short position, then back to long again during the correction in June. At the peak, the single moving average system reversed from a long to a short position *ahead* of the dual moving average system. This is because the price reversal was especially fast, and in such situations, a swift signal is required. However the short-term moving average, which represents price, lags price slightly and thus delays the signal.

The reverse is true for the low of $340. As price reversed, stalled in a correction, then continued higher, it gave the shorter-term moving average in the dual moving average system a chance to catch up and signal a reversal ahead of the single moving average system. A mixed success can therefore be seen depending on the type of market move. Next, we examine the behavior of each system during consolidating markets. This is seen in Figure 2.11.

The dual moving average system signals more trades as compared to the single moving average system. Remember that

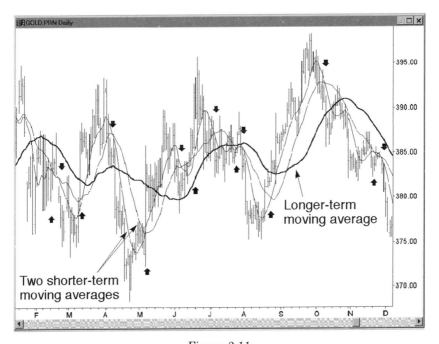

Figure 2.11
Comparison of a single moving average and dual moving averages in a consolidating market to imply trend reversal.

we are measuring the single moving average system based on price *closing above or below* the moving average and using the closing price to calculate the average values. (Hence we will not know the final value of the moving average until the close). In most cases, the shorter-term moving average performs slightly better than the dual moving average. However, there is still a large degree of "give back" and too many occasions when a loss is generated because of a late signal. In one or two cases, a profit is generated when the single moving average would have returned a loss.

Triple Moving Averages

In the first two moving average strategies, we saw how price volatility (which caused too many entries during periods of consolidation) was tackled using a second moving average to represent price behavior. But the effect of increasing the time period of the moving average caused "give backs" when price reversed quickly, and we still saw too many instances of losses during price consolidation.

The introduction of a third moving average is an attempt to reduce these losses. The third moving average is used to take profits slightly earlier and to reduce the number of loss-making trades in consolidation. The strategy works as follows.

The three moving averages used are the short-, medium-, and long-term moving averages. Positions are established when the shorter-term moving average crosses the longer-term moving average. The position is squared when the shorter-term moving average crosses back through the medium-term moving average. In this way the entry is slightly delayed to confirm a change in price direction, but exits earlier by crossover of the shorter-term moving average through the medium-term one, which is far quicker than waiting until the shorter has crossed back below the longer.

The other benefit of this is during consolidation there are periods when no position is taken and this reduces the instance of loss-making trades (see Figure 2.12).

Figure 2.12 shows that there are more trades but only by virtue of the fact that some of the trades are exits rather than reversals seen previously. It can also be seen that occasionally the shorter-term moving average reverses through the

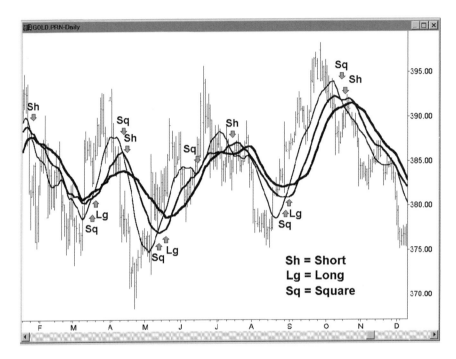

Figure 2.12
A triple moving average system with implied trades marked.

medium-term moving average but fails to move back through the longer-term moving average and then once again reverses through the medium-term. In this situation there is no renewal of the original position and the trader remains square until the shorter-term moves through the longer-term moving average. In some cases this looks likely to forgo some profitable trades. However, it also prevents some loss-making ones.

Four Moving Averages

Perhaps surprisingly, the use of four moving averages is not common although it represents a logical approach. Basically, the two longer-term moving averages determine the trend of the market while the two shorter-term moving averages dictate the trades taken. The idea behind this is the old maxim: the trend is your friend. When the longer-term moving averages have determined a downtrend, the two shorter-term moving averages will *only take short trades* and vice-versa. If the shorter-term moving averages are already indicating a position when the longer-term moving averages also indicate a change in trend, then that position is taken.

This way, positions contrary to the identified trend and the number of non-profitable trades during consolidation are avoided, since only half the positions are taken.

Figure 2.13 shows how this works. Notice how trades are normally taken in the same direction, with direction changing only when the longer-term moving averages also change direction. The biggest drawback of this is since the longer-term moving averages tend to react slower than the trading moving averages used in the earlier strategies using two or three moving averages, the longer-term moving averages are rather slow to spot a change in price direction and can waste potential profits at major turning areas.

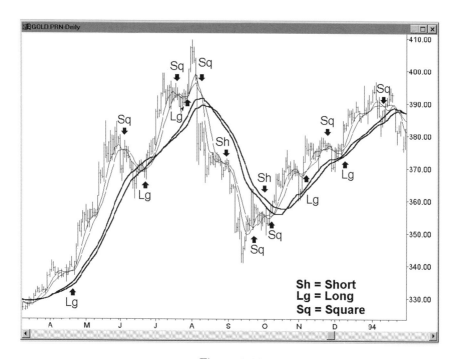

Figure 2.13
Four moving averages used to trade. The two shorter-term moving
averages trade only in the direction of the trend indicated
by the longer-term moving averages.

CHAPTER 3

Momentum Indicators

From the time markets were established, traders have been using a variety of tools to measure the momentum of price action. Perhaps the very first were moving averages but later, as technical analysis became more accepted, a few traders began to make their own calculations to measure momentum. At first these calculations were relatively straightforward and done manually daily. But with the introduction of desktop computers, analysts have been assisted in measuring a variety of periods. And in recent years, the growth in technical analysis software has brought a surge in the ability to create new and more complex indicators to measure the momentum of price action.

Currently, there is a host of momentum indicators being used. Only the commonly used indicators will be detailed in this chapter—how they are calculated and how to use them. This should provide a basic introduction to this area of technical analysis. The next chapter will describe the methods of changing these indicators.

When using any indicator, always remember that there is no single indicator that provides consistently profitable signals. The benefits and drawbacks of the indicators will be discussed so analysts can recognize both the good and bad elements of each indicator and be aware of the problems that can arise from using them. This highlights the importance of integrating technical analysis and gives a greater insight into the strength of any individual indicator or groups of indicators.

MOMENTUM

This is the most basic of all indicators and the easiest to calculate. Momentum is the difference in price from one period to the next.

Momentum = $P - P_x$
where: P = the current period's closing price
  x = the length of the time period

For example, a five-day momentum is measured by subtracting the closing price of five days ago from today's closing price. This is repeated every day and the values are plotted—joined by a single line as seen in Figure 3.1, or quite often as a histogram.

Figure 3.1 shows the chart of the US dollar–Japanese yen currency market and its 10-day momentum plotted below. Notice that momentum oscillates around the zero line. If today's price is higher than that of 10 days ago, then momentum will be positive. Conversely, if today's price is lower than that of 10 days ago, then momentum will be negative.

What does this imply? Instinctively traders will want to sell at momentum peaks and buy at troughs. But a cursory examination of the price chart against the momentum line shows that while this concept would work in many cases, for instance at points A, B, and C, it could also lead to significant losses at other times. Notice that at point D price makes a minor peak while momentum is forming a minor trough. Why is this?

As we are analyzing the *10-day* momentum, we are looking at the difference in price over 10 days. This means that when there is a sharp decline after a rally, as the decline begins, we are subtracting from the current day's closing price (which is lower than the peak of the rally) a price before the rally peaked (which is a price *also lower than the peak*). As the correction continues, price may make a minor rally but we are measuring this against price which was *still rallying*. Only when P_x represents the peak of the rally does the momentum line normalize.

An approach I have seen traders attempt is to suggest that a sale should be effected when momentum reaches a certain level, or a purchase made when momentum reaches a certain negative level. An observation of Figure 3.1 will show that this approach will not work.

To use momentum effectively, we should look at its direction. Let us consider a series of momentum values:

0.45   0.75   1.05   1.25   0.85   0.35   −0.25   −0.50   −0.75

Clearly this would be a line which rises and then falls below the zero line. What can we deduce from these values?

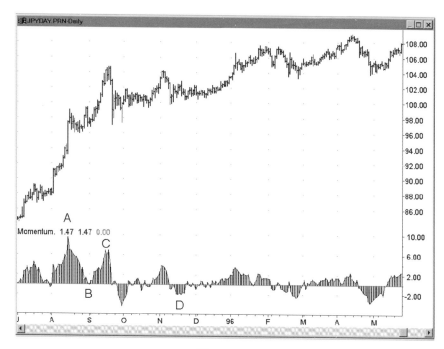

Figure 3.1
Daily USDJPY market with momentum applied.

Not only is price rising, but it is rising at a faster rate each day, i.e. $P - P_x$ is increasing each day. Then, when momentum peaks at 1.25, it starts its decline. This momentum peak does not imply that price has peaked. If $P - P_x$ gives a positive, it means that over a period of x, the price is still rising. What we can surmise from this is when momentum is increasing above the zero line, price is *accelerating* higher. When momentum decreases but is still above zero, price is rising but at a slower rate. The opposite is true for momentum rising but below zero.

Perhaps the most used signal indicated by momentum is the crossover of the line from negative to positive and from positive to negative. Theoretically this should imply that when momentum crosses from negative to positive, price momentum is strong and thus should rally, and vice versa. But even this does not give consistent results. Momentum is therefore best used as a supporting indicator with other momentum tools.

RELATIVE STRENGTH INDEX

The Relative Strength Index (RSI) was developed by J. Welles Wilder, Jr. who has contributed a number of commonly used tools. Wilder was frustrated by the fact that momentum could not identify overbought or oversold conditions and so set out to develop an indicator which signaled trading opportunities. He did this by comparing positive and negative closing prices in momentum and then normalizing them in a scale between zero and 100.

The formula he derived is:

$$RSI = 100 - \frac{100}{(1 + RS)}$$

where:
$$RS = \frac{\text{running average of n period's up closes}}{\text{running average of n period's down closes}}$$

n = number of periods used in the calculation

Relative Strength (RS) is calculated by taking the arithmetic average of up closes during the last n days and dividing it by the arithmetic average of down closes during the last n days. An up close occurs when the current period's close is higher than the close of the previous period. A down close is the opposite. Wilder aimed to measure the ratio of positive movement to negative movement. If the average up value is greater than the average down value, the RS value will be greater than one and RSI close to 100. Conversely, if the average down value is greater than the average up value, the RS will be less than one and RSI close to zero.

According to Wilder's guideline, prices generally reach overbought levels when RSI rises above 70 and prices reach oversold levels when RSI declines to below 30. Figure 3.2 gives an example of RSI drawn below a chart of US dollar–Japanese yen currency market.

In Figure 3.2 we see Wilder's RSI trading guideline works very well for most part and would have yielded good profits with only one or two losses. The risk-reward ratio looks acceptable too.

One of the most frequently asked questions is what length of period should be used in the calculation of the RSI. There is no right answer to this question as it depends on which market is being analyzed as each reacts differently with various lengths of period. Most traders use the trial-and-error method to find a period length that gives the best signals.

Wilder was a strong believer in cycles/periods. The best RSI length is generally half the cycle length of the underlying price chart. (Chapter 7 describes cycles in greater depth.)

Does Wilder's 70–30 guideline work consistently? Unfortunately this does not prove to be the case. Looking at Figure 3.3, which shows the US dollar–Japanese yen currency market, we see that if we had traded according to Wilder's 70–30 guideline, we would have made considerable losses. In this situation, the initial sale would have yielded a reasonable profit. But all except the last buy signal would have resulted in losses.

Why does the guideline succeed in Figure 3.2 with RSI indicating profitable trading signals while in Figure 3.3 these same signals prove disastrous? Examine both charts again. What is the difference between the two?

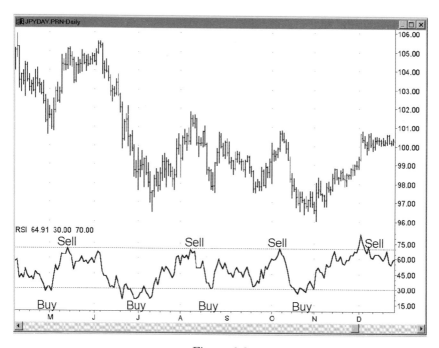

Figure 3.2
Daily USDJPY currency market with RSI and overbought/oversold levels applied.

Notice that in Figure 3.2 price was moving in consolidation sideways while in Figure 3.3 price was in a long downtrend. Wilder had spotted this diverging performance of RSI and its reactions in different types of markets.

Basically, RSI (along with other momentum indicators) is best applied in a consolidating market. When the market is trending, extreme RSI readings (and other momentum indicators) should be ignored and trending indicators used. Because of the trending nature as seen in Figure 3.3, we should be cautious of market commentators who state: "RSI is at its most oversold state in 4 weeks..." and interpret the statement as "the market is very bearish...".

Despite this, momentum indicators can be applied to a certain extent during trends—more accurately be used to determine when the momentum of the trend is slowing prior to reversal. This event is called price/momentum divergence and is a frequent occurrence at the completion of a trend. Figure 3.4 illustrates this. Charts (a) and (b) show price action while

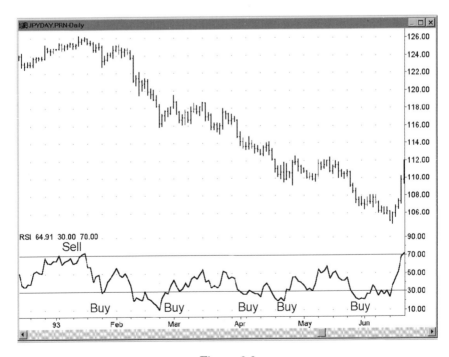

Figure 3.3
Daily USDJPY currency market with RSI and overbought/oversold levels applied in a trending market.

charts (c) and (d) show the corresponding momentum indicator. (Most momentum indicators display similar characteristic.)

Notice how price in chart (a) rises to new highs but the corresponding momentum indicator in chart (c) fails to reach new highs—each new price peak is matched by a lower momentum indicator peak. This is called bearish divergence. Chart (b) shows price action descending to lower troughs but the corresponding momentum indicator in chart (d) fails to reach new troughs—each new price low is matched by a higher momentum indicator trough. This is called bullish divergence.

Figure 3.5 illustrates the bearish and bullish divergences on a chart of the US dollar–Japanese yen currency market. Note firstly how, as the dollar rallied to marginal a new price high of 101.50, RSI failed to match these new peaks, and secondly, after the dramatic downtrend, RSI failed to match the new price low at 79.75.

Price/momentum divergence does not occur at every significant turning point, but occurs frequently enough to make it a powerful signal. It does not, however, signal any *price level*

Price

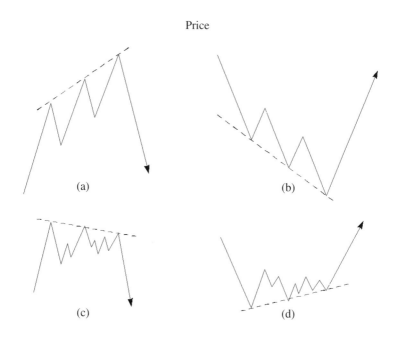

Figure 3.4
Bearish and bullish divergences of price and momentum.

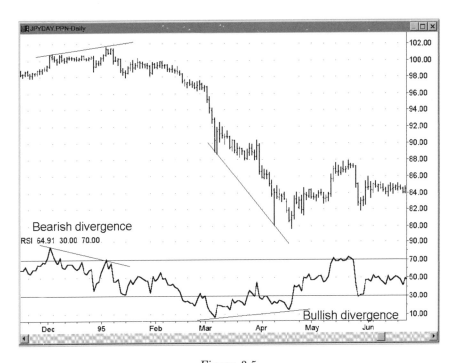

Figure 3.5
Daily USDJPY currency market with RSI and overbought/oversold levels
applied, and displaying bearish and bullish divergences.

at which reversal will occur. This must be ascertained by other analysis methods. The integration of technical analysis gives more powerful signals and this forms the basis of this book. The integration methods will be covered in Chapter 9, after other different methods of analysis are considered.

An infrequent use of momentum indicators but one that can provide useful indications of breaks in consolidation or trend is drawing trendlines on momentum indicators.

Generally, when prices have been moving in a consolidation pattern, or even in a trend, it is often possible to see a similar trend in momentum. Often it is difficult to ascertain if price trend has changed direction. But if a break in price trend is accompanied by a similar break in the trend of its corresponding momentum, then a stronger signal is generated. This is seen in Figure 3.6 which shows the price chart of the US dollar–Japanese yen currency market and its corresponding RSI.

We can see a few signals in price action in Figure 3.6. First, bullish divergence developed at point A, followed by an uptrend to new highs. A trendline can be drawn under this uptrend in price. Similarly, a support line can be drawn below the RSI troughs. But note how the RSI support line was penetrated two days before the break in the price support line at point B. It is common for the momentum indicator to anticipate a break in price trend in advance of the occurrence. Even if the trader wishes to be cautious until actual break of the trendline, he has advanced warning and can be ready for the event.

In Figure 3.7 the same currency market saw a long period of consolidation that broke downwards to around 96.50 (as indicated on the far right of the chart). Note how during this long consolidation, RSI rallied slowly in a mild uptrend channel and the channel base broke a day before price action confirmed a breakdown. After a brief consolidation, price declined to new lows.

Figure 3.6
Daily USDJPY currency market displaying an uptrend in price matched by an uptrend in RSI. Note how the break of the RSI support line at point B preceded the break of the price support line by two days.

Figure 3.7
Daily USDJPY currency market displaying a sideways consolidation
with RSI rising in a mild uptrend. Note how the RSI support broke
two days before price.

It is this type of advanced warning that gives traders an edge over other market participants and ensure that they enter a position in advance of the main move.

Another example is shown in Figure 3.8. Here we see that Brent Crude Oil rallied well, and its corresponding RSI also rose in a clearly defined uptrend below which a support line could be drawn. It is interesting to note that the RSI trend support broke at point A but the price support line was only retested. As price rose to retest the previous high, fail then decline, *RSI rose to retest the trendline* and failed at point B. This would provide a clue to the trader of the potential reversal and breach of the price support line would have been a strong sell signal. Note how price then declined along with RSI until RSI reached an oversold position.

This section has covered RSI and has introduced several uses of momentum indicators. All of these principles can be applied with other momentum indicators and will be noted in examples illustrating the following indicators.

STOCHASTICS

George Lane, another pioneer of technical analysis, developed stochastics in the late 1950s. Stochastics is based on the concept that as price rises, the closing price will rest towards the top of the recent range. Conversely when price declines, the closing price will rest towards the bottom of the range. Lane developed a series of three values, K%, D%, and Slow D%, that measures this occurrence.

$$K\% = \frac{100 \times (\text{Close} - \text{Lowest low for n periods})}{\text{Highest high for n periods} - \text{Lowest low for n periods}}$$

Assume we have seen a bullish move and current price is reaching the high of the recent range. This will give similar values for the close and the highest high for n periods. Hence, in such a situation, the numerator will be of a similar value to

Figure 3.8
The Brent Crude Oil market with RSI and overbought/oversold levels applied. Note how retest of the previous RSI support line matched the peak at point B.

the denominator, which results in K% being close to 100. (Note that the close can never be higher than the highest high for n periods.)

Now assume the opposite where we have seen a downward movement in price and the close is reaching the lowest low of the recent range. In this situation, the close and lowest low for n periods will have similar values and the numerator will have a much lower value than the the denominator. Hence, K% will have a value close to zero.

Thus, we see that as price rises, K% will rise towards 100 and as price falls, K% will fall towards zero.

As K% is highly volatile, Lane developed two other values that are derived from K%. The first is D% and is similar to a three-period simple moving average of K%.

$$D\% = \frac{\text{Sum 1}}{\text{Sum 2}}$$

where:

$$\text{Sum 1} = \begin{matrix}\text{Three-period} & - & \text{Lowest low} \\ \text{sum of Close} & & \text{for n periods}\end{matrix}$$

$$\text{Sum 2} = \begin{matrix}\text{Three-period sum of} & - & \text{Lowest low} \\ \text{Highest high for n periods} & & \text{for n periods}\end{matrix}$$

A second value Lane derived from K% is an even slower indicator called SlowD% where:

SlowD% = Three-period simple moving average of D%.

Normally, stochastics is used in pairs—K% with D% or D% with SlowD%—in a combination of overbought and oversold readings that are generally at levels of 80 or 20 respectively, together with the crossover of the faster line across the slower line. The concept of divergence can be used in stochastics, and in some circumstances trendlines on stochastics can be drawn. But due to its more volatile nature, this is not often possible.

Figure 3.9 shows K% being used with D% for the US dollar–Canadian dollar currency market. Notice the volatility of K%, often with rapid direction changes up on rapid price reversal. Unfortunately, K% is often very volatile that the simple use of crossover or overbought and oversold positions

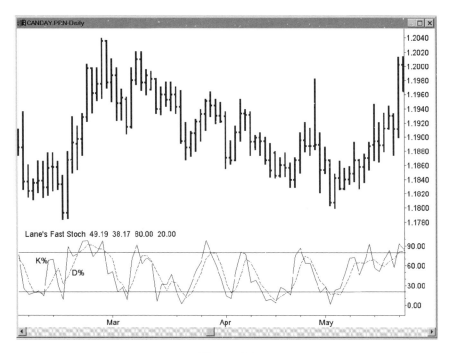

Figure 3.9
Daily Canadian dollar market with K% and D% applied along with
overbought/oversold levels.

becomes less accurate. In such situations it is often better to utilize D% with SlowD%. Figure 3.10 shows the chart of the US 30-Year Bond Yield with both fast and slow stochastics for comparison.

Notice that K% reacts too sharply, and on four occasions could have caused whipsaws in a crossover system or overbought and oversold systems. This is because K% tends to reach an extreme, reverse briefly, and then move back to the extreme.

The guideline for the number of periods to use to calculate stochastics should be based on the underlying cycle—use a period of half the length of the cycle.

Figure 3.11 shows another example of the use of stochastics, this time with the Japanese Nikkei. It shows that slow stochastics would have worked quite well in the overbought and oversold, crossover, and divergence systems.

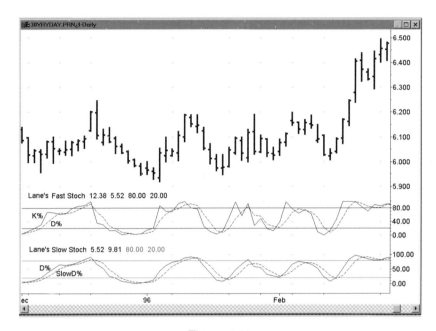

Figure 3.10
Daily US 30-Year Bond Yield with both fast stochastics (K%, D%) and slow stochastics (D%, SlowD%) applied.

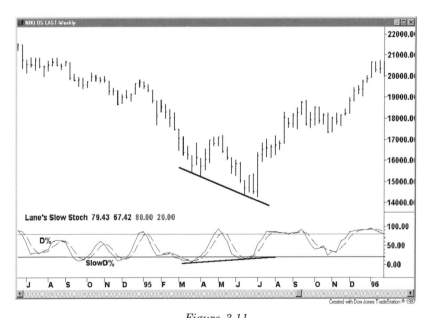

Figure 3.11
Daily Japanese Nikkei Index with slow stochastics (D%, SlowD%) applied. Both crossovers of D% and SlowD%, with divergence, perform well here.

CHAPTER 3: Momentum Indicators 53

MOVING AVERAGE CONVERGENCE AND DIVERGENCE

Moving average convergence and divergence (MACD) is a popular analytical tool because of its easily recognizable underlying concept. Although it is not strictly a momentum indicator, because it is based on moving averages, it fits into the momentum indicator category well. The concept of using the crossing of two moving averages to generate buy and sell signals is well-known and quite popular.

MACD measures the degree of fluctuation between two exponential moving averages. This value is calculated by measuring the spread between a shorter-term and a longer-term exponential moving average. MACD is therefore measured in points. To create buy and sell signals, an exponential moving average is calculated on the MACD.

MACD = Short-term EMA − Long-term EMA
Signal = EMA of MACD

where: EMA = Exponential Moving Average

Standard period length for MACD are 12 and 26 periods with the signal line being a nine-period exponential moving average of the MACD.

Some traders misinterpret this believing that MACD represents the crossing of two averages. In fact it is measuring the potential for two exponential averages to cross, thereby attempting to predict this crossover before it occurs. In this way, MACD can provide a crossover closer to actual price peak or trough. Figure 3.12 shows a chart of the Dow Jones Industrial Average with 12- and 26- period exponential averages and the relevant MACD shown below the chart. At point A, MACD crosses below the signal line suggesting an end to the immediate trend. MACD continues lower to reach point C upon which it starts rising. The two averages actually cross downwards at point B and do not cross upwards again until *after* point C. Clearly MACD has outperformed the average crossover. This situation occurs again at points D and E, and at points F and G. In all three occasions, MACD has correctly anticipated the moving average crossover and prevented the "give-back" of profit—a common problem of following simple crossover of moving averages.

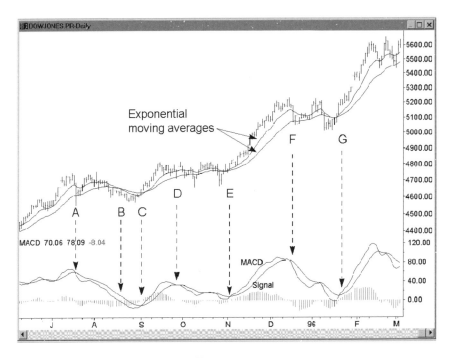

Figure 3.12
Daily Dow Jones Index with 12- and 26-period EMA applied with
MACD, showing how MACD anticipates price reversal ahead of the
moving averages.

It seems that MACD provides the perfect solution for trading. Unfortunately, this is not the case as no single indicator can cover all market conditions. Looking at Figure 3.13, a chart of the Dow Jones Industrial Average, we have sold at point A. A good downtrend is then established and we take profit at point B. Price, however, sees only a brief correction before the main downtrend continues. But look at the two averages. Although the downtrend continues, the speed of the downtrend is not sufficient initially to cause the averages to diverge. Because of this, MACD and the signal continue to rally, reversing lower only at point C where we would have suffered a loss. From there, price declines for a few days only and then sharply rallies. But MACD does not signal a reversal higher until some periods later where we again would have suffered a loss. This situation is repeated between points D and E, and between E and F, where we would have lost money on our trades yet again.

The point here is MACD is measuring the convergence and divergence of two exponential averages. If the trend is not strong *then the averages can diverge even if they are pointing in the same direction* since the speed of the trend is decreasing. In many ways this signals a potential trend reversal and clearly, we can see that a bullish divergence has developed between points B and F.

It can be seen from this last example that MACD, just as with the moving averages themselves, copes badly with rapid price direction changes. As the moving average is a lagging indicator, MACD is therefore a lagging indicator. This is especially true during the consolidation of a particularly volatile market such as the Gold market. An example of this is seen in Figure 3.14 which shows how MACD performs in the Gold market.

Nearly every trade produced a loss, and this is because gold is more volatile than the Dow Jones Index. The Gold market shows reversals that are too rapid for moving averages

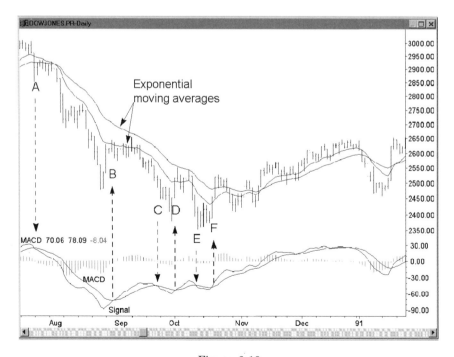

Figure 3.13
Daily Dow Jones Index with 12- and 26-period EMA with MACD. Note how MACD can cause false signals in sustained trends.

which smoothen such quick changes in price. This does not mean that MACD is ineffective, but rather that a trader should pick an indicator with care, bearing in mind in which market he is trading.

PARABOLIC

Parabolic is another of J. Welles Wilder, Jr.'s indicators, created primarily to cope with the large degree of "give-back" which occurs with moving average trading systems. Wilder offered this indicator as both a position-entering system as well as a position-exiting system. It is also known as Stop and Reverse (SAR) and is plotted on top of price.

The formula looks quite complex but is straightforward:

$$SAR = SAR[1] + \{\text{acceleration factor} \times (\text{extreme price} - SAR[1])\}$$

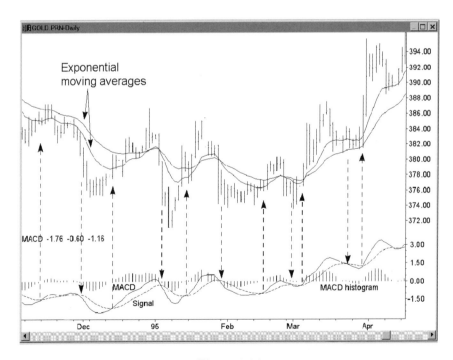

Figure 3.14
*Daily Gold market with MACD applied. Note how MACD signals lag
behind the Gold market's volatile price reversals.*

where: SAR[1] = value of the SAR one period ago
acceleration factor = method of moving the SAR closer to
price in a trend

The formula creates a series of values that moves behind price action until the high (in a downtrend) or the low (in an uptrend) penetrates the parabolic. Effectively, the parabolic can be considered a "stop loss" value that changes every day. Once price penetrates the stop loss, the position is exited and a new position in the opposite direction is established. When this change in direction occurs, the first value of the parabolic is either:

• the highest high in the preceding rally, upon a downward reversal, or

• the lowest low in the preceding decline, upon an upward reversal.

Once the first value of the parabolic is obtained, the SAR formula may be used. The "extreme price" is either the highest high in the rally, or the lowest low in the decline. The acceleration factor begins at a value of 0.02 after the first parabolic in the current position, and then increases by 0.02 each time a new price extreme is recorded, up to a maximum of 0.2. (These are the recommended parameters set by Wilder.)

In this way as prices accelerate (to record new extreme price), the speed at which the parabolic moves with price action will tend to increase, thus making the stop loss tighter. Hence, instead of allowing a position to "give back" large profit, parabolic will accelerate with price action. And as more profit is made, parabolic will protect this profit with an increasingly tighter stop.

In Figure 3.15 we see the progression of price data over a short period of time. To the left of the chart a price low was recorded at 118.05. Three days later, price rallied above the existing parabolic value. Since price has penetrated the parabolic value, its position changes to the extreme low of the previous move lower – 118.05. On this day the market recorded a high of 119.71. The next day the market rallied to a new high of 120.00. The parabolic for the current day is calculated as:

Parabolic = 118.05 + {0.02 × (120.00 − 118.05)} = 118.08

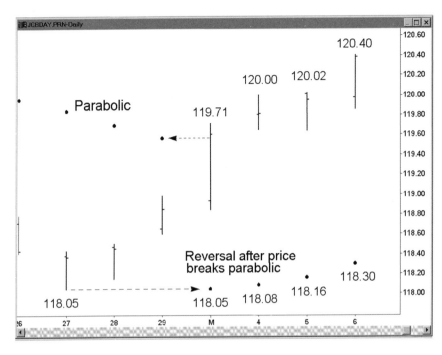

Figure 3.15
Daily Japanese Government Bond Futures market with parabolic applied.

The following day saw a marginal new high at 120.02 that would have made the acceleration factor increase to 0.04 and the parabolic would be calculated as:

Parabolic = 118.08 + {0.04 × (120.02 − 118.08)} = 118.16

Once again, the following day sees a new high to 120.40; the acceleration factor rises to 0.06 and the parabolic would be calculated as:

Parabolic = 118.16 + {0.06 × (120.40 − 118.16)} = 118.30

This calculation would continue to form a series of values. Should the trading day not record a new price high, the acceleration factor would stay at the same level. When acceleration factor reaches 0.20, it remains at that level until price reversal penetrates the parabolic level, and the same process occurs but in the opposite direction.

The parabolic is illustrated in Figure 3.16, a chart of the Japanese Government Bond Futures, which is one of the few markets that still trades well with simple moving average crossover signals. It can be seen at A that parabolic signaled an end to the downtrend much earlier than the moving averages themselves. This situation is more pronounced at B where significant savings would have been achieved. In both situations, parabolic could have been used for both entering and exiting positions, with a good deal of profitability. An additional point to note about moving average crossovers is since they are calculated using the close of each time period, no action can be taken until after the close itself. Therefore the opening price of the next bar should be used to mark trades.

As with all indicators, the parabolic does not provide a universal solution. Figure 3.17 shows the market seen in Figure 3.16 some months later. It shows how the profitable trading strategy becomes a losing strategy in a sideways

Figure 3.16
Daily Japanese Government Bond Futures market with two moving averages and parabolic. Note how parabolic reversals occur earlier than the reversals implied by the moving averages.

market. Like moving averages, parabolic works well in trends but tends to perform badly during consolidation.

Thus, it can be argued that parabolic offers a good exit signal after trends have developed, and should be used in this way rather than as Stop and Reverse. In some markets, a judicial combination of moving averages and parabolic can produce excellent results in trending markets, but this should be avoided in sideways or consolidating markets.

MOVING AVERAGE ENVELOPES

The moving average envelope is not a true momentum indicator. It is introduced at this juncture as it fits in with the general topic of using mathematically derived values in a trading strategy. The concept of envelopes is price tends to vary within a certain percentage of an average price and thus, it is generally possible to suggest that selling at the band high and

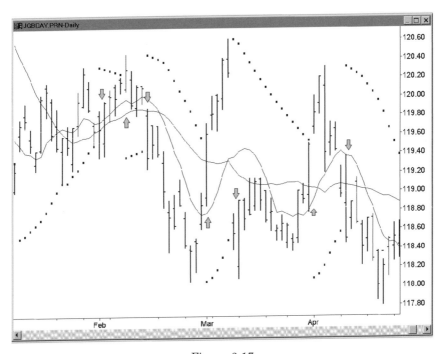

Figure 3.17
Daily Japanese Government Bond Futures market with moving averages and parabolic applied. The arrows indicate reversals implied by the parabolic. Note how parabolic does not perform well in non-trending markets.

buying at the band low will produce profitable results. The bands are calculated in the following manner:

Upper Band = SMA + (SMA × X%)
Lower Band = SMA − (SMA × X%)

where: SMA = Simple Moving Average

Figure 3.18 shows how this would work for the daily US Treasury Bond Futures. A 15-period simple moving average has been used, and around this, two bands have been drawn at 1.25% above and below the moving average. In general, it is seen that price tends to hold this band. It would be possible to trade in the direction of a break in one band. That is, if the higher band is broken, take a long position and continue long until the simple moving average has been penetrated in the opposite direction. Reverse the position only if the opposite band is penetrated. If the other band holds the correction, a further break of the original band would signal a new position.

This strategy works profitably in Figure 3.18 where the market has been trending. Since moving averages work best with a trending market, the results look good.

Figure 3.19 shows a consolidating market. Here the strategy should be to sell at the upper band and buy at the lower band. However, there are instances where one of the bands is penetrated suggesting a trending move, but this quickly reverses. It is possible to use the simple strategy of buying as the market approaches the lower band, then reversing to a short position as it closes below the lower band, thus taking a loss in favor of a trend, but then taking a further loss as price reverses to above the simple moving average.

This situation could have occurred during later stages; the problem here is knowing whether a break of a band confirms a trending move. There are other indicators that mathematically measure the strength of a move in one direction. This will be covered in a later section. Certainly the moving average bands look reasonable if we accept the above problems. This highlights the importance of integrating your analysis techniques.

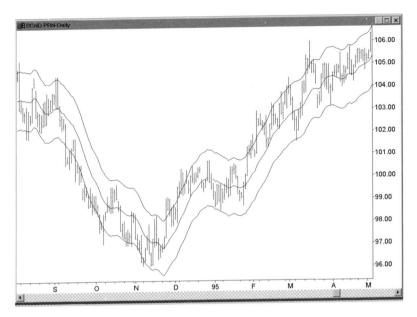

Figure 3.18
Daily US T-Bond Futures market with a 15-period simple moving average
with an upper band of 1.25% (of close) above the average and a lower
band of 1.25% (of close) below the average.

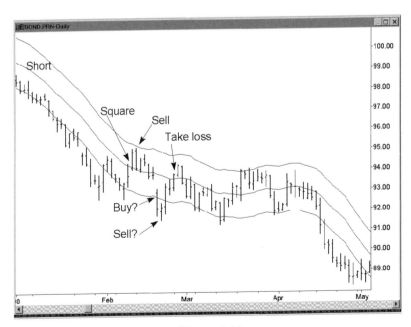

Figure 3.19
Daily US T-Bond Futures market with a trading strategy applied.

BOLLINGER BANDS

Bollinger Bands were introduced to the market by John Bollinger who considered that prices would stay within a certain range dictated by the range of recent price action. In many ways the concept is the same as that of moving average envelopes, except that Bollinger created his bands using standard deviation, a method of measuring volatility. Hence as volatility increases, the bands move wider apart; and as volatility decreases, the bands move closer to each other. Bollinger Bands are calculated as follows:

Upper band = 21-period SMA + (2 × Standard Deviation)
Lower band = 21-period SMA − (2 × Standard Deviation)

where: SMA = Simple Moving Average
Standard Deviation = Standard deviation of price against average over the same period as the moving average

Figure 3.20 shows Bollinger Bands on a chart of the US Treasury Bond Futures market. It can be seen that Bollinger Bands work in a similar manner to moving average envelopes except that the bands here vary in distance away from the moving average. Price remains within the bands during consolidation and frequently provides a barrier for prices as they approach. On the break on either side of the bands, a trend is established. A similar trading strategy can be used but the same advantages and disadvantages can be seen. These dictate that other indicators should be used to confirm or contradict any Bollinger signal.

Bollinger Bands are also an indicator of volatility. If the bands move farther apart, they indicate increasing volatility. If they move closer to each other, they indicate that volatility is decreasing. Hence if price approaches one band while the bands are diverging, there is a strong chance of a trend developing. This would suggest that the initial trade should not be to buy an approach to the lower band as the bands are diverging, but to wait and see whether the lower band is penetrated.

Although the next suggestion is more suited to integrating analysis, I shall include it here as it is about using Bollinger Bands twice. One of the disadvantages of Bollinger Bands is

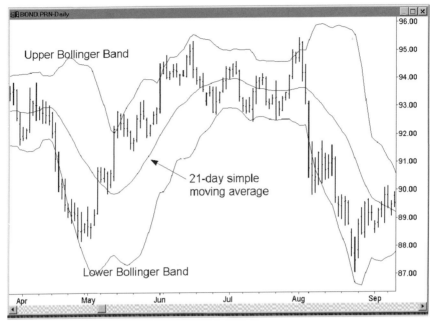

Figure 3.20
Daily US T-Bond Futures market with Bollinger Bands applied.

they do not generally provide good signals at the end of a trend. That is to say, after a trending move there is no early indication of when or where that trending move will end. However, it must be remembered that in many instances traders will be concentrating on their own trading time frame. This may be intraday where the trader tends to look at five-minute or hourly charts, or take a longer view and trade for several days. In each time frame, support and resistance arise. Thus indicators of the next longer time frame should be analyzed to establish where the larger support and resistance lie. Bollinger Bands can help in this respect.

Figure 3.21 shows the daily Gold market. This chart shows two sets of Bollinger Bands. The inner pair is calculated from daily prices, and in several instances these bands are broken and a trend develops. Looking only at these daily bands there is no indication of when price reversal can be expected. The outer (thicker) bands are calculated from weekly prices. When used with the daily bands, a stronger picture of when daily price reversal can be expected is seen.

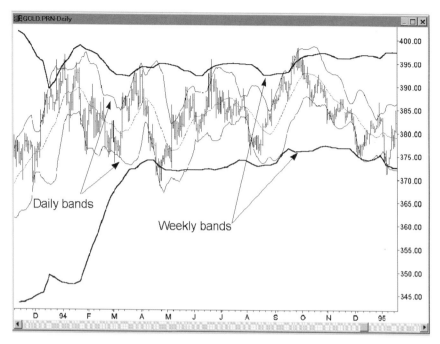

Figure 3.21
Daily Gold market with daily and weekly Bollinger Bands applied.
The weekly bands are in bold.

AVERAGE DIRECTIONAL INDEX

We have covered moving averages and momentum indicators, and concluded that moving averages perform best in trending markets (and badly in consolidating markets) while momentum indicators perform well in consolidating markets (but badly in trending markets). Obviously they should be used in their respective market conditions. But how do we know when a consolidating market has broken sufficiently to change into a trending one? And just when can we judge the end of a trending market? Often we see the break of what we think is an important level and assume that we should see a good move in one direction, only to see it reverse as we enter the market. On the other hand, how often have we seen a correction to a trend and think that the entire move has completed, only to see the trend resume?

These were also questions faced by Wilder. So he devised the Average Directional Index (ADX) to identify a sustained movement in one direction. He did this by first measuring the

directional movement and then dividing it by the true range of
the underlying price. Directional movement indicates the
underlying movement of each day. Figure 3.22 shows how to
calculate directional movement.

Wilder was observing if movement was continuing in one
direction. So he measured the *additional* movement seen in one
day. In Figure 3.22 we see that on Day 1, price saw a range
defined by the bar. On Day 2, price moved to a higher high but
the low of Day 2 was within the range of Day 1. Wilder
considered the degree of movement that was within the
previous day's range unimportant—it was an area of price in
which the market had already traded and therefore provided no
indication of which way the market would move. Wilder
considered that a new area of price implied that price
equilibrium had moved higher. He therefore took the difference
between the high of Day 1 and the high of Day 2 and called this
"positive directional movement".

Figure 3.22 also shows Days 3 and 4 in similar situations
as Days 1 and 2 but with price moving to a lower low. In these
situations, Wilder measured the difference between the lows of
Days 3 and 4 and called it "negative directional movement".
Note that if an outside day (where the current period records
a higher high *and* a lower low than the previous day) is seen,
the larger of the two measurements is taken since this
represents the area of price to which the market was being
attracted. If there is an inside day (where the current period

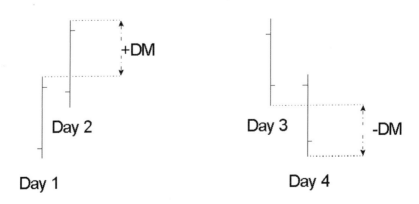

Figure 3.22
Directional movement (DM) – the additional price movement seen outside
the previous day's range.

records a narrower range than the previous day), then there will be "zero directional movement".

Wilder then divided the directional movement (positive, negative, or zero) by the true range for the day. True range is the greater of the following:

(a)   the difference between today's high and low.
(b)   the difference between today's high and yesterday's close.
(c)   the difference between today's low and yesterday's close.

The measurement in (a) is straightforward. The measurements in (b) and (c) are shown in Figure 3.23. Wilder was looking for what he thought was the effective traded range for the day. In Figure 3.23 Day 1 price rises from an open around the day's low and closed towards the high of the day. On Day 2, the market opened *above* the high of Day 1 and continued higher. Wilder considered the fact that when Day 2 opened higher than the high of Day 1, it implied intrinsic strength and therefore, the actual range of trading should be from where prices concluded the previous day to the high of Day 2. Days 3 and 4 are the reverse of Days 1 and 2, and the actual range should therefore be from the conclusion of trading on Day 3 to the low of Day 4.

Dividing directional movement by the true range will give either a positive or negative value that represents a ratio of

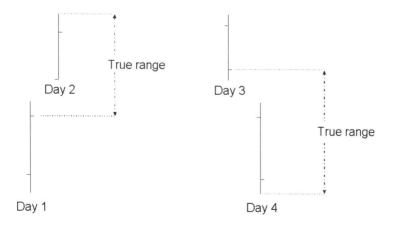

Figure 3.23
Calculation of true range.

additional movement to total movement each day. Over a 14-day period, the positive values are recorded and a running average is calculated—this is called Positive Directional Indicator (+DI). A similar calculation is made for the negative values—this is called Negative Directional Indicator (−DI). The two directional indicators represent an average of how much the market has seen additional movement that has been positive or negative. If there are more occurrences of +DI rather than −DI over the 14-day period, we can deduce that the market should have moved in a positive direction, and vice-versa.

With these values we can calculate the Directional Movement Index.

$$\text{DMI} = \frac{+\text{DI} - (-\text{DI}) \times 100}{+\text{DI} + (-\text{DI})}$$

ADX = 14-day running average of DMI.

The absolute values of DMI and ADX are used. That means that any negative value becomes a positive value. The numerator represents the difference between positive and negative movement (i.e. net movement) while the denominator represents total movement. Thus whenever price travels more in one direction (either upwards or downwards) the numerator becomes larger. We can thus deduce how strong price movement has been in one direction. By taking an average of this, we get a running average of the movement over 14 periods.

A further value called ADXR can be obtained by adding the current day's ADX to that of the previous 14 periods and dividing it by 2. The ADXR represents a slower measurement of ADX and smoothens out some of the volatility in a choppy market. ADXR values of below 20 are considered to be indicative of an extreme non-trending market.

Note that Wilder rounded off the ADX and ADXR values to whole numbers. His experiments showed that this rounding-off produced better results since there were occasions where ADX dropped by a value less than one decimal place and then resumed the previous direction. I have used ADX in many trading systems and have come to exactly the same conclusion.

Wilder's book, *New Concepts in Technical Trading Systems*, gives more detail about applying ADX and ADXR in trading systems. A guideline that I use is when ADX rises above 30 and continues to rise there is a sustained movement in one direction, that is to say, a trend. By looking at whether +DI is above −DI or vice versa, we can mathematically deduce whether it is an uptrend or downtrend. In practice, I find that some markets are intrinsically more volatile than others and so it is safer to assume a lower level of ADX to indicate a trend is developing, while other markets may require ADX higher than 30. This is a matter of personal experience and observation. It is also possible to look at the point when +DI and −DI cross; a positive cross indicates an uptrend and vice versa. It is also important to consider the position and direction of ADX at the crossover. It may also be advisable to wait until ADX begins to rise before assuming that a trend has taken hold.

Now that we understand how ADX is calculated let us look at an example. Figure 3.24 shows the Dow Jones Industrial Index with RSI and ADX. We can break this chart into a series of sections and look at the implications at each point. Point A marks where ADX dipped after having risen above 28. (In the chart, the level of 28 represents a good pivot level for ADX.) If ADX declines further, it implies that the sustained movement has come to an end, either permanently or temporarily. It is therefore better to use momentum indicators at this point. Thus, assuming we had been in a long position, we would exit the position as ADX turned down. At point A, it would not have been advisable to take a short position since RSI was already quite low. However, at point B we see RSI rising from just below the oversold line and by this time, ADX has declined to below 28. We can therefore feel safer with taking a long position at point B.

Although there is a slight dip in RSI a little later after marginally penetrating the overbought level, I would suggest that the decline is not strong enough at that point (imagine an average of RSI that has to be penetrated as a signal). Subsequently, we see price rally to point C where RSI has reversed sufficiently to indicate a reversal while ADX continues to remain below 28. By point D, RSI once again reverses from the oversold level, thus giving a further "buy" signal. By point

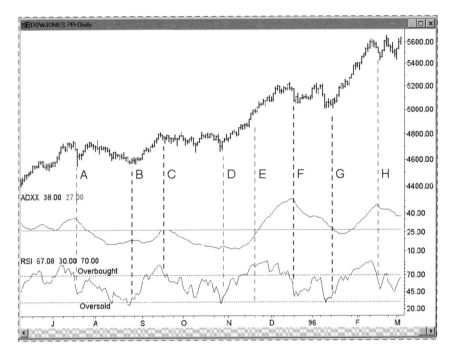

Figure 3.24
Daily Dow Jones Index with RSI and ADX applied.

E, RSI has not reversed significantly while ADX rises once again above 28, thus indicating a trend. We can therefore stay in a long position until ADX declines at point F. Again, a short position is not recommended as RSI is already low at this point (note the bearish divergence at the peak). At point G, RSI reverses sufficiently from the oversold level to go long. By the time we get to overbought on RSI, ADX has once again indicated a trend and we can take profit at point H.

From the illustrations, we can see how well ADX assists in determining whether to use RSI and prevents us from early or late entries and exits. Obviously, as with all indicators, ADX is not perfect. Despite this, it can be a very effective tool in the trader's toolkit—one that allows the trader to squeeze extra points from markets.

CHAPTER 4

Manipulating Pre-programmed Momentum Indicators

In the previous chapter, some of the original and commonly used indicators were described. We must remember that while they change the way the market regards technical analysis, the formulae are not set in stone.

Many analysts have developed new momentum indicators, some of which are based on the original few, while other analysts, such as Tom de Mark, have approached the subject of indicators to help the trader recognize market behavior from a new perspective.

This section will show how to change the indicators found in technical analysis software, such as Omega Research's Supercharts and TradeStation, to enable users to create custom-made indicators.

MOMENTUM

Momentum, a basic form of indicator, gives the difference, in points, between the current period's closing price and that of a number of periods ago. In Chapter 3 we saw that when momentum is rising and above zero, price is usually accelerating higher. And when momentum is declining but still above zero, price is usually still rising but at a slower rate. The converse is true for momentum below zero. We also saw in Chapter 3 that it can be difficult to use momentum as a signal because only one period is observed. Let us consider a combination of three periods to calculate momentum.

$$\text{Combination Momentum} = \frac{\text{Period A momentum} + \text{Period B momentum} + \text{Period C momentum}}{3}$$

By using a combination of three periods, we are considering a more informative picture of momentum. For instance, when price change over 10 days, we are ignoring events of the past, say, 20 or 30 periods. If price is in an uptrend, although there is a correction and the 10-day momentum dips below zero, the upward move may not necessarily be over. By adding the longer-term momentum valuations, it would prevent momentum dropping below zero and signal an uptrend. Similarly, when price acceleration begins to slow down, all three periods of momentum will show signs of a start of reversal. Hence, this type of momentum does not lag greatly in normal markets. Figure 4.1 compares a 10-day momentum with a three-period combination momentum (comprising 5-, 13-, and 34-day momentums). Notice how the combination momentum shows a lower tendency to cross the zero line and keeps to one direction longer.

In a volatile market, the combination momentum measurements reacts more slowly. Hence, a weighted combination momentum may be introduced. In a weighted combination momentum, the shorter-term momentum is multiplied by a weight of three, the longer-term momentum by

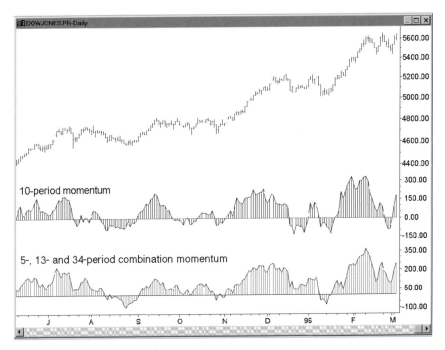

Figure 4.1
Comparison of a single-period momentum with a three-period combination momentum.

a weight of two, and longest-term momentum by a weight of one. The weighted combination momentum is calculated thus:

$$\text{Weighted Combination Momentum} = \frac{\text{Period A momentum} \times 3 + \text{Period B momentum} \times 2 + \text{Period C momentum}}{\text{Total of weights}}$$

A comparison of the simple 10-day momentum, the three-period combination momentum, and the weighted combination momentum is seen on a chart of the Dow Jones Industrial Index in Figure 4.2.

Notice that the weighted combination momentum gives the first signal of weakness at point A, followed by the 10-day momentum and soon after, the three-period combination momentum. While the 10-day momentum shows the reversal at point B slightly earlier than the other two momentum types, the weighted combination momentum is one day ahead of the

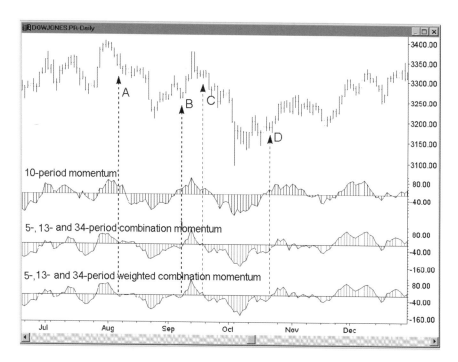

Figure 4.2
Comparison of a single-period, three-period combination, and three-period weighted combination momentums.

combination momentum. This is seen again at points C and D. In conclusion, in this market it can be seen that while the 10-day momentum is occasionally quicker to signal change in direction, the weighted momentum follows closely.

Another example is shown in Figure 4.3, with the three indicators set in a chart of the Hang Seng Index. The 10-day momentum does quite well, but at times signals change too early, while the three-period combination and weighted combination momentums tend to stay with a trend better and therefore signal profit opportunities better. The combination and weighted combination momentums may not work with every market, but they can provide better signals in some markets and are worth considering.

RELATIVE STRENGTH INDEX

The Relative Strength Index (RSI) is probably the most popular indicator used by traders today. To me, this is a reflection of the quality of the ideas of J. Welles Wilder, Jr, combined with the concepts of overbought and oversold, which can be assimilated easily by observing the line generated. But I find that the RSI is often less reliable these days, possibly due to its popularity and because price momentum is not so easily interpreted using this signal. Is there a way of changing this indicator to improve its performance for different markets? Let us look at the basic formula:

$$RSI = 100 - \frac{100}{(1 + RS)}$$

where:
$$RS = \frac{\text{running average of n period's up closes}}{\text{running average of n period's down closes}}$$

n = number of periods used in the calculation

An area we can examine is the reason why Wilder averaged the up and down closes. Wilder's argument was that if the ups and downs were not averaged, the current value of RSI would be affected by the events of the previous n periods. So, if we used a 14-period RSI and one period posted an abnormal increase, the RSI would record a higher value. Then 14 periods later, RSI would show a sharp decrease as the

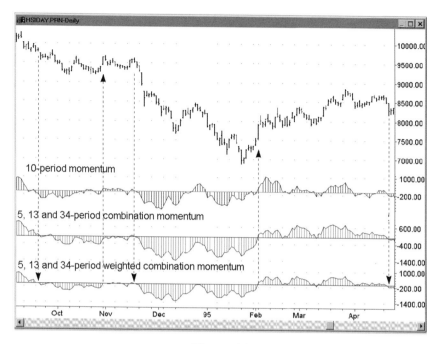

Figure 4.3
Comparison of a single-period momentum with three-period combination
and weighted combination momentums. Note how the weighted
combination momentum stays with the trend slightly better than
the other two momentums.

abnormal up closing price dropped out of the equation and the
other prices moved reasonably during that period. Wilder
argued that we should not get a large rise in value on the first
occasion since it was possible that this would bring an
overbought condition, and if there were further rallies, the RSI
would indicate an overbought position too early.

Another analyst, Stephen Cutler, reasoned differently. In
my interpretation of his reasoning if we use a period that is
half the length of the underlying cycle to measure RSI, then
time has an important influence on price. Thus, assuming we
have chosen the correct period length for RSI, the fact that it
declines when using the cycle-related period is important.

Using Cutler's principle, we can reconstruct RSI without
averaging the up and down closes but by using the sum of the
up and down closes over the period of measurement. The
outcome is shown on a chart of the US dollar–Japanese yen

currency market in Figure 4.4, which also shows Wilder's RSI of the same period length. Both Wilder's and Cutler's RSIs have been calculated for a period of 14 days as there is a strong underlying $27\frac{1}{2}$-day cycle in this market.

Note how Cutler's RSI tends to reach overbought and oversold levels more accurately than Wilder's RSI although Cutler's RSI tends to reverse to the other extreme quickly too. But remember that ADX should be used with RSI to determine when to utilize the extreme readings of the RSI. Despite this, Cutler's RSI will certainly make trading decisions clearer in most cases. Another example, seen in Figure 4.5, shows the two RSIs in the weekly US dollar–Japanese yen currency market. Since a 44-week cycle can be observed in that market, a 22-period length is used to calculate Cutler's RSI. Note how Cutler's RSI tends to reach extremes more frequently than Wilder's RSI. In fact, during the decline from 160.20 in April 1990, Wilder's RSI never reached overbought levels while Cutler's RSI reached these levels on three occasions.

Figure 4.6 shows the Dow Jones Index from late 1987 to start-1988 and includes the October 1987 crash. A 13-period

Figure 4.4
Comparison of Cutler's RSI and Wilder's RSI.

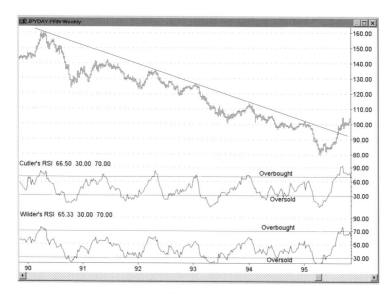

Figure 4.5
Comparison of how Cutler's RSI reaches overbought levels regularly in the
long decline from the 160.20 peak in 1990 while Wilder's RSI fails to
provide such readings.

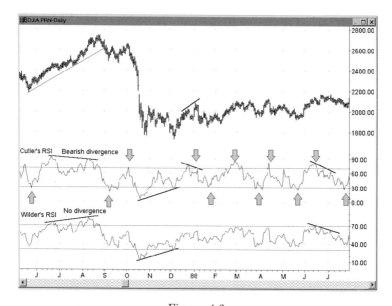

Figure 4.6
Daily Dow Jones Industrial Average with both Cutler's RSI and Wilder's
RSI applied. Note how Cutler's RSI forms a bearish divergence before the
October 1987 crash, and during the subsequent consolidation, regularly
reached overbought and oversold levels.

length is used to calculate Wilder's and Cutler's RSIs, and the difference between them is quite pronounced. Note the number of occasions when Cutler's RSI reached the classic overbought/ oversold extremes, even at the corrective high just before the crash, when Wilder's RSI did not. Both RSIs displayed a bullish divergence at the absolute low. But Cutler's RSI signaled a bearish divergence on the subsequent rally, the first peak in Cutler's RSI rising above the overbought zone whereas Wilder's RSI failed to approach this zone. Subsequent price action till July 1988 shows how Cutler's RSI continued to outperformWilder's RSI.

Figure 4.7 shows another example of how Cutler's RSI outperforms Wilder's RSI, in the US 30-Year Bond Futures contract market. Note how Cutler's RSI regularly returned to the oversold extreme during the uptrend, seen to the right of the chart. Slightly to the right of center, Cutler's RSI also formed a bearish divergence while Wilder's RSI merely moved to a new high.

The fact that Cutler's RSI can outperform the original RSI does not imply that Wilder's formula is incorrect or that it is no longer applicable. It does, however, highlight that with the increased use of common analytical indicators, the effect of these indicators may be diluted with time. More importantly, it demonstrates that although Wilder's original concept shows great insight, there is no reason why his formula should be cast in stone or that other derivatives should not be considered. I believe that minor changes in formulae that reflect the underlying nature of markets can often bring new powerful signals.

There are many other ways of changing the calculation of RSI, all of which would change the final appearance though the basic structure stays the same. Readers may wish to experiment with different styles for the market in which they trade. It is possible, for instance, to take a simple average of the ups and downs, or take an average price of (High + Low + Close)/3 for the measurement instead of the close value. It is also possible to create an RSI of the highs or the lows, and compare the two. Basically, there are no hard and fast rules. The basic theory behind RSI provides a valuable clue to trading. All that is needed is experimentation to develop a suitable value on which to work the RSI formula.

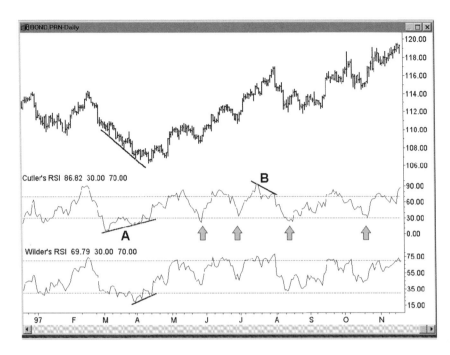

Figure 4.7
Daily US T-Bond Futures market with Cutler's RSI and Wilder's RSI
applied. Note how Cutler's RSI gives a stronger signal at A with a
pronounced bullish divergence, and also displayed a bearish divergence at
B. This is not seen in Wilder's version. It can also be seen how Cutler's
RSI regularly returns to the oversold level in the long uptrend.

STOCHASTICS

There are a few ways of changing stochastics, mainly to slow the signal. First, let us recap George Lane's formula for calculating stochastics.

$$K\% = \frac{100 \times (\text{Close} - \text{Lowest low for n periods})}{\text{Highest high for n periods} - \text{Lowest low for n periods}}$$

In one of Lane's derivations, K% was slowed down to give D%. This is done by taking the 3-period sum of the numerator of K% and dividing by the 3-period sum of the denominator. This was slowed even further to obtain SlowD% by taking a 3-period simple moving average of D%. The underlying concept was to see the closing price of the current period near the top of the recent range in an upward move and near the low of the recent range in a downward move. Stochastics oscillate between values of zero and 100, with 80 and 20 representing overbought and oversold levels respectively.

The basic calculation for K% represents the concept of stochastics. K% measures the current price in relation to the recent range. The calculations of D% and SlowD% are methods of slowing the K% signal to a less volatile line. We can also slow K% in other ways. For instance, it is possible to calculate D% by using the exponential moving average of K%. The outcome of this is shown in Figure 4.8 in the weekly US dollar–Japanese yen currency market. I have used one-quarter of the cycle length of a period of 11 weeks. Region A shows where Lane's stochastics has more crossovers than the alternative version of stochastics. The effect of using an exponential moving average often delays the crossover until a better signal is achieved. Although only one such region is highlighted in Figure 4.8, looking at the rest of the chart situations similar to A can be found on many other occasions. This would trigger fewer false signals than Lane's stochastics.

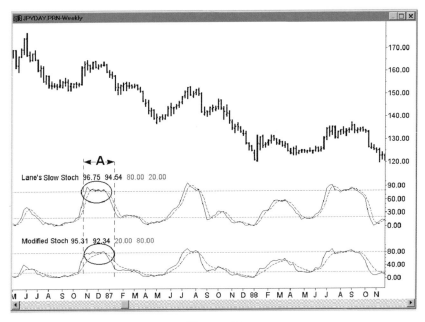

Figure 4.8
Comparison of Lane's stochastic and an alternative version.

However, the indicators created from this method of slowing down are still volatile. There is yet another method of slowing down the signal to give a more flowing indicator with fewer crossovers. By slowing the original value for D% using a simple moving average, a smoother line is achieved. Then using a short simple average of this derivative, a signal line can be created. This is shown in Figure 4.9 of a weekly chart of the Japanese Government Bond Futures contract market. The upper stochastics shown at the bottom of the figure is Lane's original version while the lower stochastics shows the new derivative.

Figure 4.10 shows the US dollar–German Deutschmark currency market in a rally from the end of 1992 to the beginning of 1993. While the initial rally, from its start to the 1.6175 high, would have caused ADX to rise, the subsequent wedge-type rally would have caused a dip in ADX and encouraged the use of momentum indicators. Using Lane's D% and SlowD%, there would have been several occasions where whipsaws could have confused the signals. However, by smoothing SlowD%, we would arrive at the higher of the two stochastics shown. Note how these smoother stochastics suit such a market by reversing very close to the market extremes. In fact, this form of stochastics performs exceptionally well during this period by providing a number of accurate signals.

However, in a volatile market, these slower forms of stochastics tend to lag behind price action, causing whipsaws as they fail to react quickly enough to market reversals.

Figure 4.11 shows the Japanese Government Bond Futures market with two alternative stochastics applied. The upper stochastics chart consists of a five-period D% and a SlowD% that is an exponential moving average of D%. The lower stochastics chart also consists of a five-period D% but with the SlowD% calculated using Lane's formula. Notice how the exponentially-calculated SlowD% is slow to react and often lags behind the D% line, causing a late signal. On the other hand, Lane's SlowD% tends to stay close to the D% line, thus providing earlier signals.

Thus there is no single solution to the type of stochastics that should be used. A better approach would be to use different types of stochastics depending on the market characteristic at the time. One method would be to use slower stochastics in trending markets to avoid early signals, and

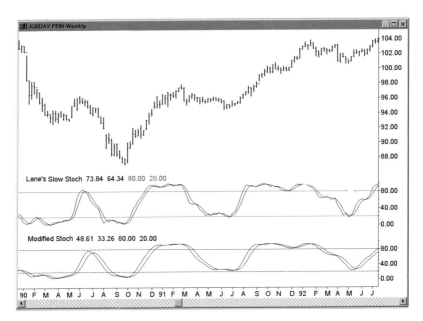

Figure 4.9
Lane's slow stochastics compared to a slower version calculated
with moving averages.

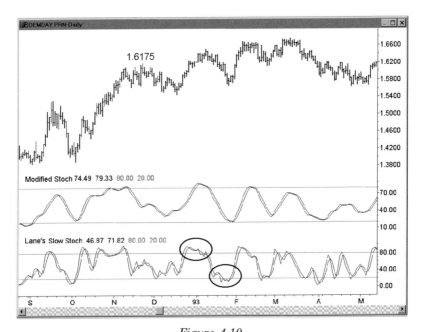

Figure 4.10
Comparison of slow stochastics (created using the moving average) of D%
and Lane's D% and SlowD%.

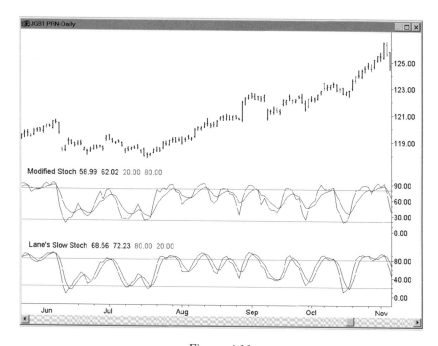

Figure 4.11
Comparison of Lane's D% and SlowD%, and slow stochastics created using an exponential moving average of D%. Note how the EMA-created SlowD% tends to lag behind Lane's D% by a margin larger than the lag of Lane's SlowD% behind D%.

shorter-term stochastics when a corrective market is anticipated.

MOVING AVERAGE CONVERGENCE AND DIVERGENCE

The MACD is a popular tool because it uses moving averages. However, just as moving averages are most profitable during trending markets, MACD generally performs better during trends. As moving averages suffer from weaknesses, so, too, does the MACD. MACD tends to be a lagging indicator and in order to provide a good signal, it needs to see the market consolidation before reversing trend. This will allow the signal line to follow upwards, behind the MACD line, and then crossover towards the high of the market. Unfortunately, it is common for the market to reverse quickly, resulting in "give back" of profit being common. It can also cause whipsaws during particularly volatile markets, especially during consolidation when market conditions often become confused with strong and conflicting opinions and sharp reversals. Hence, the opposite trend is normally established before any reversal signal is given.

Figure 4.12 demonstrates these problems on a chart of the US dollar–German Deutschmark currency market. MACD with the standard default of 12- and 26- period exponential moving averages has been applied. The chart shows approximate buying and selling levels implied by the crossover of the MACD line over the signal line. In most cases, the market reverses quite a considerable way before the crossover occurs. This can cause poor profitability at the very least, and possibly a loss-making situation over the length of the trading period.

So how can we change MACD to provide a more timely signal? Let us recall the formula for MACD.

MACD = Short-term EMA – Long-term EMA
Signal = EMA of MACD

where: EMA = Exponential Moving Average

Calculating further,

Fast MACD = MACD – Signal.
Fast Signal = Exponential average of Fast MACD.

This is a commonly used indicator and analysts refer to it by various names, including MACD Histogram, (as referred to by Alexander Elder). It provides a signal more sensitive to changes in price direction. Therefore, it can assist in identifying and taking advantage of reversals much earlier. As with any indicator, it has its drawbacks and these should be understood. Since we are creating a more sensitive indicator it can suggest a reversal of price direction a little too early— crossing higher (or lower) only to see the original trend continue. However, with a little care and analysis with other indicators, MACD signals can prove timely and provide more profit opportunities.

Figure 4.13 shows the same chart as seen in Figure 4.12 with the addition of the Fast MACD. We see that the Fast

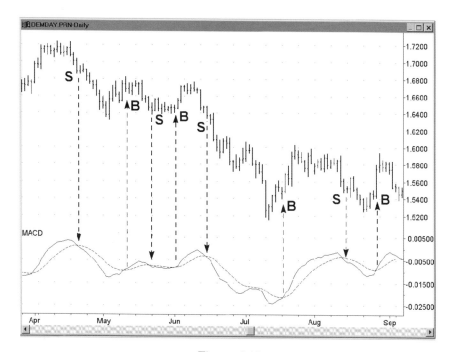

Figure 4.12
Buy and sell signals generated from MACD crossover.

MACD frequently outperforms the ordinary MACD except where price action develops in the middle of the chart. Notice how the Fast MACD has signaled an earlier start (than the ordinary MACD) to the downtrend but suffers a little whipsaw during the overall downtrend as it was too sensitive to the brief correction. Once again at the end of the downtrend it provides a more timely reversal higher.

The Fast MACD on its own, as with all technical indicators, is insufficient to provide consistent results. But when used with a combination of analytical tools, it can prove valuable in pinpointing price reversal in a timely manner.

RELATIVE SPREAD STRENGTH.

Relative Spread Strength (RSS) is an indicator that I created when I moved to Japan where I noticed a number of traders using moving averages as their main source of technical signals. I have never been comfortable using moving averages since my early days as an analyst when I made several bad

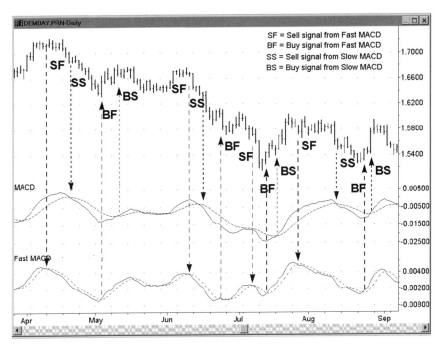

Figure 4.13
Comparison of signals generated by MACD and by the fast MACD.
SF = Sell signal from Fast MACD.
BF = Buy signal from Fast MACD.
SS = Sell signal from Slow MACD.
BS = Buy signal from Slow MACD.

miscalculations trying to apply them. But there are many traders who make good profits from using moving averages. From that perspective, moving averages should be considered.

Fully aware of the slowness of moving averages, I set out to create an indicator that would signal the crossovers and therefore allow me to anticipate the Japanese traders' actions.

I began by calculating the spread between two moving averages. I was trying to find a method of anticipating the strength of how moving averages moved apart or together. So I decided to pass the spread through the RSI formula, the idea being that I would be measuring the strength of the degree of the spread. The outcome was averaged over three periods to smoothen the resultant indicator, the RSS.

Figure 4.14 illustrates the RSS. Notice that the RSS runs smoothly in a range between zero and 100 (essentially an RSI range) and matches the broad swings in price action. While there are no specific buy or sell signals, my guideline is: when RSS rallies above 80, traders should look for reasons to sell, and when RSS falls to below 20, traders should look for reasons to buy. This may sound slightly vague but it falls in with the topic of this book on integrating analysis.

The chart in Figure 4.14 shows the weekly US dollar–Japanese yen currency market. Generally when RSS is above 80, the daily chart should be observed for signs of potential reversal. Similarly the daily chart should be consulted when RSS falls below 20. More of this will be covered on integrating analysis.

Figures 4.15 and 4.16 show two more examples of RSS, in the Japanese Government Bond Futures market (where moving averages are used heavily) and the Hang Seng Index. From observation, RSS works best on longer-term charts that are less affected by short-term speculation, and so reflects the larger and more basic swings in investor sentiment. After experimenting with several period lengths of moving averages, I find that lengths of 10 and 40 periods appear to give good results over a broad range of markets where moving averages are used heavily.

STANDARD DEVIATION BANDS

Standard deviation bands were introduced by John Bollinger and are commonly called Bollinger Bands. The bands are calculated thus:

Upper band = 21-period SMA + (2 × Standard Deviation)
Lower band = 21-period SMA − (2 × Standard Deviation)

where: SMA= Simple Moving Average
            Standard Deviation = Standard deviation of price against average over the same period as the moving average

With a little thought, other ideas that use the concept of standard deviation can be generated. Bollinger Bands use a constant number of standard deviation—generally around two. A single standard deviation has a probability of containing 65%

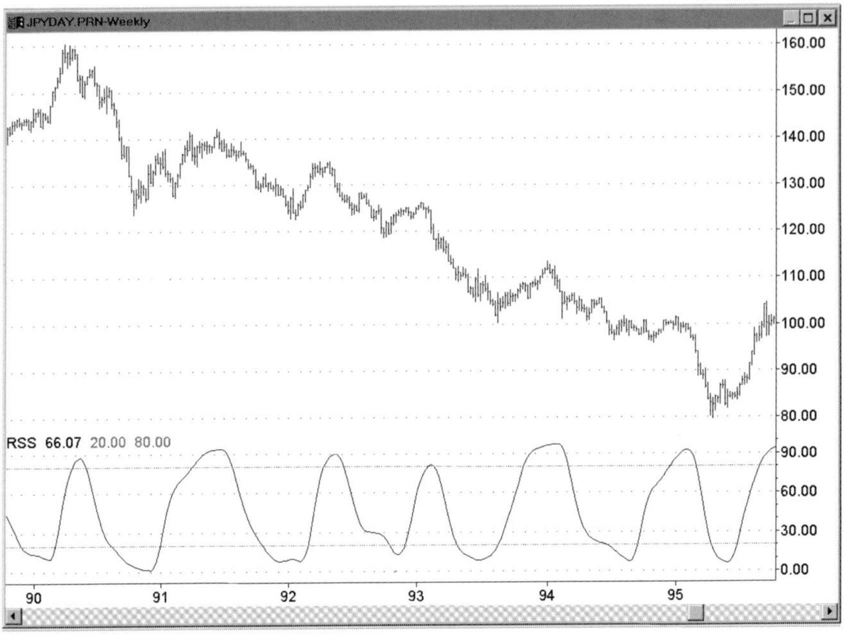

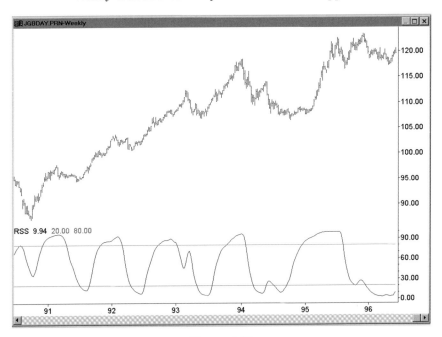

Figure 4.14
Weekly USDJPY currency market with RSS applied.

Figure 4.15
Weekly Japanese Government Bonds Futures market with RSS applied.

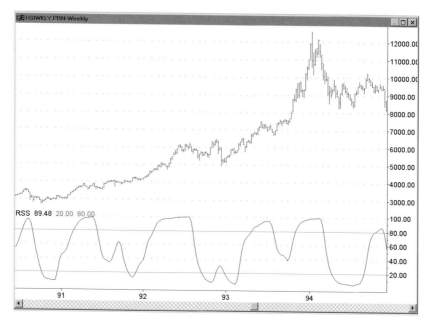

Figure 4.16
Weekly Hang Seng Index with RSS applied.

of subsequent price movement while two standard deviations has a probability of containing 90% of subsequent price movement.

Markets, however, are dynamic and their volatility changes constantly. We can, therefore, devise a method of changing the number of standard deviations used. So in consolidating markets, we can reduce the number of standard deviations to less than two and in volatile markets, we can increase the number of standard deviations. Wilder had his own form of measuring volatility—Average True Range. True range was explained in the section Average Directional Index in Chapter 3. Average true range is the average of the true ranges over a chosen period. We then use average true range to construct bands on either side of a moving average. Price lies between these bands most of the time.

If we measure average true range as a percentage of underlying price, we obtain an average percentage variance from an average price. This percentage generally varies between 1.5% and 2.5% depending on volatility. Using this average percentage variance in the calculation of standard deviation, we derive standard deviation bands that vary with the volatility of the market. When the market is quiet, the bands will move closer to price. When the market is more volatile, the bands will move away from price action.

Figure 4.17 illustrates this on the Japanese Nikkei-225 Index. At first glance, the bands do not offer much guidance to the trader—price breaks above the bands in an upward move and vice versa. But the bands do give an earlier signal of when price is moving in the opposite direction. What we need to do is attempt to approximate the limits of these price breaks above and below the bands. My idea then was to add Bollinger Bands (being a deviation of price from a central moving average) as a standard measure of extreme price movements.

Figure 4.18 shows the addition of Bollinger Bands (in bold lines) and bands calculated from percentage variance (in thin lines). The outer bands (Bollinger Bands) provide a better indication of extreme price as at point A, while the inner bands (percentage bands) give an earlier indication of price reversal

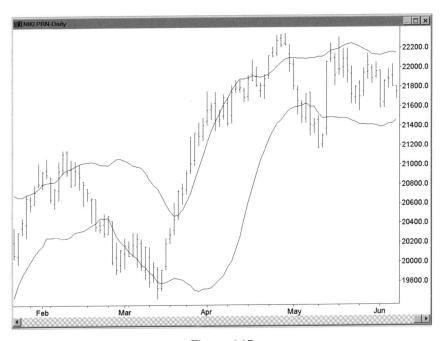

Figure 4.17
Daily Japanese Nikkei Index with standard deviation bands applied.
The value of the deviation varies according to the average true range
as a percentage of price.

as at points B and C. Moveover, observe that during the rally from the low just before point C to where price broke the inner bands, the percentage bands tend to contain price lows in an aggressive move higher. As the momentum of the rally decreased, price retraced to levels that dipped lower than the percentage bands, as at point D.

I also attempted to find a method of drawing bands that would contain price at these times. I experimented with some ideas and developed retracement bands which were calculated using the values I had obtained earlier. I took the spread between the two sets of bands (Bollinger bands and inner bands) and made two calculations. First, the Low Spread was added to the lower inner band, and the Low Spread was subtracted from the base moving average. The maximum value of the two was chosen. Second, I subtracted the High Spread from the higher inner band and added the High Spread to the base moving average. The minimum value of the two was chosen. The calculations are as follows:

Bollinger Bands

Upper = Average(Close, 21) + Standard Deviation(Close, 21) × 2
Lower = Average(Close, 21) − Standard Deviation(Close, 21) × 2

Percentage Deviation Bands (Inner bands)

Band High = Average(Close, 21) +
               Standard Deviation(Close, 21) × X
Band Low = Average(Close, 21) −
               Standard Deviation(Close, 21) × X

where: X = Average({100 × Average True Range[21]/Close}, 7)

Retracement Bands

Upper = Min {[Average(Close, 21) + High Spread],
           [Band High − High Spread]}
Lower = Max {[Average(Close, 21) − Low Spread],
           [Band Low + Low Spread]}

The retracement bands are drawn in dotted lines in Figure 4.19. The rejection of price at point A is a safer call since we had already seen price dipping further just before it had

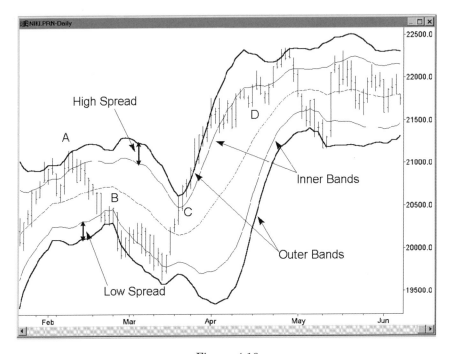

Figure 4.18
Daily Japanese Nikkei Index with two sets of standard deviation bands.
The outer bands (bold lines) are Bollinger Bands while the inner bands
(thin lines) are those calculated by a variable deviation seen in Figure
4.17. A moving average (dashed line) has also been applied.

penetrated the higher retracement band. As price declined from
point A through both retracement bands down to the lower
Bollinger Band (bold line), we see retracements contained by
the dotted line at B and the lower Bollinger Band tested for
several days. Subsequently, a rally began from close to the
lower Bollinger Band, penetrating the first retracement line,
signaling an end to the decline. Upon penetration of the inner
band at C, we look for the potential for further moves higher.
As the rally continued through the upper Bollinger Band,
retracements were contained by the inner band until, as
momentum slowed, the inner band was penetrated but
contained by the higher retracement line. While this higher
retracement line remained untouched we can imply that
further moves higher would be seen. This eventually occurred,
and only when the higher retracement line was broken did we
see a deeper correction to the lower bands.

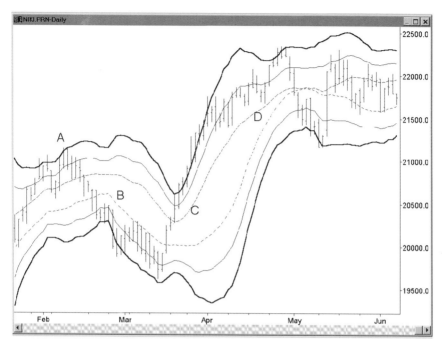

Figure 4.19
Daily Japanese Nikkei Index with the same bands as in Figure 4.18 and
retracement bands (dashed lines).

Now, there are a set of guidelines for these bands. To check that they work effectively we should look at another section of price action to test their validity. Figure 4.20 shows the period of price action preceding Figure 4.19. We see situations similar to Figure 4.19 during this period. At point A, notice that the lower band has been penetrated, and we are, therefore, looking at a short position. However, in retrospect we know this would have made losses. Can we spot this at an early point? In the previous example (Figure 4.19), a break of the upper Bollinger Band saw an aggressive rally which was contained by the inner band. Can we suggest that once the outer band is penetrated we require the inner band to remain intact to maintain our position? If we had taken this strategy in Figure 4.20 we would have made a small loss at point A and again at point B, but one bar later we would have entered a good trending move that was initially contained by the higher inner band. Then, as the trend was established we saw a correction that was contained by the higher retracement band

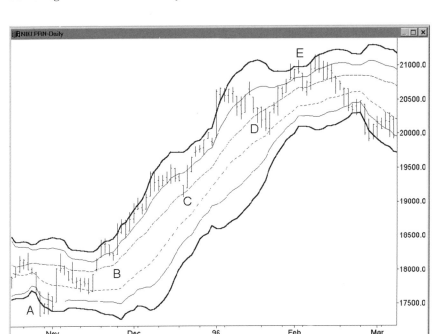

Figure 4.20
*Daily Japanese Nikkei Index with the same bands as in Figure 4.19, but
shown on a different section of price.*

at point C, and the trend continue. At point D we see that the
upper retracement band was penetrated and we would have
taken profit at this point. However, the move was contained by
the lower retracement band and this was a suggestion that as
price reaches the outer bands once again we could establish a
short position since the momentum of the trend had
deteriorated. This short position would have been taken at
point E and after a minor new high, we saw price reverse
through the inner band, both retracement bands, to move
towards the lower Bollinger Band. Price then holds below the
lower retracement band.

Now that we have put together an idea that appears to
work well in one market, we should test it on another market
to see if the same logic applies to other markets. Figure 4.21
shows the Dow Jones Index between October 1995 and March
1996. This chart has the same three sets of bands used in
Figure 4.20. In addition weekly Bollinger Bands are also drawn
in. The chart begins with a narrow trading range. Price has

bounced between the daily Bollinger Bands, which is based on price high and low, with a rally from the bands at point A. At this point there is no other indication that profits will be seen above the upper daily Bollinger Band. However, the band is tested at point B, with support supplied by the upper retracement band. We then see price penetrate the upper daily Bollinger Band at point C. As price rallied the uptrend was contained once again by the upper inner band until penetration at point D. This would have given a good opportunity to secure some of the profits of a long position. Price was then supported by the lower inner bands around point E. A small consolidation is seen before a decline to the lower daily Bollinger Band at point F. Since we have seen the weekly Bollinger Band resistance broken (also at point C), the potential for further profits is anticipated and therefore a rally from point F is a safer forecast. This was confirmed after the penetration of the upper retracement band at point G and the subsequent rally being supported by the upper inner band. This support was broken at point H.

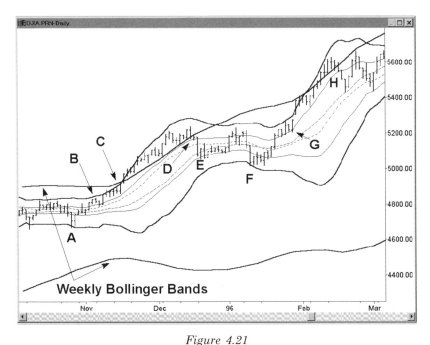

Figure 4.21
Daily Dow Jones Industrial Average with the same set of bands applied as in Figure 4.20, but with the addition of weekly Bollinger Bands.

Figure 4.22 shows the subsequent price development. It shows the break of the upper inner band at point H and the resultant decline to the upper retracement band at point 1, followed by a rally to a new minor high, but contained by the weekly Bollinger Band. Given the greater volatility, the rejection from the upper weekly Bollinger Band was again a safer call, and it can be seen that a longer correction has resulted. Within this longer sideways move I have counted the number of times the bands have provided highly accurate levels from which a reaction can be anticipated. While a new minor high was seen after penetration of the daily Bollinger Band at point 13, a rapid penetration of the upper inner band signaled an end to this, and a retracement to the inner band and retracement band is seen at point 14. The correction continued until we finally see price test the lower weekly Bollinger Band at point 16. Although the subsequent price action is not shown in Figure 4.22, the break at point 16 indeed provoked a new rally above the weekly Bollinger Resistance.

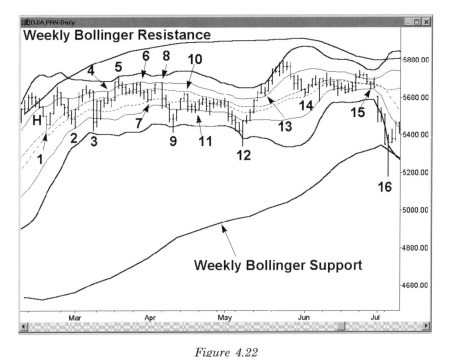

Figure 4.22
Daily Dow Jones Industrial Average with the three sets of bands as in Figure 4.21 and weekly Bollinger Bands applied to a period of consolidation.

From the examples seen in Figures 4.21 and 4.22, we see that these bands appear to work well for both the Nikkei and the Dow Jones Indexes. They may not work on other markets but other parameters can be developed to form a trading strategy. What I hope to have achieved by this exercise is to demonstrate the method of developing ideas that others have used and creating indicators that prove more useful to the markets being analysed. As the standard indicators are found on all technical analysis software, other traders are looking at the same signals. Manipulating these ideas and developing new derivatives of these standard indicators can often give you the edge over the other players in the market.

MOMENTUM BANDS

Momentum Bands is another one of my ideas. It was developed in a background of traditional technical analysis, with specific techniques of measurement in terms of price repetition. What I wanted to achieve was a graphical representation of traditional analytical techniques along with those specific techniques which suited my own outlook on price behavior.

Let us begin with a few observations of various analytical techniques:-

- Support or resistance, when revisited, will provide support or resistance again.
- In reaction to events, market behavior tends to repeat itself.
- Price behaves in two ways—it forms trends (uptrends or downtrends) or it consolidates.

These logical observations form some of the basic tenets of technical analysis. The market tends to "remember" where profits or losses were made, and these are frequently at support and resistance levels where a break has caused a fresh trend to develop. Patterns are a reflection of collective market attitude—a general repetition of excess at market extremes causing reversal patterns or confusion in continuation patterns. Finally, a basic fact—the market either trends or consolidates.

Let us also consider typical market phrases that represent the attitudes or emotions of market participants:

- The trend is your friend.
- Prices have gone too far, too fast.
- Price action is stuck in a range.

These phrases may be considered clichés but they actually represent the thoughts of traders and other market participants. In an attempt to take this line of thought further, let me declare that one of my favorite forms of analysis, in spite of all its debatable strengths and weaknesses, is the Elliott Wave Principle. Without describing the concepts in any depth (the Elliott Wave Principle, is covered in Chapter 5), we can identify some points that most traders will acknowledge:

- Price behavior develops either as a trend or correction.
- Price behavior develops in recognizable sequences (or patterns). In Elliott Wave terms, this will be as five-wave trending moves or as three-wave corrections (or a series of three-wave corrective moves.)
- Price movements have a tendency to be equal in length.

My objective for developing Momentum Bands therefore was to represent these thoughts in their entirety and in a measurable manner, and to develop a graphical way of displaying the market reactions and emotions as represented by these various statements. Let us now consider the various aspects of market behavior and how they are traditionally measured.

Basic Price Behavior

Trends

A trend is a sustained movement in one direction, frequently initiated by a break in consolidation and often accompanied by a breach of a support or resistance level. Perhaps the most common measurement of a trend is the moving average, though the actual period of the average may differ with various markets and, indeed, may differ between different trending moves in the same market.

Consolidation

Consolidation is a period of general volatile price behavior, accompanied frequently by either strong conflicting opinions among market participants or general confusion over price direction. Clear support and resistance levels often develop during periods of consolidation. The favored tool to measure price behavior during consolidation is momentum or a derivative of momentum.

Resistance

Resistance is a level that price finds difficult to penetrate during an upward move. Resistance may cause a complete reversal in price movement or a pause, sometimes a series of pauses, before the upward move continues. There is no favored tool to measure resistance, though a calculation of recent highs would be the most accurate representation.

Support

Support is the opposite of resistance with a similar but converse occurrence; a level that price finds difficult to breach during a downward move. Support is best represented by a calculation of recent lows.

Calculation of Momentum Bands

- Add the respective highest price for five periods and for 13 periods, then divide the result by 2. This represents average resistance in the recent past.
- Add the lowest price for five periods and for 13 periods, then divide the result by 2. This represents average support in the recent past.
- Add the average resistance and support and divide the total by 2. This represents an "equilibrium" around which the market has traded. It is also a form of moving average, a trend indicator.
- Measure the five-period momentum (price change) and register the largest positive and the largest negative movements seen during this time frame for the past 13 periods. This represents the largest upward and downward movements the market has been comfortable with recently.
- Calculate the smallest five-period momentum seen during the past eight periods, whether positive or negative. This

represents a form of "nervousness" in reaction to larger trending moves.

Note that the periods used for these calculations are Fibonacci numbers (which are discussed in Chapter 5).

With these results I have created the following bands:

Corrective Resistance (CR)

The average of recent   +   the smallest five-period
highs   momentum

Trend Resistance (TR)

The equilibrium + the largest positive momentum

Corrective Support (CS)

The average of recent   −   the smallest five-period
support   momentum

Trend Support (TS)

The equilibrium − the largest negative momentum

Note that calculations for the previous period are made based on the previous period's values but are plotted one period ahead so that their values are not affected by the current period's price action.

Use of Momentum Bands

If a market is correcting in an otherwise larger trend, we would not expect price action to retrace further than the CR and CS. Hence, if we break through one of these levels it suggests that the market may be trending. While we are trending, we would not expect the market to retrace more than the extent of the largest positive (or negative) momentum from the equilibrium (i.e. TR and TS).

Figure 4.23 shows the Dow Jones Industrial Average with the weekly chart on the left and the daily chart on the right. The thinner bands in both charts are the Trend Support/ Resistance bands while the thicker bands are the Corrective Support/ Resistance bands. As with every other analytical

method, always consider charts of different time frames—if
there is a break of daily support or resistance, refer to the
weekly chart to see where the next larger support or resistance
lies. This principle applies to Momentum Bands too.

We begin our analysis of Figure 4.23 with the test of CR
at point A on both the daily and weekly charts. Resistance is
represented by both the weekly and daily CRs. There is a great
deal of movement sideways that is broadly held by CS before
price rallies and breaks both the weekly and daily CRs at point
B. This break of recent weekly and daily resistance suggests
that we should see the resumption of an uptrend. We should,
therefore, examine the daily TS for signs of the trend ending.
TS works well, rising behind price and providing support
around point C before stalling at point D. This type of pattern,
where price makes a small correction then continues the trend
to retest the CR and rejection, is common at trend reversals. It

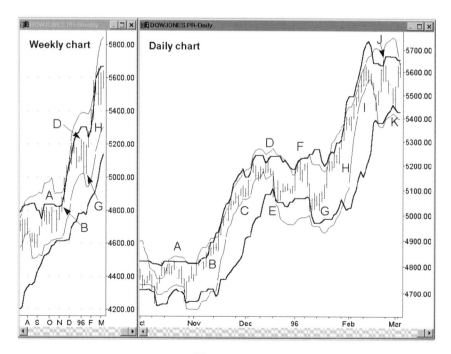

Figure 4.23
*Weekly Dow Jones Industrial Index shown on the left with the daily index
shown on the right. Both charts have Momentum Bands applied. The bold
lines represent Corrective Support and Resistance while the thin lines
represent Trend Support and Resistance.*

would be good at this juncture to look for bearish divergence in momentum indicators to confirm our analysis.

After rejection at point D we see the break of TS, and a swift decline to test and marginally break below the CS at point E. This is followed by a retest and rejection of the CR at point F, followed by a second decline, down to point G. This once again produces a marginal breach of CS. But notice on the weekly chart how this corresponds with the weekly CS holding at point G and then we see a further move higher. This rally breaks both the weekly and daily CRs at point H. We can now anticipate a further rally and therefore watch the daily TS again. We finally see breach of the daily TS at point I, which suggests that we will see a test of the daily CS. After a second test of CR at point J we see a decline to point K on the daily CS. This has held and price then retests the daily CR. Note that we still have not seen the breach of the weekly TS, and until this occurs we should consider the larger trend to be higher. Risk therefore favors the next test of the daily CR to succeed and the daily uptrend continue.

Within this picture, we should remember that the intraday chart should be consulted and that Momentum Bands work within this time frame. Thus it can be seen that Momentum Bands tend to show graphically the underlying momentum picture by highlighting areas of support and resistance in all time frames.

Figure 4.24 shows a similar situation in the US 30-Year Bond Yield. Both weekly and daily charts start with the test of the weekly and daily CRs at point A. Following this, we see a test of the daily CS, brief rejection, then breach to confirm further softness. This softness continues lower, controlled by the daily TR, which sees rejection at B. By this time we have also seen breach of the weekly CS and thus the potential for further weekly losses. Soon after point B, we see a break above the daily TR, implying a test towards the daily CR. But while price remains below the weekly TR we shall remain bearish. CR is tested at point C and rejected, causing the downtrend to resume with the breach of the daily CS. We then look at the daily TR to control price and this occurs around point D, but soon after breaks, suggesting a move back to the daily CR—this occurs at point E, which also corresponds to a test of the weekly TR. Another move lower tests CS again causing a marginal

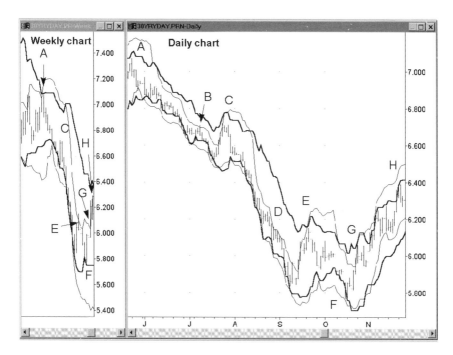

Figure 4.24
Weekly US 30-Year Bond Yield on the left with the daily chart on the right. Corrective Support and Resistance are in bold lines while Trend Support and Resistance are in thin lines.

breach. But we see the classic reversal pattern on the weekly chart, with a test and rejection of the weekly CS, which has turned flat by this point.

A reversal tests both the daily CR and the weekly TR at point G. The breach implies a test at the weekly CR and this occurs at point H.

The last two examples show how examining more than one time frame assists in obtaining a "feel" for momentum on all scales and in identifying the underlying momentum picture. Some markets are too volatile for Momentum Bands. But for markets that are less volatile, Momentum Bands provide a useful addition to a complete set of analytical tools.

CHAPTER 5

The Elliott Wave Principle

The Elliott Wave Principle is either loved or hated. It is a form of analysis where basic concepts I find to be in total accordance with the principles of technical analysis.

It is widely accepted that current price reflects market knowledge, both fundamental and technical, and therefore, any new information will affect price. Central bank and government policies are seen to be part of that information. In short, market behavior is a reflection of the collective action and thoughts of the participants. These participants include the central banks, governments, fund managers, investment managers, professional traders, and private traders. Even the public is a participant as their reaction to interest rates, exchange rates, and inflation is the response to government policy and policy changes aimed at voters.

The Elliott Wave Principle considers the collective emotion of the market and its participants. These participants react in similar ways and these reactions, according to the basic tenets of technical analysis, tend to develop in recognizable patterns. Just as some traders accept the possibility of trendlines, triangles, and head and shoulders, there should be no difference in their attitude towards the Elliott Wave Principle. This analysis method tries to recognize the different characteristics of trends and consolidation, and arranges them in order. So, if we can recognize the most recent pattern (emotion), we have a better chance of recognizing the next emotion and thus identify the next move. Furthermore, when linked with Fibonacci's theories, the Elliott Wave Principle can often predict the degree of price movement with great accuracy.

The biggest drawback of the Elliott Wave Principle is its complexity—wave counts are subjective rather than objective. When used with care, the Elliott Wave Principle can be one of the most powerful tools of technical analysis. However, it cannot be learnt overnight or just by reading this book. It takes some years of experience and practice to be able to integrate it within your technical analysis without making too many mistakes.

With this in mind let us examine the principle and see how we can profit from its use.

THE BASIC WAVE STRUCTURE

Elliott proposed that price develops in an eight-wave structure. The first five waves define the main trend of the move. Within these five waves are three *impulsive* waves separated by two *corrective* waves. Subsequent to a five-wave structure, the market will correct in a three-wave structure in the opposite direction. This correction usually comprises two impulsive waves (which are counter-trending) separated by one corrective wave.

Figure 5.1 shows the basic Elliott Wave structure. Waves 1, 3, and 5 are *impulsive* waves while waves 2 and 4 are corrective waves. Hence, the ABC wave structure can be described as corrective. For now we will concentrate on the impulsive waves first, while the characteristics of the corrective waves will be discussed later.

Figure 5.2 is a chart of the Singapore Gas Oil contract. It serves as a good example of a downward impulsive wave. Note how the two perfect-looking three-wave corrective wave structures, 2 and 4, break up the main thrust of the downward move.

THE COMPLEX STRUCTURE

Figure 5.1 shows how a trending (impulsive) wave develops. Note that the peak of the five waves is labeled (1), and the end of the declining corrective wave structure (ABC) is labeled (2) (upon completion of wave C). Since the impulsive waves, 1, 3, and 5 are trend-forming, they will be constructed of five waves each. Hence, usually after five waves in an impulsive wave structure, these five waves form part of a larger five-wave count i.e. wave (1). As corrective waves are three-wave structures, the ABC wave can be labeled as a correction in a larger wave count i.e. wave (2).

In Figure 5.3, the basic wave structure illustrated in Figure 5.1 forms wave (1) in the bottom left of the chart. After completion of corrective wave (2), a larger wave (3) develops in five waves. This is followed by a three-wave correction in wave (4). Finally, wave (5) progresses higher, and upon completion

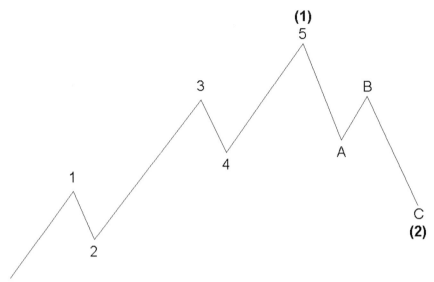

Figure 5.1
The basic wave structure. A trending move of five waves followed by a three-wave correction.

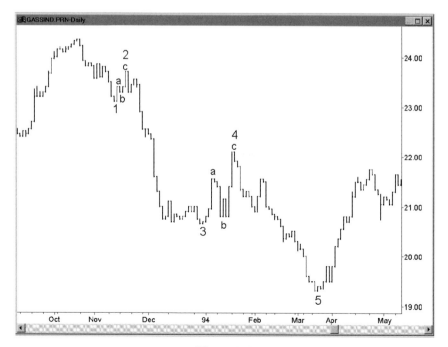

Figure 5.2
A five-wave decline in the Singapore Gas Oil contract.

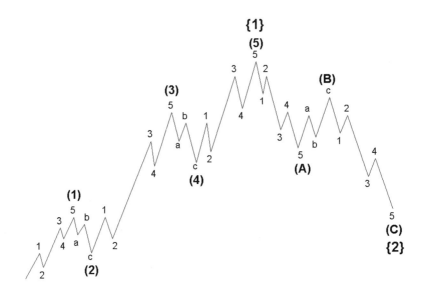

Figure 5.3
The simple wave structure seen in Figure 5.1 is shown on the left forming
waves (1) and (2). Following these, waves (3), (4), and (5) develop to
complete a trending wave labeled {1}. Wave {2} develops on (A), (B), and (C).

can be labeled wave {1} of *higher degree* (of an even larger
wave). Note how the subsequent three-wave correction pulls
price back lower in a correction. In this case a three-wave ABC
pattern is formed, with waves (A) and (C) constructed of five
waves each, and wave (B) constructed of three waves.
Corrections can be far more complex as will be discussed later.
This three-wave correction is labeled as wave {2} of higher
degree. Let us now look at some practical examples.

Figure 5.4 shows the basic wave structure of the Singapore
Gas Oil contract in a five-wave decline that is broken into a
series of five waves within each impulsive wave. The
subsequent correction comes in three waves, with waves (A)
and (C) comprising five waves and the intermediate wave (B)
developing in a triangle. (Triangles will be discussed in a later
section within this chapter.)

Figure 5.5 shows the gold market during a large rally from
$325 to $409. Within each impulsive wave, five waves can be
seen, and within each corrective wave, three waves can be seen.
After completion of wave (5) at $409, a three-wave correction
developed within which waves (A) and (C) comprising five

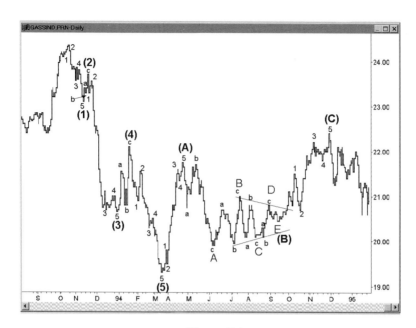

Figure 5.4
A five-wave decline in the Singapore Gas Oil contract market followed by a
three-wave correction (A)(B)(C) within which wave (B) is a triangle.

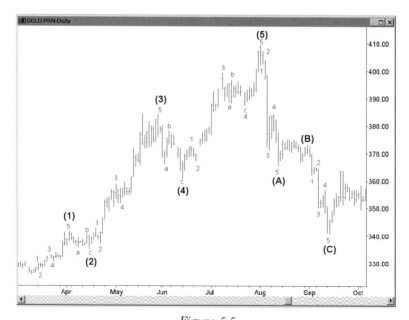

Figure 5.5
A five-wave rally in the gold market followed by a three-wave
corrective decline.

waves each. In this example, it is difficult to see the three-wave pattern in wave (B) but it is usually visible in charts of shorter time frame.

UNBREAKABLE RULES

Elliott placed only three rules on the wave but these rules are unbreakable.

Rule 1: Wave 2 can **never** retrace more than 100% of wave 1.

Figure 5.6 illustrates this situation and the wave count shown is therefore incorrect. Should the following wave be 100% of the current wave, a different wave count system would have to be applied.

Rule 2: Wave 3 is **never** the shortest of the three impulsive waves, 1, 3, and 5. Usually it is the longest, but this is not always the case.

In Figure 5.7, waves 1 and 5 are both longer than wave 3, thus violating this rule. Hence, the wave count shown is incorrect and an alternative wave count system would have to be used.

Rule 3: Wave 4 (in an impulsive move) **never** retraces to a level below the peak of wave 1 in an uptrend or above the trough of wave 1 in a downtrend.

(The reference to an impulsive wave is intended to show that we are referring to trending waves which come in five distinguishable waves. Occasionally a trending wave can develop in three waves as seen later.)

The wave count in Figure 5.8 is therefore incorrect and should be relabeled using a different system.

EXTENDING WAVES

Frequently, impulsive waves tend to extend, that is, they tend to develop into longer structures in which five additional waves can be seen in one of the wave positions, thus making the entire structure look to consist of nine waves. Figure 5.9 illustrates the extending wave.

Notice how between waves (2) and (3), an additional five waves develop—wave (2) is followed by a second wave 1 which

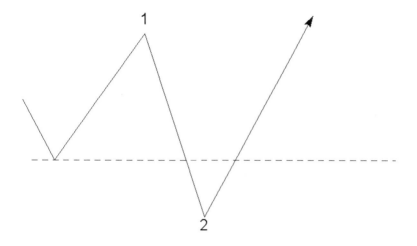

Figure 5.6
Unbreakable Rule 1: Wave 2 can never retrace more than 100% of wave 1.
The wave count shown is incorrect.

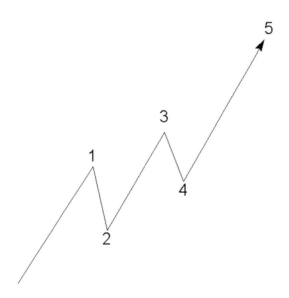

Figure 5.7
Unbreakable Rule 2: Wave 3 is never the shortest of the three impulsive
waves 1, 3, and 5. The wave count shown is incorrect.

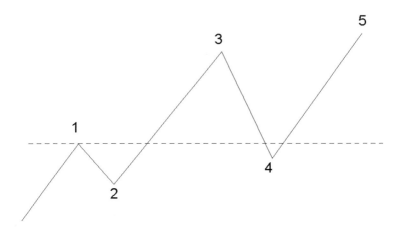

Figure 5.8
Unbreakable Rule 3: Wave 4, in an impulsive move, never retraces below
the peak of wave 1 in an uptrend or above the trough of wave 1 in a
downtrend. The above wave count is incorrect.

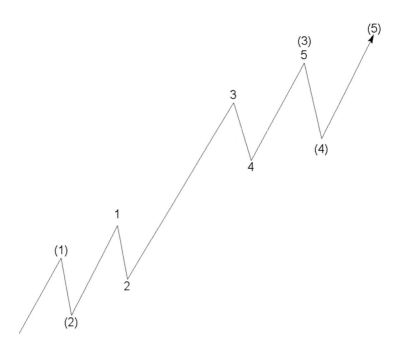

Figure 5.9
A wave extension in wave (3).

is developed through to completion of wave 5, itself the termination of wave (3). This is followed by waves (4) and (5).

In many ways the extending wave concept is similar to impulsive waves developing further in five waves. The difference is, in the complex wave structure, each major impulsive wave is constructed of five waves of *lesser degree*— meaning they are basically constructed of smaller waves— while in an extending wave, the five additional waves are of *the same degree* or of similar size.

Extending waves can appear in any of the impulsive waves, although statistically, wave 3 sees most extensions, followed by wave 5, with extensions in wave 1 relatively uncommon in my experience. Figure 5.10 shows an extending wave in a wave 3 position in the US dollar–German Deutschmark currency market.

Clearly, the main wave structure consists of five waves labeled (1) to (5), and wave (3) develops in five waves labeled 1 to 5, with each wave being of the same degree as the major waves.

A complication of extending waves is they can develop as "double extensions". That is to say, not only does one wave

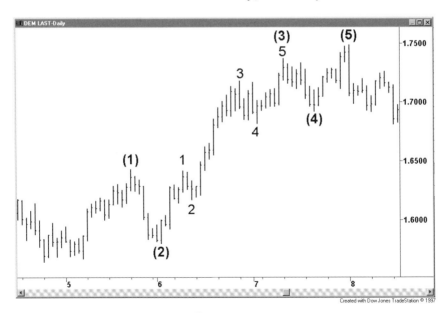

Figure 5.10
Example in the USDDEM currency market of an extending wave (3),
itself developing in five waves -- 1, 2, 3, 4, and 5.

extend in waves of the same degree, but the third wave of the extension can develop in waves of the same degree. Figure 5.11 shows how this may develop.

Note how wave (3) develops in five waves labeled 1 to 5, and within this five-wave structure, wave 3 develops in five additional waves labeled (i) to (v). These extending waves are of the same degree. Double extensions normally develop within a particularly aggressive phase of the wave development when volatility is high. Figure 5.12 shows how this occurred in the US dollar–Japanese yen currency market.

The entire wave began with mild downward movements, which accelerated after the completion of wave (ii), and then wave (iii) began. Subsequently, we saw a runaway downward move in distinct waves. Here, wave (3) comprises waves 1, 2, 3, 4, and 5, and wave 3 comprises waves (i), (ii), (iii), (iv), and (v).

The question usually asked at this point is: how do we know when a wave will extend? There is no definite answer but later, the Fibonacci relationship in waves will be used to explain extensions. Fibonacci often helps in identifying which waves are related, thus assisting in clarifying a wave structure.

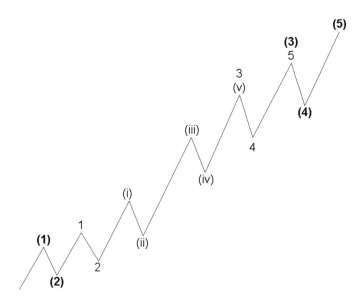

Figure 5.11
A double-extension in wave (3). This shows a wave 3 that is part of an extending wave and is itself an extending wave comprising waves (i), (ii), (iii), (iv), and (v).

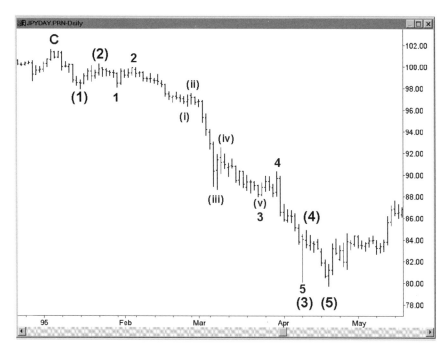

Figure 5.12
A double-extension in the USDJPY currency market.

Always view the wave in its entirety, including its multi-extensions, and understand how the entire wave should labeled.

Figure 5.13 shows examples of extending waves and their position within the larger wave structure. In the left chart, we see the development of the monthly market of the US dollar against the Japanese yen from 1969 to 1986. During this period, the yen began to strengthen from the 360 level set in the 1940s with a decline in a five-wave structure down to the 180 level by late 1978. As this is a five-wave structure, another five-wave structure must develop lower after a three-wave correction has been completed. We therefore label the first five-wave structure as either wave {A} or wave {1}—at this juncture we do not know which it will be. From the completion of wave [5] to 1982, a three-wave corrective rally occurred and it remains below the wave [4] peak. This corrective wave is labeled wave {B} or wave {2}.

From this point, we are looking for a five-wave decline that should move lower than the first decline (at around 180) and

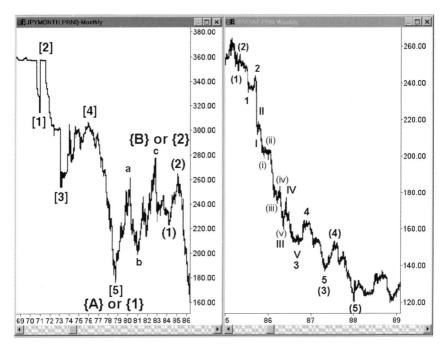

Figure 5.13
An initial five-wave decline in the USDJPY market, labeled {A} or {1}.
This is followed by a three-wave correction labeled {B} or {2},
which does not breach the previous wave (4). Subsequently breach of the
180 level confirms the decline seen on the right within which a triple
extension can be counted.

probably decline around the same length as the first wave {A} or wave {1}, that is a length of just over 180 yen (360–180). Since wave {B} or wave {2} ended at around 280, we have a target level of around 100. From this peak of 280, we see that an initial wave is completed, followed by a corrective wave to around 265. These we can confidently label as waves (1) and (2). Thus we are looking for a wave (3) that should decline towards our target, but not reach it since we are looking for a wave (3) decline to be followed by a wave (4) and wave (5).

Now looking at the right chart which shows the decline from the 265 level, we see how the market declined initially in several short moves, then became stronger. Where we labeled waves (1)-(2)-1-2 without any prior information, we might have been tempted to call these waves 1-2-3-4 to be followed by a wave 5. However, remember that we are looking for a decline that will break below 180 at least and probably decline towards our targeted 100 level. As these declines begin, since we are entering a wave 3, we must be aware of the strong possibility of an extending wave that should decline towards our target. An extending wave did indeed occur, and in fact developed in a triple extension as seen in the right chart. Our wave structure finally ended at 120. As a matter of interest, the 120 level was implied by taking the wave 1 and multiplying by 2.618, a Fibonacci projection level. This will be covered towards the end of this chapter.

EXTENDING FIFTH WAVES

Impulsive

We have seen how extending waves develop in the third wave position (and potentially in the first wave position). It is also worth noting the types of extension that can be expected in the fifth wave position as they can produce some confusion during development. Fifth waves can develop in three types of extended waves: impulsive, diagonal triangles, and expanding triangles (occasionally known as expanding wedges).

Figure 5.14 shows how a standard impulsive extending fifth wave develops. It is the same as any other extending wave in that it has individual waves of the same degree as waves (1) to (4). The problem with this type of extension is its capability to confuse even the experts. After identifying four waves ending at wave (4), it is possible to count five smaller waves to where i is labeled. We could have labeled the fifth small wave as wave (5) since we have seen five waves to complete it. Initially all is well as we see a decline (wave labeled ii in Figure 5.14). But this reverses and climbs to new highs (to wave iii) making it apparent that wave i is not wave (5). Hence we label the waves following wave i as waves ii and iii. We may, during this process, look for an expanded flat correction (discussed later) but the move continues and develops, as shown, to complete wave v of (5). As can be seen there are no clear rules on how to anticipate an extending fifth wave except to follow the earlier explanation of looking at the wave structure of one larger degree and developing on where potential targets may be.

Figure 5.15 shows a series of extending fifth waves, with an extending wave (v) within the extended wave 5 which in

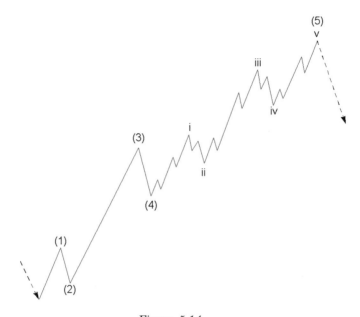

Figure 5.14
An impulsive extending wave (5). The initial minor five waves in wave i
may be misconstrued as the completion of wave (5). However, after the
reversal at wave ii and move to new highs at wave iii, the extension
becomes apparent.

turn is within an extended wave (5). This may look very
complicated, but the eventual low at wave (5) to complete wave
{C} is very close to wave equality with wave {A}. Indeed, such
an event of multiple extensions is unusual, but single
extensions can occur quite frequently. Other examples will be
seen as we progress with other parts of the wave structure.

Diagonal Triangles

The observant reader would have noticed that when describing
an extending fifth wave I used the term "impulsive" extending
fifth wave. Also, in stating the third unbreakable rules (refer
back to the section Unbreakable Rules), it may have created a
slight uncertainty in that I had described the five-wave
structure as impulsive with each of waves 1, 3, and 5 as
impulsive waves. It would therefore follow that wave 4 is
within that structure and thus the mention of "impulsive move"
would not be necessary.

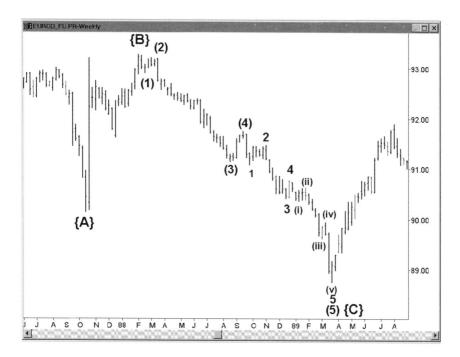

Figure 5.15
Two extending fifth waves, wave (5) and wave 5, in the
Eurodollar Futures market.

However, there is just one exception. Fifth waves can occasionally develop as diagonal triangles, or in classic technical analysis terms, "wedges". Within a diagonal triangle are five waves depicting the underlying trend, two of which are intervening corrective waves. But each of these five waves are constructed of a *three*-wave structure (not five). Figure 5.16 shows how a fifth wave should develop in a diagonal triangle. Wave (3) in its final stages and wave (4) are shown. The final five waves in wave (5) develop in a series of three-wave structures starting with wave (i) and ending with wave (v). Within a diagonal triangle it is permissible for the peak (trough) of wave (i) to overlap with the trough (peak) of wave (iv).

The illustration in Figure 5.16 is a perfect wedge that develops between two converging trendlines. This is not always necessary. Diagonal triangles can also develop between two parallel trendlines; waves (i) and (iv) do not necessarily need to overlap; or the entire structure can develop without trendlines, with or without overlap.

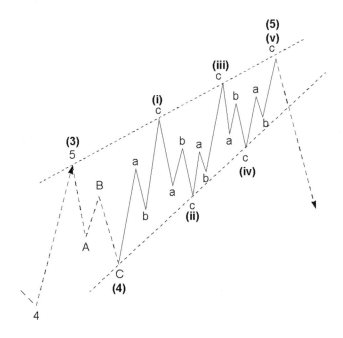

Figure 5.16
A rising diagonal triangle in a wave (5) position. Although it has been shown as developing within two converging trendlines, this need not necessarily occur.

Figures 5.17 and 5.18 show practical examples of diagonal triangles. Figure 5.17 shows the US dollar–German Deutschmark currency market in a rally from 1.3865 in September 1992. The third wave rallied in a perfect five-wave structure with the fifth wave developing as a wedge-shaped diagonal triangle. Notice also how the subsequent retracement dropped to the first "touch" of the wedge support line - a classic analysis guideline. Figure 5.18 shows the final wave in the Japanese Government Bond Futures market developing in five waves. The final wave came as a diagonal triangle, completing the larger three-wave structure, (A)(B)(C), and suggest a reversal in the fortune of the Japanese Government Bonds.

Expanding Triangles

Expanding triangles are a complex pattern that can confuse during analysis. Figure 5.19 shows how an expanding triangle should develop. It shows the end of the waves (3) and (4) after

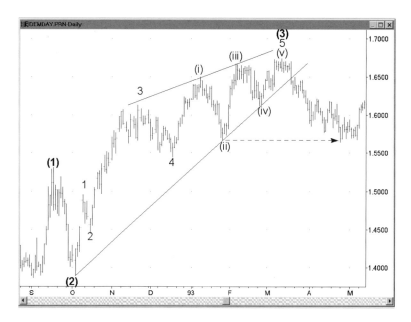

Figure 5.17
A diagonal triangle in the USDDEM currency market in the wave 5
position and labeled (i), (ii), (iii), (iv), and (v).

Figure 5.18
A declining diagonal triangle in the Japanese Government Bond Futures
market in a wave (5) position and labeled (i), (ii), (iii), (iv), and (v).

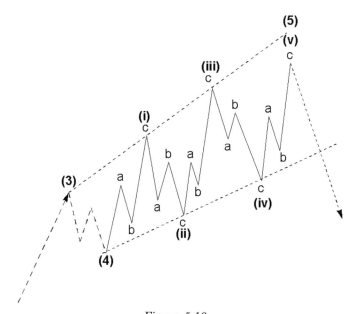

Figure 5.19
*A rising expanding triangle in a wave (5) position, labeled (i), (ii), (iii),
(iv), and (v).*

which five upward waves develop in a similar fashion to a
diagonal triangle. But here, the trendlines are diverging rather
than converging. Each of the five waves develops in three
waves with overlapping peaks/troughs. In general, there is a
strong underlying sentiment in the market in the direction of
the trend, and the expanding triangle tends to confuse market
participants who are looking for an aggressive move. After
completion of the pattern, reversal is normally very strong.

Fortunately expanding triangle patterns are not very
common and the example in Figure 5.20 is one of the very few
examples I have of expanding triangles. In this case, the
underlying sentiment was exceptionally strong in the US
dollar–German Deutschmark market. The dollar had rallied
aggressively from the low at 1.5020, peaked at 1.6355 after
which it consolidated for a long period. When the uptrend
resumed, the underlying sentiment was very bullish, and I
remember the lowest target being quoted was 1.72, followed by
predictions of 1.84, 2.04, 2.46, and even 3.46 by one aggressive
Elliottician. However, it became quite obvious after a while

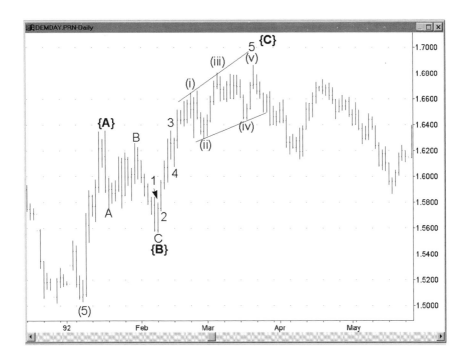

Figure 5.20
A rising expanding triangle in wave 5, labeled (i), (ii), (iii), (iv), and (v).
Note how after the pattern completed, price formed a strong reversal.

that this move was not living up to expectations. While I was equally confused, I finally spotted this particular pattern developing and called a top on the day it occurred. This points to a factor that should not be forgotten. Often, finding the correct wave count is difficult since there are many different types of structures that can occur. However, with a degree of dedication, a lot of analysis and consultation of other indicators, the correct structure can be discovered in time to make a trade that could make the annual budget! In fact, in the example shown, the wave {A} and wave {C} are of equal length, and at the peak, bearish divergences were forming, thus warning of a reversal. The dollar eventually declined to a new historic low of 1.3865.

Failed Fifth Waves

Failed fifth waves are a frustrating part of Elliott Wave

counting. Occasionally you will spot the development of a five-wave structure, seen the end of wave 3 and counted wave 4. Happy that this has been one of the easy counts, you carry on to count five intermediate waves higher but this stops short of the wave 3 peak (or trough). In most circumstances, you will decide that this is wave (i) of wave 5, or believe that you have counted incorrectly and that it is part of a larger corrective structure. However, what has really happened is the fifth wave has stalled just before the peak or trough of wave 3, and that completes the structure. The subsequent reversal is normally sharp and aggressive since it is a sign of the market's underlying weakness (in the case of a rising five-wave move).

There is no rule to help determine when this can occur. The guideline I usually recommend is if wave 3 meets the overall target you had measured, then there is a risk of seeing a failed fifth. It can confuse the subsequent wave count since it looks like part of a correction. As Rule 2 disallows wave 2 from retracing more than 100% of wave 1, you have to count waves 4 and 5 as waves A and B, making the count look corrective and not impulsive.

Figure 5.21 shows how a failed fifth wave develops and Figure 5.22 shows how this looks in practice, with the potential error in subsequent counts. In Figure 5.22 I have shown the "obvious" wave count which shows the decline from the peak on the left in an ABC pattern ending at the lowest low. Subsequent to this low, we see a sharp rally which is followed by a decline to just above the previous low. The market again experiences another strong rally. This would then have been labeled 1, 2, 3, 4 as shown (although the 4th wave would have been unusually low). We would then be looking for a five-wave rally to complete wave 5. After completion of that fifth wave, we would have been looking for a correction either in wave 2 or B, and then another rally to new highs. By taking the correct count, shown on the right chart, with the first rally (wave 1 in the left chart) as a wave 4 followed by a wave 5 to complete the ABC pattern lower, we would have then counted the move to 1.6355 as wave -A-, the correction as wave -B- and then we would have expected a five-wave rally in wave -C-. *The important point here is that subsequent to that wave (C), we would have known that the move higher was a correction only and thus looked for a move to new lows.* In fact, referring back

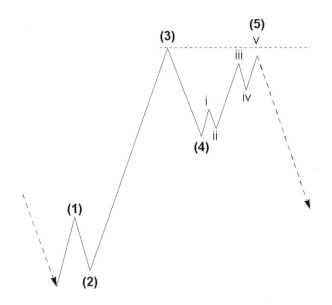

Figure 5.21
A failed fifth wave. Note how the extreme of wave 5 fails to penetrate
the peak of wave (3).

to Figure 5.20, the example of the expanding triangle (the subsequent wave structure), we would have been given much better warning that a strong decline was coming (also seen later in Figure 5.24).

ELLIOTT'S GUIDELINES

Elliott's guidelines for wave counting are not rules, but helpful hints useful to note. They can assist greatly in clarifying a wave count, potential targets, or where reversals can potentially be expected. Two of these guidelines cover corrective wave structures, which we have not covered yet, but the term should be remembered when reading the following pages.

Alternation

Elliott noticed a strong tendency for the corrective waves in an impulsive structure to alternate in complexity. In other words, if wave 2 is simple in structure (an ABC zigzag), then wave 4 will be complex (triangle, expanding flat, triple three). If wave 2 is complex, then wave 4 is likely to be simple.

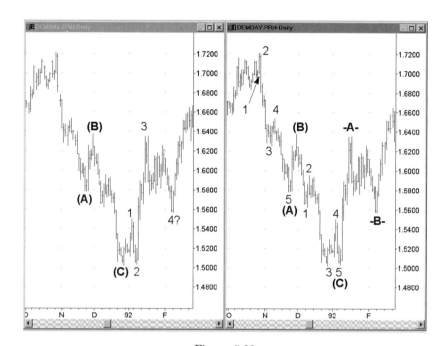

Figure 5.22
Example of how a failed fifth can confuse. On the left, the initial decline is
labeled (C) from which waves 1, 2, 3, and 4 are used to count a rally.
However, counting the decline on the right as a failed fifth can change the
labeling of the subsequent rally and the expectations of price during this rally.

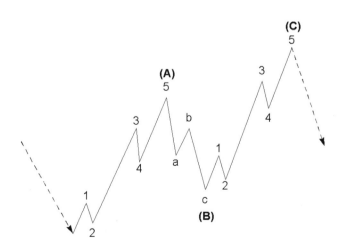

Figure 5.23
A simple zigzag correction labeled (A), (B), (C) within which waves (A) and
(C) comprises five waves, and wave (B) comprises three waves.

B Waves

After the completion of a three-wave move, there is a tendency for the peak or trough level of the intermediate B wave to provide support or resistance. This may be temporary or for a long period, but when spotted, the B wave gives a good opportunity to make a short-term profitable trade.

Wave 2 of an Extending Fifth Wave

Where an extending fifth wave has been seen, the initial correction will normally move directly to the extreme of the second wave of that fifth.

Examples to illustrate these three guidelines will be included in later examples of corrective wave structures.

CORRECTIVE WAVE STRUCTURES

Although the impulsive wave structure has its complications, most students of the wave principle can overcome these complications. On the other hand, corrective wave structures tend to be more complex, with several potential structures being possible, making its interpretation more difficult. It is this that gives rise to confusion and doubts over the Elliott Wave Principle, sending some students to search for a simpler form of analysis. But, if considered in the right perspective, several controlling guidelines can be applied to the interim wave structure that is difficult to interpret. These guidelines will help users gauge when the interim wave structure is complete and when the next move in the larger degree begins. Together with Fibonacci measurements and other indicators, it is often possible to identify the end of the interim wave structure and make profit from the subsequent move.

Zigzag

The zigzag is the most simple corrective ABC pattern. Figure 5.23 shows how the zigzag develops in three waves, two of which are impulsive waves separated by a three-wave corrective wave. Waves A and C are impulsive waves since they form the direction of the *counter-trend* with wave B correcting the first counter-trending move. Often this is referred to as a 535 move. After the ABC pattern, the main trend will resume.

Figure 5.24 shows the US dollar–German Deutschmark currency market between the failed fifth low at 1.5020 and the expanding triangle fifth at 1.6865. In this rally, price action rose in an ABC pattern where waves (A) and (C) developed in five-wave structures and wave (B) in three. Note that in this structure, waves (A) and (C) are of equal length. Observe how the wave pattern follows Elliott's guidelines with the first rally (wave (A)) ending at 1.6355, which also marked the end of a previous wave -B-. After completion of wave (C), the first decline to wave -1- came towards the trough of the preceding wave 4 of lesser degree.

Flat Correction

The zigzag pattern displays the simplest correction form. It occurs when wave A develops in five waves. Unfortunately, wave A often develops in three waves, thus implying that the

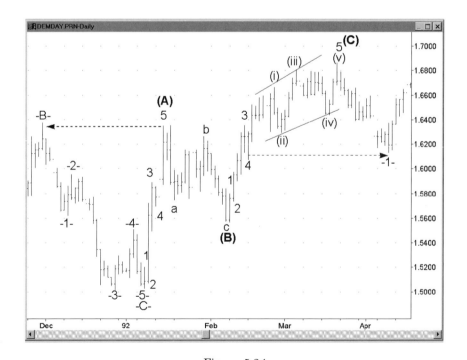

Figure 5.24
A zigzag rally in the USDDEM currency market labeled (A), (B), (C). Note how wave (A) developed in five waves, wave (B) in three, and wave (C) in five with the fifth as the expanding triangle shown in Figure 5.20.

wave structure will develop in one of three patterns. The first of these is the flat correction. Figure 5.25 shows how a flat correction should develop. Note how wave (A) develops in three waves, followed by wave (B), which also develops in three waves, and finally, wave (C), which develops in five waves. In this structure, wave (B) retraces back to the level of the end of the major trending move. Wave (C) will then move back to the level of the end of wave (A). In this way the complete wave structure looks flat, and after this the major trend will resume.

Figure 5.26 shows the development of the market for the US dollar against the Japanese yen after the low of 96.50 in July 1994. This is an interesting example as there are two flat corrections within this period. The entire flat correction can be seen and ends in the labeled five-wave move, completing close to the peak of wave (A) at 101.80 and after a five-wave move from the wave (B) low of 96.05. Looking at the development of wave (B), notice how it comes in a three-wave pattern but with the middle wave B coming as a flat correction abc. During development of this correction, there was little indication of how each wave would develop. However, after the develoment

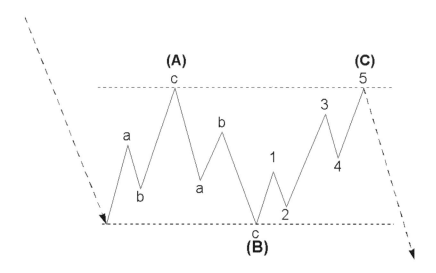

Figure 5.25
A flat correction. Note how wave (B) ends at around the same level
as the end of the trending wave (dashed lines) and wave (C) ends
at around the same level as wave (A).

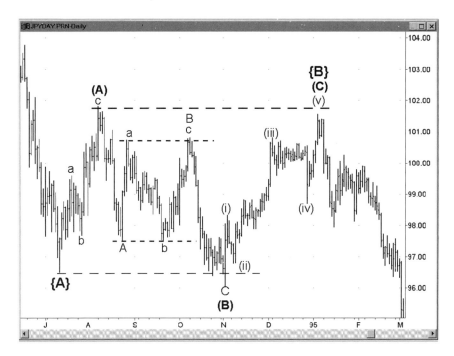

Figure 5.26
Two flat corrections in the USDJPY currency market. Note how wave
(B) ends just below wave {A} and wave (C) then rallies to complete
at the same level as wave (A). Also, within wave (B), wave B
comprises a flat correction abc.

of final wave (C) to 101.55, it becomes obvious what the pattern
is, and therefore provided an excellent opportunity to sell
dollars with a relatively tight stop-loss.

Expanded Flat Correction

The second type of correction that can develop when a three-
wave structure A occurs, is an expanded flat. This is shown in
Figure 5.27. After the end of the trending move, a three-wave
correction develops (wave (A)), after which a second three-wave
move develops to form wave (B). Wave (B) descends to below
the low of the intermediate trend (or the high of an uptrend),
then reverses higher in five waves to form wave (C) at
approximately the same level as the peak of wave (A). This
pattern normally signals that the trend will resume in an
aggressive manner.

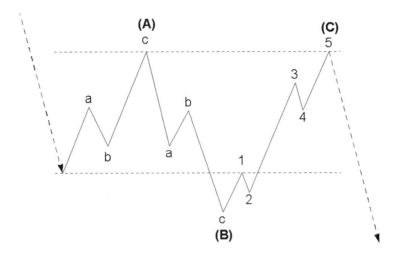

Figure 5.27
An expanded flat. Note how wave (B) (part of the correction) declines
below the trough of the declining trending move (left dashed line) and
wave (C) rises to the peak of wave (A).

Figure 5.28 shows an expanded flat in a wave (2) position. Note how wave B of this wave (2) rallies above the peak of the wave (1), then declines back to the level of the first wave A correction. Following completion of this expanded flat, we see a strong wave (3) develop higher in five waves. In accordance with Elliott's guideline of alternation, wave (4) is short and shallow following the complex wave (2). Similarly, notice how the decline from the peak of wave (5) fell to just above the base of wave 4.

Triangles

The third and final pattern that can develop should wave A come in three waves is a triangle. In a triangle, the correction will develop in a series of five three-wave moves which are contained within converging lines. After completion of the fifth three-wave move, the underlying price direction will continue, as seen in Figure 5.29. This type of correction is commonly taught as a basic continuation pattern. But, the Elliott Wave Principle gives the development of a triangle a little more structure and assists in highlighting when a triangle is complete.

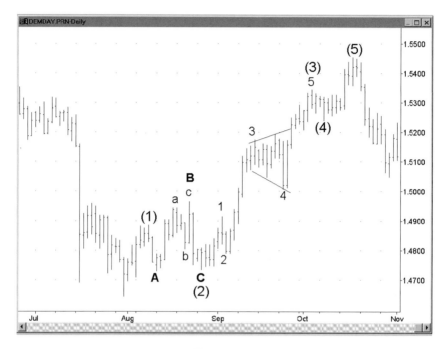

Figure 5.28
An expanded flat wave (2) within a rally in the USDDEM currency
market. Note how wave B completes above wave (1) and wave C declines
back to the level of wave A.

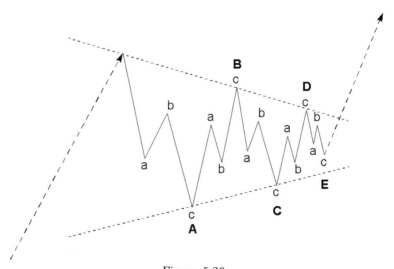

Figure 5.29
A triangle. Note how the triangle develops in five waves, each
comprising three waves.

Figure 5.30 shows an ABC structure in the Singapore Gas Oil contract market with wave (B) developing as a triangle. Notice in the triangle, the separate waves of three converging between two lines. Subsequently, the overall price move continues in wave (C) comprising five waves in a diagonal triangle.

There are some concepts that should be understood before we continue with corrective wave structures. Look back at all the examples shown of the type of corrections that can develop when wave A consists of three waves. First, where a three-wave structure is expected, it can occur as any three-wave structure or *multiple* of it. For instance, in Figure 5.26, the wave (B) developed as a zigzag pattern with wave B coming as a flat correction, while in Figure 5.30, wave (B) developed as a triangle. In fact, wave B after a three-wave A can be some of the most complex and confusing waves, and where possible, should be avoided when considering trades.

We have also seen in all the previous examples that wave C will *always* develop in five waves. These five waves may be

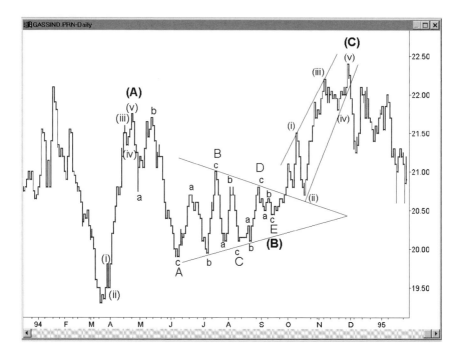

Figure 5.30
A triangle as a wave (B) in the Singapore Gas Oil Futures market.

either impulsive or form a diagonal triangle. Rarely do they develop as a triangle. Thus, when a wave C is anticipated, always look for it to develop in five waves, and after those five waves, look for the underlying price direction to resume.

Note on the Three-Wave Wave A.

Many traders begin to question the validity of the Elliott Wave Principle at this point, asking how they can tell whether after three waves, the structure completes a zigzag or is just part of a more complex structure. Frankly, there is no answer. But, it must be remembered that these are potential structures, and once they are recognized, the completion of the pattern can frequently be anticipated, thus enabling a profitable position to be taken. The guideline I use is if we see a five-wave move lasting perhaps one year, and a three-wave correction occurs within two weeks of it, then it is unlikely that we have seen the entire correction but a small part of a more complex correction. We should also bear in mind the levels implied by Fibonacci retracements, which will be discussed a little later.

It is vital that the Elliott Wave Principle forms only a part of your analysis, with other means of identifying the underlying momentum and trend of the market. Cycles and momentum can contribute to a powerful combination of analysis techniques, and this will be discussed a little later.

Wave A Diagonal Triangle – "Type Two"

Robert Prechter noticed a new derivative of a diagonal triangle in the 1980s, see Figure 5.31. It is basically the same as a diagonal triangle in a wave 5 position except that it is constructed of *impulsive* waves rather than of a series of three-wave moves. Prechter noticed this occurred only in wave A positions. Note that this is an exception when waves (i) and (iv) may overlap. Also when this structure (waves of five, three, five, three and five, in that order) occurs, the count anticipated should be for a subsequent wave B followed by a wave C.

Double Zigzags

Again, unfortunately, we must accommodate other complex corrections such as the double zigzag. The basic formation of

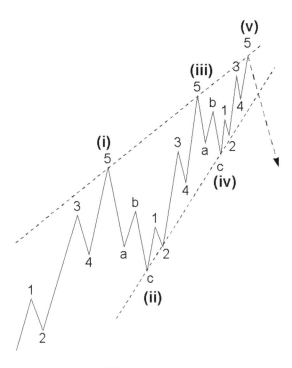

Figure 5.31
A diagonal triangle type 2 as identified by Robert Prechter. Note how each
wave in the direction of the underlying trend is constructed of five waves
instead of three.

the double zigzag is similar to that of the simple zigzag except it is repeated. Figure 5.32 shows the simple zigzag followed by a three-wave correction and then another zigzag. The first ABC pattern is completed and the intermediate three-wave correction is labeled as wave X. Note that wave X normally fails to breach the extreme of wave B of the first zigzag. This is in line with Elliott's guideline which states that wave B will either provide support or resistance when revisited. Similarly, the wave counter may see a three-wave correction that suggests that the overall trend may have resumed. However, the wave B extreme should be approached with care since a correction of some kind is likely, even if brief. After the wave X is completed, a further ABC pattern comprising waves -A-, -B-, -C- can develop.

Figure 5.33 shows how gold rallied in a double zigzag from the $340.80 low in September 1993 to a peak of $396.65 in

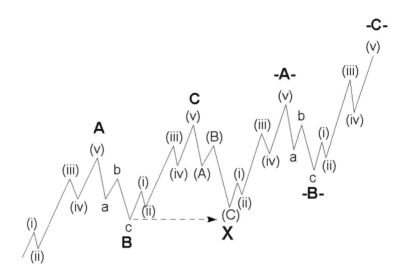

Figure 5.32
*A double zigzag. After completion of the initial ABC move, a wave X
(comprising three waves) develops but does not breach the extreme of wave
B. A further -A--B--C- move then develops.*

Figure 5.33
A double zig-zag in the gold market.

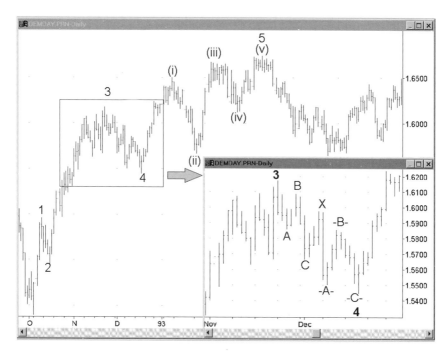

Figure 5.34
A wave 4 comprising a double zigzag in the USDDEM currency market.

January 1994. Figure 5.34 shows the market of the US dollar against the German Deutschmark in a wave 4 correction in December 1992. This developed as a double zigzag before resuming the uptrend in a diagonal triangle wave 5.

Triple Threes

The triple three can develop in basically the same way as the double zigzag. But after the second ABC zigzag is completed a *second three-wave correction* is seen—another X wave—subsequent to which a third ABC pattern is seen. This is quite annoying at times, and once again, there is no rule which dictates when a triple three can be seen. In such situations, I use time and price extent as a guide as used in the three-wave wave A—if we have seen a trend lasting one year, it is unlikely that we shall see a correction lasting only two weeks. In addition to this rule, since with double zigzag and triple three we continue to see deeper corrective moves as each ABC pattern normally (but not always) reaches new corrective peaks or troughs, we can use the Elliott guideline that after a wave 5, the market normally retraces to the span of the preceding wave 4 of lesser degree and usually to the level of the extreme of the wave 2 of the previous wave 5.

Figure 5.35 shows the development of a triple three. Note how the intermediate X waves generally fail to breach the extreme of the previous wave B and the next ABC pattern can develop. Triple threes can be seen in very choppy price behavior and a general confusion will be noticeable in market sentiment with differences in opinion over whether the main trend has ended or whether it will continue. However, there is a positive point to note—there is no such thing as a "Quadruple Three". In other words, after a triple three ends with a further X wave, it is followed by another ABC pattern. Therefore, if a triple three is seen, it is safe to assume that the main trend will resume and a good profitable trade can be entered.

Figure 5.36 is an example of how a triple three developed in the British pound–US dollar currency market. Note that it is a very complex structure accompanied by confusing market behavior. After the triple three is completed we see price reversal. It is important to note that where a three-wave pattern is expected, any form of corrective pattern can be substituted. In the case of Figure 5.36, the second wave -X- comes in the form of a triangle—five waves of three—a triangle

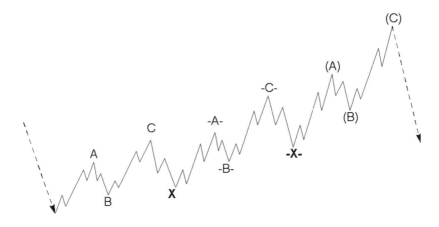

Figure 5.35
A triple three. After a double zigzag is completed, a second wave -X-
develops and it does not breach wave -B-. A third zigzag then develops.

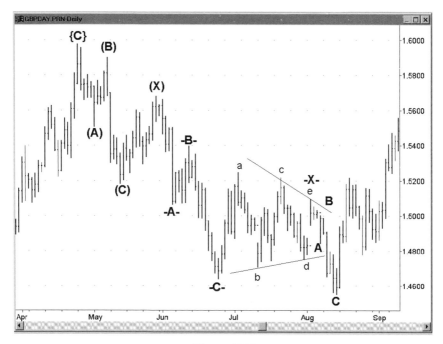

Figure 5.36
A triple three in the GBPUSD currency market with the second -X- wave developing as a triangle.

being a corrective pattern. The second X wave can also be formed in a zigzag or double zigzag patterns, or even a triple three itself.

This concept also applies to B waves. Perhaps B waves are the most complex and difficult parts of the wave structure in which to trade because there are so many combinations of three-wave structures that can develop that there must be a great deal of uncertainty. Again, we should bear in mind Elliott's guidelines and also the time and price guidelines I follow vis-à-vis price retracement in both extent and time.

FURTHER COMPLEX CORRECTIONS

To complete the description of corrective price patterns, I shall add a selection of complex corrections, all valid within the rules of the Elliott Wave Principle and substitute a variety of three-wave patterns where they can develop. This often produces some complex patterns and in the majority of cases, with corrective patterns, it is almost impossible to predict how the correction will develop. However, there is a guideline that should be remembered: always have in your mind the wave structure of one larger degree. When applying Elliott's guidelines on retracements, always bear in mind where the extreme of the previous wave 4 or wave B lies. Keep in mind also Fibonacci projections, and regularly browse through the wave structure to find Fibonacci relationships that will guide you through some difficult times. Finally, the most important thing to realize is not necessarily being able to predict each stage of the correction, but being able to identify its completion. Often a long and complex wave development can confuse you and cause you to reconsider whether to continue using the Elliott Wave Principle. With constant application and analysis, the identification of the completion of a complex correction can bring remarkable rewards by taking advantage of a new trend that the rest of the market has not anticipated.

The following are examples of the types of correction that can develop. Often, they occur in very short-term markets (intraday) as these reflect a combination of all lengths of trading, from the short-term scalpers to long-term players hedging their exposures. Remember that where an ABC pattern is expected, any three-wave pattern or group of three-wave patterns (double zigzags, triple threes) can be substituted. In a simple ABC pattern (but not in triangles), wave C always develops in five waves. The following are some examples that illustrate this.

Figure 5.37 shows a zigzag with wave B as a triangle.

Figure 5.38 shows a zigzag with the wave -B- coming as a flat. Wave B of the flat develops as a zigzag with wave b as a triangle.

Figure 5.39 shows a zigzag labeled -A--B--C- with wave -B- as an expanded flat. Within the expanded flat, wave (B) comprises a zigzag. Wave B is also an expanded flat. Wave (C) rallies back to the high of wave (A) from where wave -C- declines to new lows.

Figure 5.40 displays a zigzag with wave (B) as a double zigzag. Within wave (B), wave X is a triangle and the following wave (b) is a flat.

Figure 5.41 displays a triple three. After the first five waves that form the first wave (A), wave (B) develops as a

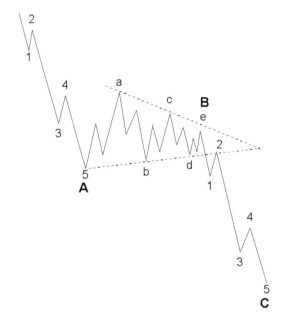

Figure 5.37
Complex corrective patterns. A zigzag with wave B as a triangle.

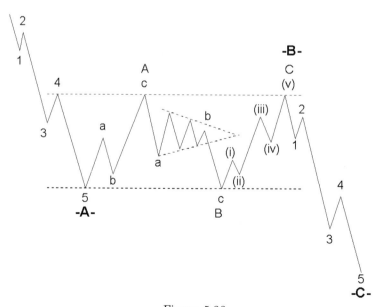

Figure 5.38
Complex corrective patterns. A zigzag with wave -B- developing as a flat.
Wave B of the flat is a zigzag within which wave b is a triangle.

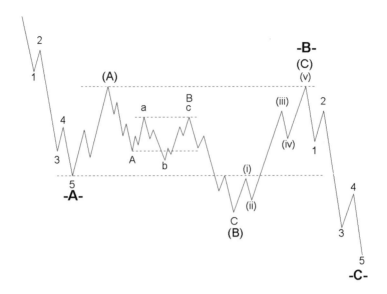

Figure 5.39
Complex corrective patterns. A zigzag (waves -A-, -B-, -C-) with wave -B- as
an expanded flat. Within wave (B), wave B is also an expanded flat.

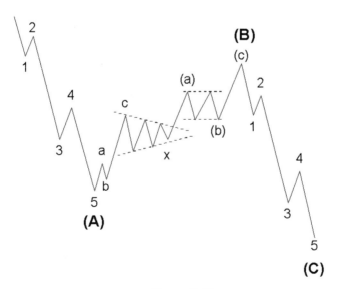

Figure 5.40
Complex corrective patterns. A zigzag with waves (A) and (C) comprising
five waves each and wave (B) comprising a double zigzag. Wave X is a
triangle and wave (b) is a flat.

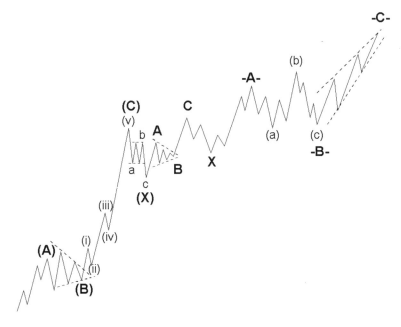

Figure 5.41
Complex corrective patterns. A triple three with wave (B) as a triangle,
wave b of (X) as a flat, wave B as a triangle, wave -B- as an expanded
flat, and wave -C- as a diagonal triangle.

triangle where the b wave is expanded. The subsequent wave
(C) develops with an extended wave (v). Wave (X) has a flat
wave b and the subsequent ABC pattern is quite short. After
the second intermediate wave X, we see a further wave -A-,
which is followed by an expanded flat wave -B- where the wave
(c) retraces to the extreme of wave (a). This is then followed by
a wave -C- as a diagonal triangle to finish the entire pattern.

While Figure 5.42 is a complex pattern, frequently the
individual waves can be identified by applying Fibonacci ratios.
It is here that the wave structure of one larger degree is
important in order to identify what is expected. In this
complete structure, it would be easy to miscount wave (C) as a
third wave, and misidentify the subsequent confusing structure
as a diagonal triangle. This complex pattern would indeed
create a great deal of uncertainty in the market but upon
completion it would signal a good (and probably unexpected)
reversal.

Figure 5.42 shows a flat correction with waves (A) and (B) as a flat. Within wave (B), wave -C- develops as a diagonal triangle, as does wave (C). Wave (IV) of the wave (C) diagonal triangle develops as a triangle.

Figure 5.43 shows a zigzag with wave (B) as a triangle. Within the triangle, the final wave E develops as a triangle. This pattern is generally associated with a confused market where opinions are clearly divided between bulls and bears. The subsequent break is generally swift and decisive with a large number of incorrect positions being squared by stop-losses.

Figure 5.44 shows a zigzag but with wave (B) as an expanded flat. Within this expanded flat, wave B develops as a triple three. The triple three has its own complex three-wave patterns, with the first wave -b- as a flat, the second wave (b) as an expanded flat, and a triangular wave (x) before a final zigzag, with wave b again as a flat. Wave C within wave (B) rallies in a regular impulsive five-wave move before the final wave (C) declines in five waves, but with wave (5) coming as an extended fifth. Within the extended fifth, wave 5 comes as a failed fifth.

Fibonacci Ratios

Within the description of the Elliott Wave Principle, I have frequently referred to the wave structure as having Fibonacci

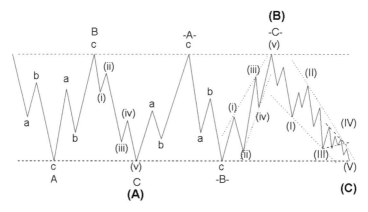

Figure 5.42
Complex corrective patterns. A flat correction with waves (A) and (B) as flats, and a diagonal triangle in wave (C).

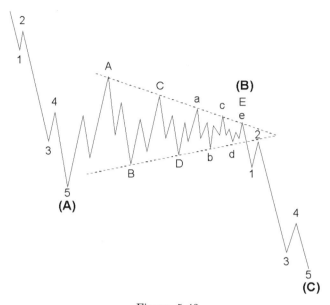

Figure 5.43
Complex corrective patterns. A zigzag within which wave (B) develops as a
triangle and wave E of the triangle also develops as a triangle.

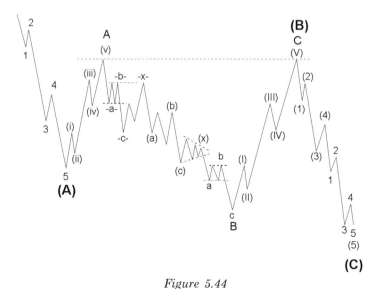

Figure 5.44
Complex corrective patterns. A zigzag with wave (B) as an expanded flat.
Within wave (B), wave B comprises a triple three, with wave -b- is a flat,
wave (b) an expanded flat, wave (x) a triangle, and wave b a flat. Wave
(C) develops with an extended wave (5).

relationships. Many traders are aware of Fibonacci retracement levels but there are other relationships that become evident when applying Elliott Wave analysis to markets. Before describing common wave relationships, I will explain how Fibonacci ratios are calculated.

Fibonacci begins with the creation of a sequence of values that are calculated from previous values in the sequence. The sequence runs as follows:

$$1, 1, 2, 3, 5, 8, 13, 21, 34, 55, 89, 144, 233, \ldots$$

Each number is calculated by the addition of the previous two numbers in the sequence. For example, $1 + 1 = 2$; $2 + 1 = 3$; $3 + 2 = 5$; $5 + 3 = 8$; $8 + 5 = 13$; and so on.

Interestingly, if two adjacent numbers are used and one is divided by the other, the result *always* arrives at 0.618 or 1.618. But, for the first few numbers in the sequence, this is not true. For instance, 2/3 is equal to 0.667 and 3/2 equals 1.5. As we progress further into the sequence, the observation quickly becomes more accurate.

$\dfrac{3}{5} = 0.600$ $\dfrac{5}{8} = 0.625$ $\dfrac{8}{13} = 0.6153$

$\dfrac{13}{21} = 0.6190$ $\dfrac{21}{34} = 0.6176$ $\dfrac{34}{55} = 0.6181$

If we then switch the numerators and denominators we arrive at:

$\dfrac{21}{13} = 1.6153$ $\dfrac{34}{21} = 1.6190$ $\dfrac{55}{34} = 1.6176$

And we quickly come to the same ratio of 1.618.

If we now make the same calculations with values that are two positions apart within the sequence, we arrive at:

$\dfrac{13}{34} = 0.3823$ $\dfrac{21}{55} = 0.3818$ $\dfrac{34}{89} = 0.3820$

Switching the numerators and denominators around gives:

$\dfrac{34}{13} = 2.6153$ $\dfrac{55}{21} = 2.6190$ $\dfrac{89}{34} = 2.6176$

As a final example, take values three numbers apart in the sequence and we arrive at:

$\frac{13}{55}$ = 0.2363 $\frac{21}{89}$ = 0.2359 $\frac{34}{144}$ = 0.2361

$\frac{55}{13}$ = 4.2307 $\frac{89}{21}$ = 4.2380 $\frac{144}{34}$ = 4.2352

We can also derive more relationships from other Fibonacci relationships by subtracting it from or adding it to 100. For example,

100 − 23.6 = 76.4
100 + 23.6 = 123.6
100 + 38.2 = 138.2

Also, by adding the ratio sequence the results of 1/1 = 1 and 1/2 = 0.50 we arrive at a sequence of ratios:

0.236, 0.382, 0.50, 0.618, 0.764, 1.00, 1.382, 1.618, 2.618, 4.236 ...

There is another interesting feature of the Fibonacci sequence. Whether you multiply or divide any one number of the sequence by another, the result will be another number in the sequence:

Multiplication
$0.618 \times 0.382 = 0.236$ $0.618 \times 0.618 = 0.382$ $1.618 \times 0.382 = 0.618$
$4.236 \times 0.618 = 2.618$ $2.618 \times 1.618 = 4.236$ $1.618 \times 1.618 = 2.618$

Division
$0.618 / 0.382 = 1.618$ $0.382 / 0.618 = 0.618$ $1.618 / 2.618 = 0.618$
$2.618 / 1.618 = 1.618$ $1.618 / 0.382 = 4.236$ $0.382 / 0.236 = 1.618$

These ratios occur in many natural events from snail shells to rose petals, from rabbit population to the relationship of parts of the body. The ancient Egyptians used these ratios to build the pyramids while the Greeks used them in the construction of the Parthenon. Can we suggest that these ratios also occur within the markets? The following are guidelines to common relationships. It should be stressed that they do not occur all the time, but the frequency of their occurrence is sufficient to make us apply them as supporting evidence of wave relationships.

Impulsive Waves

Wave 1

Has no relationship with any preceding wave as it is the first in a sequence. However, bear in mind the Elliott guidelines regarding wave B extremes or the extreme of wave 2 of the previous fifth wave of one lesser degree.

Wave 3

Usually 1.618 or 2.618 of wave 1. In an aggressive move, it can occasionally be 4.236 of wave 1.

Wave 5

Usually 0.618 of the distance from the beginning of wave 1 to the end of wave 3. Wave equality with wave 1 can also be seen. Alternatively, look at the target implied by the wave structure of one larger degree. An extended fifth wave can be 1.618 of the distance from the beginning of wave 1 to the end of wave 3.

Diagonal Triangles

Wave (i)

Has no relationship to any preceding wave. Look at the internal structure or resistance generated from historic price action.

Wave (ii)

Refer to the Elliott guidelines, in particular the extreme of wave b within wave (i).

Wave (iii)

Usually has equal length with wave (i) but can occasionally be 0.618 of wave (i).

Wave (iv)

0.618 of wave (ii).

Wave (v)

0.618 of wave (iii).

Since diagonal triangles are constructed of three-wave moves, attention should also be given to the internal structure of the waves abc (refer to the section on Corrective Wave Structures) and also to the Elliott guidelines.

Corrective Waves

Wave 2

No single relationship works well. Can be anywhere between 0.236 and 100% of wave 1. It would be wise to refer to the position in the larger wave count. If wave 2 of an A wave or the start of a bigger wave 1 higher is referred to, then close to 100% is possible. If wave 2 of a larger wave 3 is referred to, then we may only see 0.236 of wave 1. Take note of the internal relationships of the waves.

Wave 4

Most frequent is 0.382 of wave 3 (not the beginning of wave 1 to the end of wave 3). They can occasionally pull back 50% of wave 3, but one of the best guidelines is the extreme of the previous wave 4 of one lesser degree.

Wave A

Refer to the Elliott guidelines. Bear in mind the larger wave structure and whether 0.382 has any influence.

Wave B

B waves are the most unpredictable since they comprise any sequence of three-wave moves. In a simple ABC pattern, 0.50 to 0.618 of wave A is most common. Refer also to the Elliott guidelines.

Wave C

Most common relationship is wave equality with wave A, followed by 0.618 or 1.618 of wave A. However, refer to the particular wave structure—if an expanded flat, expect to retrace to the extreme of wave A.

Triangles

Wave A

No single relationship is preferred. In a wave 4 position, it can rapidly retrace 0.382 of wave 3. Bear in mind the internal construction of waves abc.

Wave B

Can develop in many different ways. Refer to the Elliott guidelines.

Wave C

Most common is 0.618 of wave A. Refer to the Elliott guidelines and look at the internal structure of the abc pattern.

Wave D

Most common is 0.618 of wave B. Refer to the Elliott guidelines and look at the internal structure of the abc pattern.

Wave E

Although the textbook suggestion is 0.618 of wave C, the problem with wave E is it can fall short of this, sometimes making only 0.382 or 0.50 of wave C. Look also at the extreme of wave b within wave D.

Expanded Flats

Usually wave B will extend 1.382 of wave A (sometimes only by 1.236). While these are not strictly Fibonacci ratios, they are the addition of two ratios. Alternatively, the extended wave B can often stall at the level of the original target of a wave 3, if this falls short of a target.

These will be covered again in the section on Integrating Analysis Techniques, but before ending this chapter on the Elliott Wave Principle, let us take a look at an example of Fibonacci working within the wave structure.

The example in Figure 5.45 is one of the best examples of Fibonacci relationships I have seen—they do not always behave this well! Figure 5.45 is the chart of the US dollar against the German Deutschmark from the 1.3865 low in September 1992 to the 1.7684 high in February 1994.

The entire wave pattern is a three-wave {A}{B}{C}.

Wave (1)	1.5310	No relationship
Wave (2)	1.3895	Also the trough of wave (ii) of wave (1).

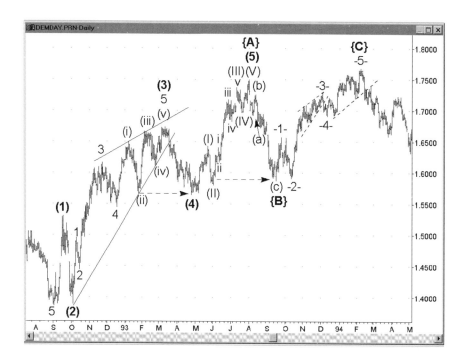

Figure 5.45
The influence of Fibonacci ratios in the USDDEM currency market. Not only do many of the waves develop with these Fibonacci relationships, but the Elliott guidelines also provide excellent clues.

Wave 1	1.4955	Approximately 0.764 of wave (2).
Wave 2	1.4445	Approximately 0.50 of wave 1.
Wave 3	1.6170	1.618 of wave 1.
Wave 4	1.5446	Approximately 0.382 of wave 3.
Wave (i)	1.6500	Wave equality with wave 1.
Wave (ii)	1.5665	0.764 of wave (i).
Wave (iii)	1.6670	Approximate wave equality with wave (i).
Wave (iv)	1.6117	0.618 of wave (ii) (meets trendline from 1.3895)
Wave (v)	1.6740	0.618 of wave (iii) (meets peak of previous wave 2).
Wave 5	1.6740	Approximately 0.618 of wave 1 to wave 3.
Wave (3)	1.6740	Unusually 2.0 of wave (1) (meets double bottom target).

Wave (4)	1.5647	0.382 of wave (3). Retraced to low of wave (ii).
Wave (I)	1.6432	No relationship.
Wave (II)	1.5805	0.764 of wave (I).
Wave i	1.6420	Approximately 0.764 of wave (I).
Wave ii	1.6177	0.236 of wave i.
Wave iii	1.7182	1.618 of wave i.
Wave iv	1.6820	0.382 of wave iii.
Wave v	1.7371	0.382 of wave i through wave iii.
Wave III	1.7371	No relationship.
Wave IV	1.6923	Approximately 0.236 of wave III.
Wave V	1.7488	Approximately 0.618 of wave I (also equal to wave v).
Wave (5)	1.7488	Approximately 0.618 of wave (1) to wave (3).

This completes wave {A}.

Wave a	1.6920	Falls to the extreme of wave IV.
Wave b	1.7263	0.618 of wave a.
Wave c	1.5875	Falls short of 1.618 of wave a, just above the extreme low of wave (II) of wave (5).

This completes wave {B}.

Wave -1-	1.6572	No relationship.
Wave -2-	1.5905	Almost 100% of wave -1-.
Wave -3-	1.7297	No relationship but meets peak of wave b within wave {B}.
Wave -4-	1.6908	No relationship.
Wave -5-	1.7684	Approximate wave equality with wave -1-.
Wave {C}	1.7684	0.50 of wave {A}.

This completes wave {C}.

Clearly, while not all follow Fibonacci ratios, there is a high degree of relationship throughout the entire structure, sufficient enough to guide a trader through this period of price action. Not all wave structures have this high level of wave relationships, but in most, there will be enough to give traders a good indication of the underlying move.

CHAPTER 6

Elliott Wave: Pitfalls and Tips

In Chapter 5 the basic principles of Elliott Wave were described. If this form of analysis was straightforward, we would all be very happy. However, as with other analysis methods, there are many occasions within the Elliott Wave Principle where the wave count is unclear, at times almost impossible to count. Some analysts tend to be over-enthusiastic about longer-term wave counts and make far-reaching projections that in many cases result in losses which could have been avoided. It is also very easy to attempt to predict tops and bottoms of markets slightly too early, thus resulting in premature taking of profit and also failure in taking advantage of resumption of trends.

In this chapter I shall attempt to describe these pitfalls of using the Elliott Wave Principle and how to overcome them. I will also share tips on how to take advantage of a greater number of situations using the Elliott Wave Principle.

BASIC TIPS

The following are basic facts about the Elliott Wave Principle that will assist in understanding the implications of future price action.

1.   There is never a complete correction comprising a single five-wave move.

If you count a five-wave move against the underlying trend, after a subsequent three-wave correction (or combination of three-wave moves), a five-wave move should be seen in the same direction of the initial five waves.

Figure 6.1 shows the weekly chart of the US dollar against the British pound with an Elliott Wave pattern of (A)(B)(C)(X) -A-? where ? is -B- or (a). This pattern counts the recovery from the 1.4070 low of February 1993 as an (A)(B)(C) correction, followed by an intermediate wave (X) in what could be a double zigzag or even a triple three. From the trough of wave (X), we

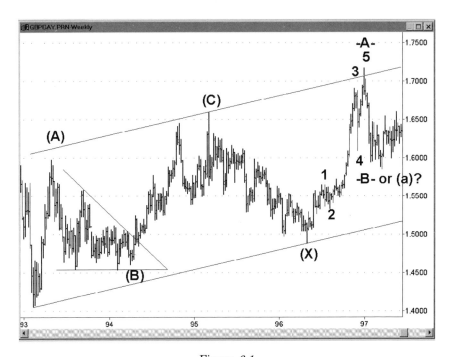

Figure 6.1
*The weekly GBPUSD currency market showing an (A)(B)(C) rally followed
by a decline in wave (X) and a five-wave rally. Since a five-wave move is
seen, we must expect a further five-wave move to new highs.*

see what appears to be a five-wave move up to the 1.7168 high
of January 1997, followed by a decline to 1.5855 in March 1997.

What can we deduce from this wave count assuming it is
correct? First, since we have seen a five-wave incline from wave
(X), we should see another five-wave move up. We are therefore
expecting levels higher than the 1.7168 peak of wave -A-. The
move down to 1.5855 represents a decline of just under 61.8%
of wave -A-. The temptation is to assume that this is an end to
wave -B-, implying that a five-wave incline should be seen
making new highs, perhaps equal in length to wave -A-, or
161.8% of this length.

We should analyse the 1.7168–1.5855 decline a little more
closely and this is shown in the daily chart in Figure 6.2. The
decline from 1.7168 is labeled and to support this wave count,
wave 3 is 261.8% of wave 1, while the wave a correction of the
triangular wave 4 retraced almost 50% of wave 3. After
completion of the triangle, price continued to decline with wave

5 equivalent to 38.2% of the distance from the start of wave 1 to the end of wave 3.

Thus, with the decline coming in five-waves we can expect the rally from 1.5855 to be purely corrective and expect a decline thereafter. The first clean move upwards to 1.6545 is labeled wave A of a higher degree wave -(b)-. This appears to be followed by a triangular wave B ending at 1.6273. From the fact that wave B developed as a triangle, we can deduce that the previous analysis calling for a three-wave incline is correct since triangles only appear as a b wave or a 4 wave. In this case, the triangle is very unlikely to be a wave 4 and is therefore wave -(b)-. If we then add to the end of wave B a figure equal to the length of wave A, we arrive at a target of 1.6963 for wave -(b)-. We could also suggest a target of 1.7389, being 161.8% of wave A. This would take us above the wave -A- peak of 1.7168, but we cannot rule out the possibility of an

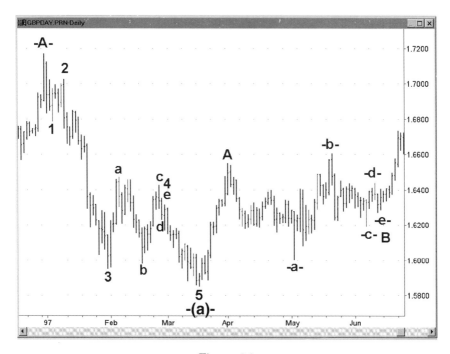

Figure 6.2
The daily GBPUSD chart showing the price decline from wave -A- seen in Figure 6.1. Note how this has developed as a five-wave decline and therefore any rally must be corrective, to be followed by a decline to a low below wave -a-.

expanded flat wave -(b)-. To confirm this, look at a Fibonacci relationship of wave -(a)- by multiplying it by 123.6% or 138.2%; we arrive at 1.7477 and 1.7669 respectively. The first level is quite close, so this should be borne in mind. Let us look at how price progressed from this point.

Figure 6.3 shows the daily bar chart comprising the entire move from the 1.7168 wave -A- peak and thereafter. Following the previous analysis, the conclusion is that one target for the corrective -(b)- wave rally should end around 1.6963 or in the event of an expanded flat, between 1.7389 and 1.7477. In fact, wave -(b)- peaked at 1.6988—only 25 points away from wave equality with wave A. The subsequent decline developed in five waves to form wave -(c)-. Within wave -(c)- we saw good Fibonacci relationships:

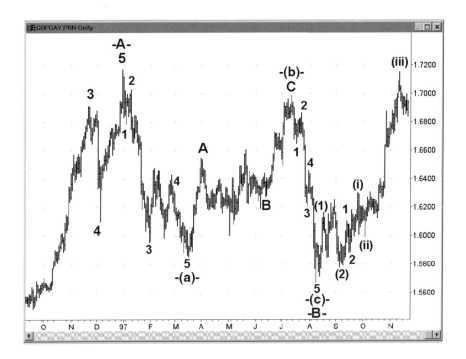

Figure 6.3
*The daily GBPUSD chart showing price action seen in Figures 6.1 and 6.2
and thereafter. Note how after the five-wave decline of wave -(a)-, a
corrective rally in wave -(b)- develops and wave -(c)- declines in five waves
below wave -(a)-. This then completes a three-wave correction and is
followed by an impulsive move upwards—which is still in progress.*

Wave 3   = 161.8% of wave 1.
Wave 4   = 38.2% of wave 3.
Wave 5   = The length from the beginning of wave 1 to the
               end of wave 3.
Wave -(c)- = Wave -(a)-.

2. **Wave C in a zigzag, double zigzag, triple three, flat,
or expanded flat will always develop in five waves—
either impulsive or as a diagonal triangle.**

This rule applies to all the waves detailed above. While
zigzags, double zigzags, and triple threes have wave A
developing in five waves, and flats and expanded flats have
wave A developing in three waves, in all these cases, the final
leg of the correction will develop in five waves which form the
counter-trend correction.

Figure 6.3 is an example of a neat ABC pattern where
waves -(a)- and -(c)- are equal, and both comprise five waves
each. Figure 6.4 shows a double zigzag in the US 30-Year Bond

Figure 6.4
*Wave (C) developing in five waves in the weekly US 30-Year Bond
Futures market.*

Futures chart starting in October 1981 and completing in September 1993. (Until wave (B) is broken, we cannot be certain that this will not continue to develop into a triple three). Let us examine the first ABC pattern.

Figure 6.5 breaks down the first ABC pattern of Figure 6.4 in the daily chart. It can be seen that both waves A and C comprise five waves each. Wave C is approximately 161.8% of wave A. Referring back to Figure 6.4 subsequent to the first ABC pattern, wave X develops and retraces back to the level of the wave B trough. This is followed by a further ABC pattern in which wave (B) is a large triangle. Figure 6.6 shows the development of price action from the end of wave (A), through the triangle, and then the breach to complete wave (C).

It is interesting to note that the triangle developed with the lengths of alternate waves being related.

Wave c = 50% of wave a.
Wave d = 50% of wave b.
Wave e = 50% of wave c.

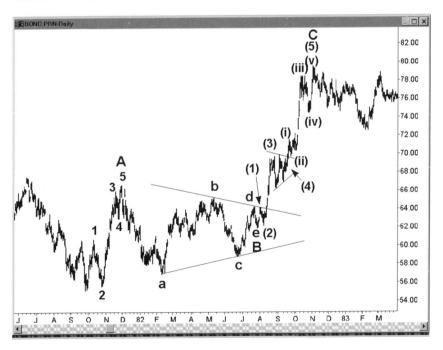

Figure 6.5
*A wave C developing in five waves in the daily US 30-Year
Bond Futures market.*

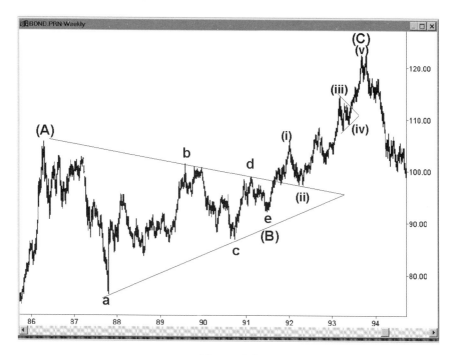

Figure 6.6
Development of price action following from Figure 6.5, again as a wave (C)
in five smaller waves.

Wave (C) then develops as a diagonal triangle with wave (iii) being only slightly longer than wave (i), and wave (v) being 61.8% of wave (iii). Finally wave (C) is approximately 61.8% of wave (A).

As a further example of wave C developing in five waves, Figure 6.7 shows the US dollar against the Japanese yen from July 1994 to January 1995 during which there was a complex flat correction. The entire correction from the initial low of 96.50 on the July 12, 1994 to the 101.55 peak on the January 4, 1995 developed as a flat correction. Within this correction, wave {B} comprises an ABC pattern where the wave (B) also developed as a flat. In this complex move, there are several C waves, of which four have been labeled—the others not being discernible from the daily bar chart. First, since a flat always begins with a three-wave A wave, there is a diagonal triangle wave C in wave {A}. Similarly, since wave (B) developed as a flat, there is also a C wave within wave (A) although this

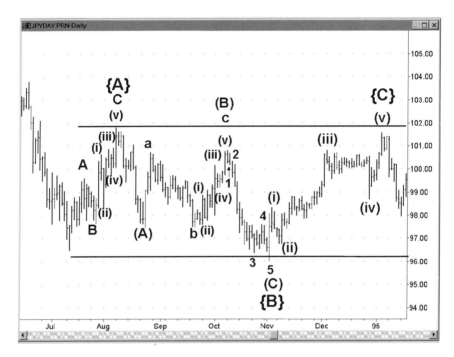

Figure 6.7
*Several C waves developing as five waves: in wave C of {A}, in wave c of
(B), and in wave {C}.*

cannot be discerned from the daily chart. There will also be at
least one C wave in wave b although this cannot be seen.
Second, wave c within wave (B) developed as a diagonal
triangle. This was followed by a decline in five impulsive waves
to form our third wave (C), which completed wave {B}. Finally,
wave {C} also developed in a diagonal triangle, completing just
below the peak of wave {A} in a classic flat.

As a final example, Figure 6.8 shows the daily chart of the
WTI Crude Oil cash market from May to December 1993. Price
had broken lower from the end of a triangle and after an initial
wave {1} decline, an expanded flat wave {2} was formed. In this
wave {2}, the market rallied in three waves to form wave (A)
within which wave C comprised a diagonal triangle. Wave C
declined sharply to complete wave (B). Price then rallied in five
waves yet again to the level of the wave (A) peak thus
completing an expanded flat correction. Subsequently price
once again dropped in a wave {3} decline.

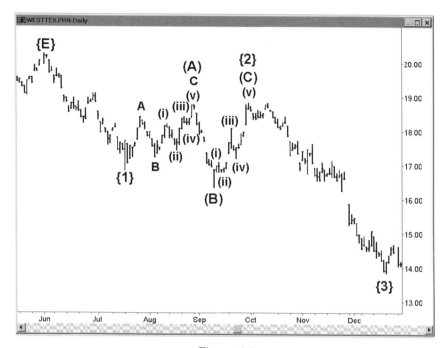

Figure 6.8
C waves developing in five waves, as seen in wave C of (A) and
also wave (C).

3. Price patterns need not necessarily be "neat" or "tidy".

Some analysts prefer patterns, such as triangles or diagonal triangles, to develop within lines that they have drawn. This is not necessary and can actually cause an incorrect wave count to be used. The most important issue is that the internal wave structures are satisfied. Let us look at examples of how some wave structures do not actually develop as their names would suggest.

Figure 6.9 shows the weekly bar chart of the US 30-Year Bond Yield in a large decline from 10.42% in December 1987 to 5.769% in October 1993. I have labeled this decline as three sets of ABC patterns that can be counted either as a declining diagonal triangle or a triple three depending on the wave structure prior to the 10.42% high marked as ??. However, within this declining structure, the initial wave (B) and the second wave X have developed as triangles that do not

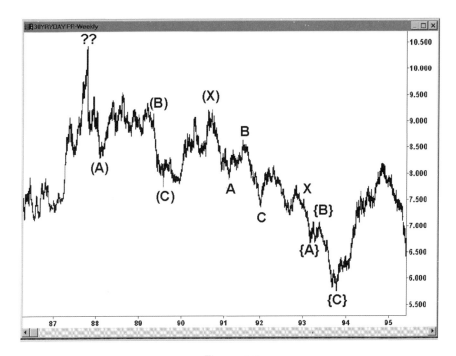

Figure 6.9
A diagonal triangle in the weekly US T-Bond Yield chart. However, it does not develop within tidy support or resistance lines.

resemble closely to what would mathematically be regarded as a triangular pattern. Nor if the entire downward move were a diagonal triangle, would this structure fit nicely into a downward declining wedge between two converging lines or a pair of parallel lines. However, I find the wave count seen in Figure 6.9 most possible due to a large number of Fibonacci relationships that occur between relevant waves. To establish these relationships, let us examine each individual sector of the decline.

Figure 6.10 shows the first ABC structure with wave (B) labeled as a triangle. This pattern does not look very much like a triangle. However, each of the individual legs of the triangle are constructed of three waves, each with the following Fibonacci relationships to support the entire structure:

In wave A,
Wave A = 61.8% of wave (A).
Wave b = 61.8% of wave a.

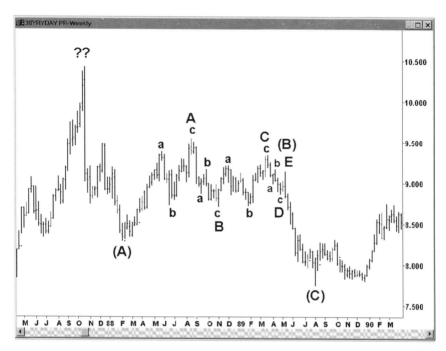

Figure 6.10
*A triangular wave (B) in the daily US T-Bond Yield chart that does not
develop within neat converging support or resistance lines.*

Wave c   =   0.764% of wave a.

In wave B,
Wave b   =   50% of wave a.
Wave c   =   61.8% of wave a.

In wave C,
Wave C   =   50% of wave A.
Wave c   =   123.6% of wave a.

In wave D,
Wave D   =   61.8% of wave B.
Wave b   =   50% of wave a.
Wave c   =   76.4% of wave a.

Wave E   =   38.2% of wave C.

Wave (C) =   61.8% of wave (A).

Thus, with the large number of Fibonacci relationships, wave (B) certainly looks to comprise five three-wave moves that, although do not conform to a triangle developing within two converging lines, certainly have the correct internal wave structures. Similarly, with waves (A) and (C) related to each other, I cannot construct a more convincing alternative.

The fact that waves A and C of Figure 6.9 are almost identical in length and that the intervening corrective wave B retraces between 50% and 61.8% (in three waves where waves a and c are equal in length as seen in Figure 6.11), supports the labeling as an ABC move. This structure is shown in Figure 6.11 with the second triangle developing as a wave X after the second ABC pattern.

The triangular wave X has the following Fibonacci relationships with other waves:

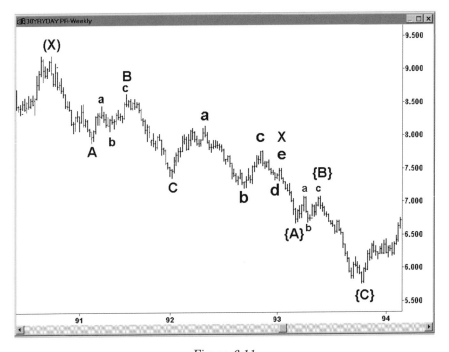

Figure 6.11
The same chart seen in Figure 6.10 but with more detail shown for the second and third ABC moves. Waves A and C are almost equal in length. Wave X forms a triangle but one that does not hold between tidy support and resistance lines.

Wave b = 123.6% of wave a.
Wave c = 0.764% of wave a.
Wave d = 50% of wave b.
Wave e = 38.2% of wave c.

To complete the downward move, wave {B} retraces 50% of wave {A} and wave {C} is 1.618% of wave {A}.

Now let us examine a diagonal triangle within the fundamentals of the Elliott Wave Principle. Wave relationships will be established and an example will be given of a pattern resembling an ascending or descending wedge, with the wave (iv) overlapping the wave (i). However, this need not necessarily be true—diagonal triangles are five waves of three and these are the only requirements for the pattern. Figure 6.12 shows the US 30-Year Bond Futures market in a rally between September 1990 and September 1993. This section of price action has been shown in Figure 6.6 when illustrating

Figure 6.12
Daily US T-Bond Futures chart displaying a diagonal triangle rally. Note how although waves (i) to (iv) remained within a rising channel, wave (v) broke through this channel before reversing.

wave C always developing in 5 waves. Figure 6.12 shows the daily bar chart thus giving slightly more detail. Note that the diagonal triangle has neither developed between two converging lines nor two parallel lines. (Although the first four waves held between two channel lines, the fifth wave broke through these.)

In support of the count being a diagonal triangle, the following relationships can be measured:

In wave (i),
Wave b   =   38.2% of wave a.
Wave c   =   Wave a.

Wave (ii) =   61.8% of wave (i).

In wave (iii), unfortunately wave a and wave b are not equal although the internal five-wave counts of each have Fibonacci relationships:

Wave b   =   61.8% of wave a.

In wave (v),
Wave b   =   61.8% of wave a.
Wave c   =   161.8% of wave a.
Wave (v) =   61.8% of wave (iii).

Note also that in this diagonal triangle, wave (iv) did not overlap wave (i). Although it has been explained that diagonal triangles provide the only exception to the unbreakable rule that waves 1 and 4 cannot overlap, it is not necessary for them to do so. There are many cases where the waves (i) and (iv) do not overlap and appear like an impulsive move. The underlying requirement for diagonal triangles is that each of the five waves comprises an abc pattern.

4.   ABC patterns and 121(2) patterns have the same wave counts.

This can be the source of one of the most frequently made errors in wave counting, even by experienced Elliotticians. Figure 6.13 shows how both structures develop and how the internal structures of both are identical. How then should we know when a correction is taking place, or is the start of an extending wave? Clearly, there are totally opposite implications implied from the two wave counts and we should be able to judge this. The easiest answer is to say that a correction can only come after the completion of a five-wave move. However, this is a rather pat answer since there will be many occasions when the internal wave count of a trending move cannot be easily labeled and there are undoubtedly times when errors can be made.

The answer, therefore, is not readily available, though with the aid of cycles, as described in the Chapter 7, we can begin to overcome this problem. However, until we have discussed the use of cycles, we must look at other guidelines that can assist us.

Figure 6.14 shows the same price action of the US 30-Year Bond Futures market as in Figure 6.12 except that I have suggested that as price was rallying higher, an incorrect wave count could have been made as shown. Thus instead of considering wave {B} as a triangle, this wave count was labeled

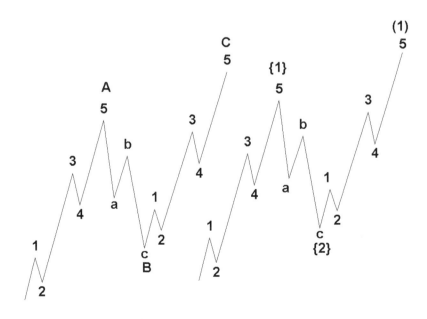

Figure 6.13
5-3-5 patterns can comprise either waves A, B, and C, or waves {1}, {2}, and (1) in an extending wave. Note how each count has opposing implications.

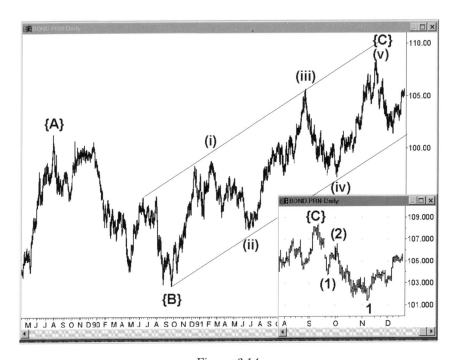

Figure 6.14
The same price action as seen in Figure 6.12 but with an incorrect wave
count suggesting that completion of a five-wave move had been seen
between a rising channel. Note price development in the inset that labels
the decline from wave {C}.

with wave B at the earlier low and a count of a diagonal
triangle made from that point. (Note that in terms of all being
three-wave structures, this does have some basis.) The
argument for this wave count may have been that we had seen
a nice five-wave move rising between parallel lines. In the
bottom right, of Figure 6.14, I have placed the count that
should then have been implied, following what had been
considered the completion of a five-wave incline.

At what point could we have known that the labeled count
was incorrect? Let us consider two of the Elliott guidelines.
First, after the completion of a five-wave move, we expect price
to retrace to the extreme of the second wave of the fifth.
Second, after the completion of a three-wave move, price
usually retraces to the extreme of the intervening wave B.
Figure 6.15 shows the the final stage of the rally along with the
decline labeled (1)(2)1.

There are several clues here. First, price indeed declined to the extreme of the second wave (although this was a second wave of a three-wave leg of a diagonal triangle) but did not decline to the extreme of the wave b. Perhaps this should not be a surprise since there is a rising support line and we may have been cautious as price approached this line. In the decline, wave 1 was just a little longer in length than wave (1), and this is not an uncommon occurrence in situations where an extension occurs. Thus, perhaps we would have been prepared for a correction but would have been anticipating a decline through the support line, perhaps a minor bounce at the wave b extreme, then the full extent of a wave 3 of an extension moving downwards. However, price rallied from the low marked as wave -1- and a count of an ABC pattern in a wave -2- would have been favored. This is where we could have known that we were wrong in our wave count.

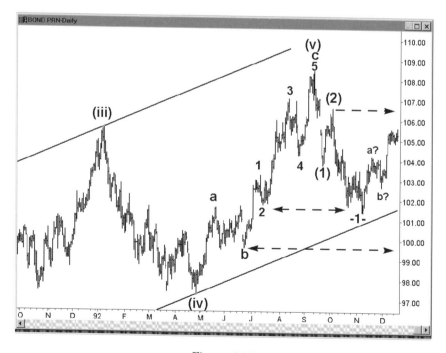

Figure 6.15
Price action as seen in Figure 6.14 is enlarged to show the final stage of the rally and the decline from wave C. Note how we may have counted this decline as waves (1), (2), -1- to imply a declining extended wave.

In this situation, a break of the wave (2) peak would not be allowed under Elliott rules. In this case, we should expect the wave c of wave -2- to be equal to the wave a. As soon as price penetrated this level, and then marked the wave -2- peak, we would have known that we had labeled the wave structure incorrectly and a more bullish alternative would have been sought.

Let us now look at another situation where 535 patterns can confuse. Instead of anticipating a reversal after a move, we instead consider the 535 structure to be merely a correction to an underlying trend, where in fact we had witnessed a 121(2) structure indicating a reversal.

Figure 6.16 shows the same period of price action in the US dollar against the Japanese yen cash market as shown in Figure 6.7. Let us assume that we had placed a wave count as shown in Figure 6.16—that we considered that we were still in the midst of a sideways correction, perhaps in the form of a

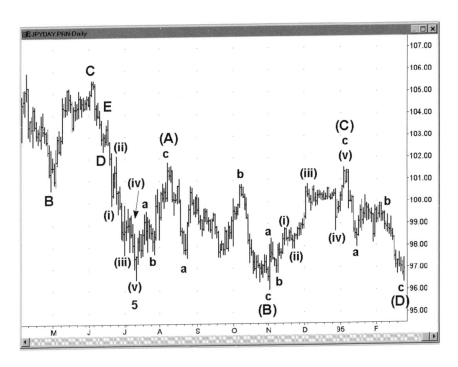

Figure 6.16
Price action as seen in Figure 6.7 with a mistaken wave count suggesting a sideways consolidation, probably a triangle.

triangle. Thus, the peak at 101.55 has been labeled as a wave (C) of the triangle and we are now looking for a wave (D) to be followed by a wave (E).

To break down the wave that has been labeled wave (D), look at Figure 6.17, which shows the completion of two nice five-wave declines from the wave (C) peak down to what has been labeled a wave (D). Clearly, the expectation from this wave count is we should see a rally above the wave (4) corrective peak and back to the wave (2) or wave -B- peaks, from where a larger decline is expected. The entire labeling *appears* to be in accordance with a series of three-wave moves. Thus the logic behind the expectation of a rally is quite valid. However, since we have seen two five-wave declines, we must also be aware that this could also be a 121 pattern and we should therefore consider the possibility of this other wave count being correct. Thus, we should always have a "reserve" wave count and be aware of the implications this reserve count could have.

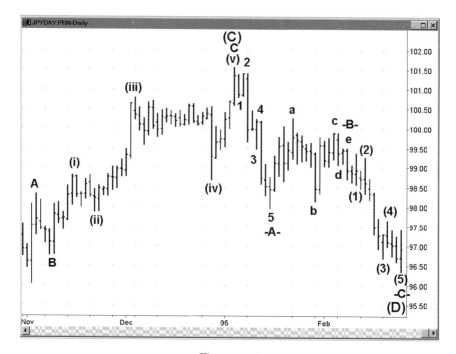

Figure 6.17
Price action as in Figure 6.16 enlarged to display the assumed wave count.

Figure 6.18 shows how a second wave count has been anticipated. It is important here to clearly label the different potential wave counts in a clear manner. Personally I use different colors to label counts on the technical analysis software I use and this enables me to follow each count without confusion. As Figure 6.18 is in black and white, the alternative wave counts can begin to look confusing. However, starting at the bottom left corner of the chart, it can be seen that I have placed B or (B) to acknowledge that perhaps we had completed wave (B) of a flat correction and this would imply a slight change in the labeling of the rally from this low to the high marked C or (C). It must be remembered that in some situations the actual internal wave count of a particular move is difficult to substantiate as a certainty and mistakes or problems of this type can arise. (In fact, the Fibonacci relationships are much more accurate with the alternative wave count).

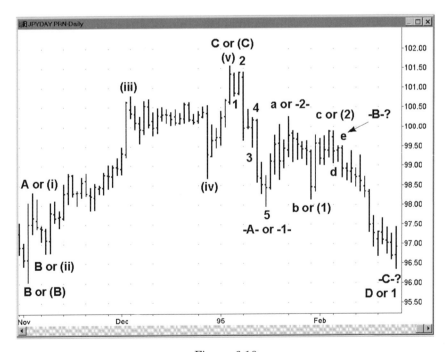

Figure 6.18
Price action as seen in Figures 6.16 and 6.17 shown here with an alternative wave count.

Thus, with the 101.55 peak labeled C or (C), we realize that this can be considered a major peak and that the subsequent declines should be labeled in an impulsive manner. The first five-wave decline is therefore quite clearly a choice between wave -A- or -1-. However, after this, we face a problem. The original count had a wave -B- developing as a triangle. As discussed earlier, triangles appear only in a wave B or wave 4 position. Thus we cannot label the original wave -B- as -B- or -2- and we should label the original wave a as A or -2-. This itself should force us to look at the subsequent decline that was originally labeled as wave b since we have here an obvious disparity of internal wave counts. B waves are comprised of three waves, while a wave 1 comprises five waves. Thus a closer look at the decline in a shorter time frame should be made in order to identify, if possible, exactly how the decline developed. In the daily chart, it would appear to resemble a three-wave decline—the hourly chart might resolve this disputed count.

It is here that we should allow ourselves some latitude. Even now I cannot identify every single internal wave count of some of the wave counts I have made. When I began practicing the Elliott Wave Principle, it caused me some doubts. However, after garnering a great deal of experience, I have discovered that where there is an element of dispute concerning internal wave counts, I give greater weight to other forms of analysis such as cycles and momentum indicators while at the same time preparing alternative wave counts with anticipated reactions implied from these wave counts.

In the situation described I would continue labeling the low (originally labeled as wave b) as wave b or (1), knowing that a wave b would imply a subsequent wave c rally, while a wave (1) would imply a wave (2) correction—in both cases the same reaction. The subsequent move up is therefore labeled c or (2). In the decline from this point, we have to decide whether the first slight move down constructed a wave d or the wave 1 of a five-wave decline. In either case, the important factor is that the following peaks declined thereby implying a downtrend. Thus we have no further problem until the final low labeled as wave D or 1.

It is at this low shown that we have a problem to solve. A wave count of wave D would imply a rally back to the wave B level while a wave 1 would imply a correction in a wave 2 before further declines. The first obstacle to overcome would be the previous wave 4 peak—price moving above this level would allow further gains, though even a wave 2 count would also allow this. We should also note that this low is only slightly above the low marked B or (B) on the far left and any break below this level would confirm the impulsive count down and cause us to be extremely bearish with the 1212 (extended wave) count implied.

The subsequent price action is shown in Figure 6.19. It can be seen that the rally from the final low shown in previous charts was very shallow and the low at 96.05 marked wave (B) was broken within days, implying the alternative wave 1212 count. Thus by preparing alternative wave counts in advance, when incorrect forecasts result (as with any other form of analysis) it is possible to rapidly anticipate the correct wave count and thus the correct development of price action from that point.

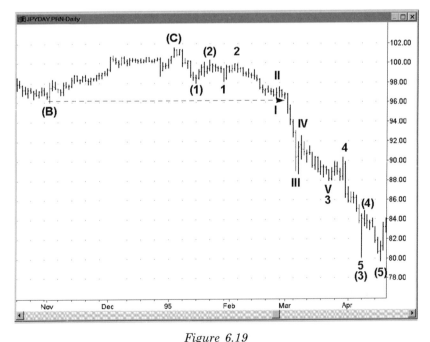

Figure 6.19
Development of price action from Figure 6.18. Price now breaks below the wave (B) level at 96.20, thus signaling that the corrective wave counts were incorrect and the impulsive counts were correct.

5. When looking at complex corrections, always refer to the Elliott guidelines.

A common source of confusion often arises when attempting to assess stalling points of complex corrections. While this cannot completely be eliminated, a useful rule of thumb is to apply Fibonacci retracement levels and also the Elliott guidelines regarding common retracement levels. There are two useful guidelines:

- After the completion of a five-wave move, prices commonly retrace to the span of the fourth wave of one lesser degree and, specifically, to the extreme of the second wave of the fifth.
- After the completion of an ABC pattern, price usually retraces to the extreme of the intervening wave B.

Figure 6.20 shows both circumstances. In the example, price is rising in five-wave moves. Notice how wave (4) remains above the fourth wave of wave (3) and the rally resumes in a wave (5) subdivided into five internal waves labeled (i) to (v). As we see the completion of the fifth wave labeled wave {1}, we

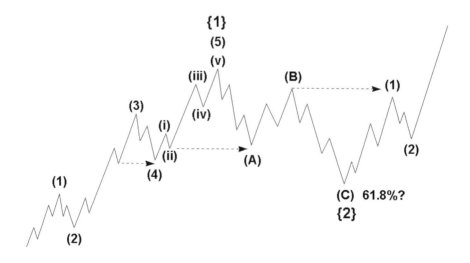

Figure 6.20
Note how in a trending move, wave (4) remains above the fourth wave in wave (3) and how wave (A) retraces to the level of wave (ii) of wave (5).

see the first five waves decline to the base of the wave (ii) of wave (5). This level can provide a base for further price gains (if a three-wave decline is seen) while in some situations it can be a temporary stalling area for a corrective rally before a second decline in wave (C) to complete the entire correction. This may equate to a Fibonacci retracement level. Then, as prices rise once again following the completion of wave {2}, we see that price stalls at the wave (B) peak.

Let us look at a couple of examples of this. Figure 6.21 shows an underlying rally in the currency market of the US dollar against the German Deutschmark from the end of 1992 to the beginning of 1993. This period of price action has been shown before but it provides an excellent example of how both Fibonacci ratios and Elliott's guidelines can be combined. We can see that the US dollar rose in a diagonal triangle to complete wave (v) of wave 5 of wave (3), then subsequently declined in a rather untidy fashion. This decline is rather difficult to label and obviously takes the form of a complex correction—probably a double zigzag. The issue we always face is whether a double zigzag completes the entire correction or whether a triple three will develop and bring one further down. However, as seen, I have added to the chart, a Fibonacci retracement tool which has been drawn to display the corrective levels of 38.2%, 50%, and 61.8% together with Cutler's RSI. Note three points:

- First, price has retraced 38.2% of wave (3).
- Second, price has retraced to the wave (ii) of wave 5.
- Third, Cutler's RSI displays a bullish divergence.

With a combination of these three factors, the suggestion that the decline has completed is much stronger.

Now look at Figure 6.22. This shows a period of the US dollar against the German Deutschmark from the end of 1991 to the beginning of 1992. During this period, the dollar developed in a broad decline that completed at 1.5010 in a double bottom, failed fifth. Note how the failed fifth reversed price rapidly and within days had retraced to the extreme of the wave B. Following this, price corrected in a simple zigzag, but with wave b developing as a complex rally. Note that waves a and c are of equal length and moved to complete a 61.8%

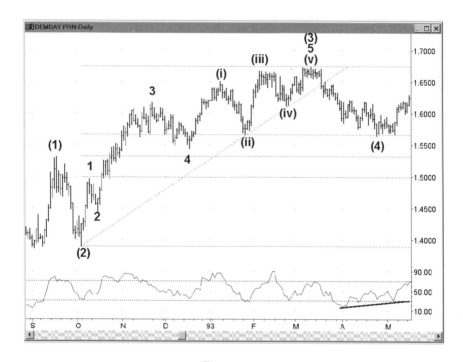

Figure 6.21
An example combining Fibonacci ratios with Elliott's guidelines to provide
a stronger picture.

correction of the original wave -A-. While no divergence is seen at this point, there are plenty of other examples in this section of price action, including the peak at wave -C- where waves -A- and -C- are equal. The entire correction actually moved to just above a 50% retracement of the entire downtrend.

6. Wave 4 or wave B will provide support in an uptrend and resistance in a downtrend.

Refer briefly to the Elliott guidelines. Basically the guideline states that after the completion of a five-wave structure, price will retrace to the span of the wave 4 of one lesser degree and usually to the extreme of the second wave of the fifth. Figure 6.23 shows how this type of price action will develop. Note how the wave 4 correction in wave (3) corrects to the span of the previous wave (iv) (this being the wave 4 of one lesser degree). From this correction, price continued higher in

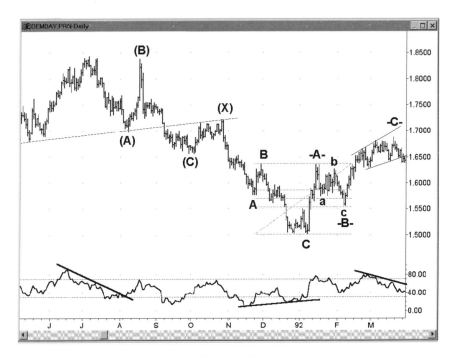

Figure 6.22
Note how at the wave C trough, bullish divergences supported a reversal
and how wave -A- retraced to the same level as wave B. A 61.8%
retracement in wave -B- then followed. Wave -C- is equal to wave -A-,
and was accompanied by a bearish rising expanded triangle and
a bearish divergence.

five waves to complete wave (5). The illustration shows how price declines to the wave 2 that rests within the span of wave (4).

If we consider the simple definition of trends, this guideline fits in very well. An uptrend is where successive highs are higher *and* successive lows are also higher. This is exactly how Elliott had suggested price action will develop. It therefore gives us some clues as to what to expect at these moments. At times, where the wave count is a little ambiguous, we can state that once the wave 4 low in an uptrend, or the wave 4 high in a downtrend has broken, there is far greater risk of price reversal.

When considering whether a correction has completed, the same thing can be said of a wave B. Double zigzags and triple threes are complex corrective patterns and the Elliott

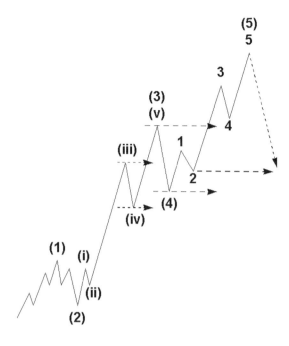

Figure 6.23
Subsequent fourth waves provide support in an uptrend and until broken,
the uptrend can be considered to continue.

guidelines on its own cannot predict whether the correction will develop into one of these patterns. Thus, looking at Figure 6.24 it can be seen that the description of a trend also fits into this situation. (Remember that part of a correction is a *countertrend*.) Thus, the correction cannot be deemed as potentially complete until a B wave has been broken.

Figure 6.25 shows the development of the US dollar against the Japanese yen after the historic low at 79.75. This is an interesting example since I have seen many different interpretations of this movement. Clearly, it is a very complex rally and although I have indicated my personal interpretation of the wave structure, I am still not certain of it. While many critics of Elliott will point to this as a failure of the principle, there are some underlying clues we can gain from Elliott guidelines. While the dramatic reversal to the downtrend could not have been anticipated from the Elliott Wave Principle, we can note that the level a around 79.00/80.00 was a valid target as it is approximately equal to the other two downward moves

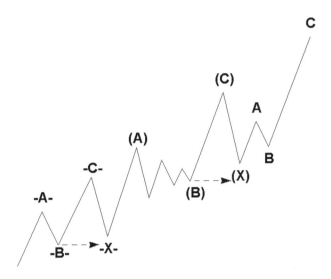

Figure 6.24
An example of how B waves provide support and until broken, a correction
can still be considered to be intact.

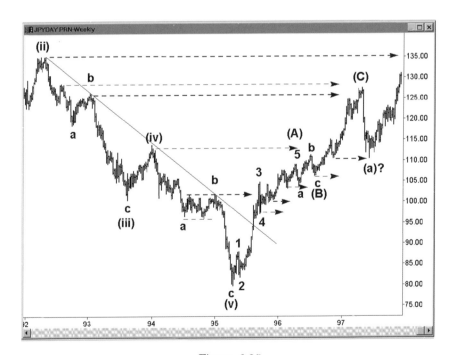

Figure 6.25
Note how the principle of support and resistance can be linked to Elliott
wave counts, and how the uptrend from the 79.75 low at wave (v)
remained intact while corrective lows did not break.

from the 160.20 peak (not shown). The break of the long-term downtrend line was a strong clue, and then break of the wave b peak at 101.55 and the peak at 113.60 that represented the previous wave (iv). Note that during this period of movement upwards, each subsequent corrective low moved higher and in several cases important resistances were broken. Since the wave structure was particularly complex, the fact that these corrective lows were never breached should have guarded against a strongly bearish forecast. These lows began with the initial wave 4, then continued with the second wave of wave 5, then the fourth wave of wave 5. Even after completion of five waves (as I have counted them), wave a failed to breach the previous wave 4 and an expanded flat correction was seen, and once again wave (B) failed to penetrate the wave 4 of wave 5. Price then continued higher to complete five waves at 127.50, which I have labeled wave (C).

The decline from the wave (C) peak was confirmed once the wave 4 of the wave (C) had been breached. The decline was sharp and made its way down to the level of the wave (B) trough but held above the trough of the wave 2 of wave (C). From there, price rose towards the peak of 135.00 of the wave (ii) of the decline from 160.20. This also coincides with a 138.2% extension of the wave (a) decline from 127.50 to 110.57.

Figure 6.26 shows a similar picture in the US dollar market against the German Deutschmark with the weekly chart on the left showing a five-wave rally and the chart on the right showing the correction from the 1.8915 peak. The rally from the low marked as wave (2)? at 1.3805 was a clear five-wave pattern with Fibonacci relationships to support it. Within this rally, we saw a wave 3 equal to 1.618 of wave 1 and wave 5 equal to 0.618 of the length of wave 1 to wave 3. Subsequent to the completion of the five-wave move, we could look at two things: one, that we expect the dollar to decline to the span of the second wave of the fifth and within the span of the fourth. If we also took a Fibonacci 0.382 correction of the entire five-wave move, we arrive at a value of 1.6962. The decline from the 1.8915 peak is quite complex and there are times when the actual wave structure becomes ambiguous. However, if we had looked at the Elliott guidelines, we would have seen that the important peaks on the way down were not broken. Even the wave (X) failed to move above the previous wave (B) and the

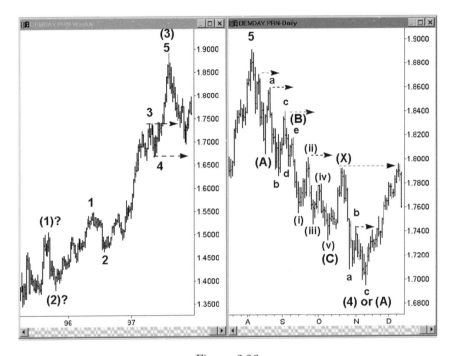

Figure 6.26
On the left is an example of an impulsive rally in the USDDEM currency
market followed by a decline from the wave (3) peak that found support in
the span of wave 4. On the right note how the decline developed, with each
corrective peak remaining unbroken.

decline continued down to 1.6950 only a few points below the
0.382 measurement and well within the span of the previous
fourth wave. The second wave of the fifth is rather difficult to
see, but the combination of the above provides a strong guide
to the subsequent upward move. Also note how in the move up
from 1.6950, price stalled just marginally above the wave (X)
peak. This suggests that further strength is possible after a
correction lower.

A final example of how a fourth wave acts as a barrier to
price is shown in Figure 6.27. This shows the Hang Seng Index
Futures market in a sharp collapse after its rally to the 16,765
peak in August 1997. Price rallied in five waves to this peak
and this rally had several supporting Fibonacci relationships.
It is interesting to note how the initial decline bounced just
above the wave 4 trough, around a level that looks to have been
the wave 2 correction. The second decline broke through this

low and declined sharply to the wave 2 low of wave (5), but within the span of the previous fourth wave. While timing requires additional analysis, the degrees of such moves are very common and provide excellent clues as to the levels to target after the completion of five waves and also control excessive bullishness or bearishness until such levels are broken.

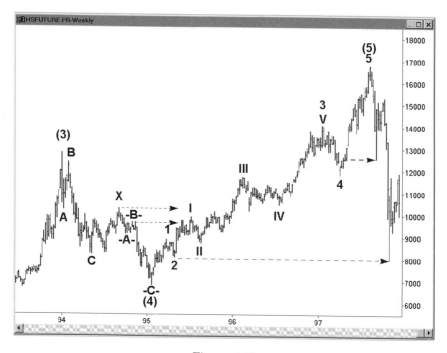

Figure 6.27
The Hang Seng Futures showing how after breach of the wave X, prices rallied and each subsequent corrective low moved higher. Note how the initial decline from wave (5) first stalled just above wave 4, then broke through to move to the wave 2 of wave (5).

CHAPTER 7

Cycle Analysis

Cycle analysis is not a widely practiced form of technical analysis but increasingly, analysts are beginning to incorporate its concepts into their forecasting while some traders appear to be using the technique as well. Cycle analysis is not a concept that can be grasped quickly, but with patience and practice, it can provide a distinctly valuable addition to the basket of analytical tools. Cycle analysis assists in identifying the approximate timing of trend reversals and general upward or downward movements. On its own, cycle analysis is valuable, but when combined with other techniques, it can contribute to profitable trades.

The basic idea behind cycles is that natural events occur in recognizable cycles, e.g. the period taken by planets to circle the Sun, Earth's revolution around the Sun which produces the four seasons, the revolution of the moon around Earth which affects the tidal patterns of the oceans, etc. Intense research into cycles has been undertaken by Edward R. Dewey, Stan Erlich, and Walter Bressert, who have noted certain cycles, such as the 9.6-year cycle in Atlantic salmon abundance, a 22-year cycle in international battles, an 11-year cycle in sunspot activity, and one that many recognize, the 60-year cycle of economic depression. We readily accept many of these cycles in our daily lives, such as the re-occurring business cycles, cycles identifying industrial expansion and recession. The same concept can also be applied to market behavior.

Some basic principles of cycles will first be discussed. This will be followed by a description of how cycles can be measured and used in a trading environment.

CYCLIC PRINCIPLES

There are four basic principles associated with cycles and an understanding of these would assist in applying cycle analysis.

- Summation   Cycles (and its associated cyclic force) can be "added" together.

- Harmonicity   Neighboring cycles are normally related by a multiple of two.
- Synchronicity   There is a strong tendency for related cycles to reach troughs at about the same time.
- Proportionality   Cycle amplitude is usually related by a multiple of two.

Figure 7.1 illustrates these four principles at work. Notice that the smallest cycle has an amplitude of X and the next larger cycle has an amplitude of 2X (principle of proportionality). Also, note that two smallest cycles (X) occur over the same time period as one of the next larger cycle (2X) (principle of harmonicity), and that the troughs of these X and 2X cycles occur at the same time (principle of synchronicity). These principles are also observed in the larger cycles—two 2X cycles occur within a single 4X cycle and two 4X cycles occur within the 8X cycle. Each larger cycle has an amplitude double

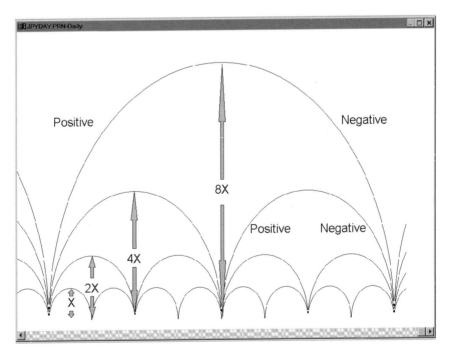

Figure 7.1
A series of cycle lengths displaying the cyclic principles of harmonicity, synchronicity, proportionality, and summation.

that of the next smaller cycle, and the troughs of all cycles converge at the same time. Finally, it is possible to suggest that when the cycle is rising, it has increasing positive pressure, and when it is declining, it reverses this pressure, becoming negative on the way down. By totaling the effects of these cycles, it is possible to see how strong the upward or downward price movement should be. This is the principle of summation.

Figure 7.2 illustrates this in another way—as sine waves that can be added together to give positive or negative values. Four cycles are shown in this illustration—a large dominant cycle, a long cycle, a medium cycle, and a shorter cycle. In reality, in addition to these four types of cycles, there would be longer and shorter cycles that would contribute to a more complex matrix of cyclic pressures. Figure 7.2 shows three examples of the summation of cycles with their individual pressures. The sum of these pressures is indicated at the base

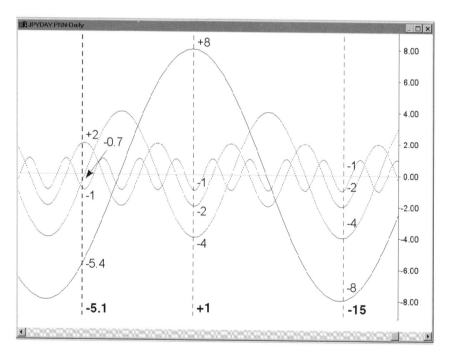

Figure 7.2
Cycles shown as sine waves to illustrate harmonicity, synchronicity, proportionality, and summation. Values are shown to display the force of each cycle, with the sum of these forces shown at the base of the chart (in bold), to highlight the principle of summation.

of the chart. The middle sum shows the largest cycle at its peak. However, because the other three have reached their troughs at this time, the total pressure from all the cycles would only be +1. Moving down the right of the largest cycle to reach its trough, the other three cycles have also found their troughs, in accordance with the principle of harmonicity, and the combined pressure would be −15. To the left of the chart is an example of cyclic pressure during an upward swing of the largest cycle which has not yet crossed to positive, and so the combined cyclic pressure is −5.1.

Note also in Figure 7.2 how the four cycles will find lows at the same time (principle of synchronicity), that the frequency of the cycles is related by a ratio of 2:1 as the cycles become larger (principle of harmonicity), and that each cycle has an amplitude twice that of the next smaller cycle (principle of proportionality).

Figure 7.3 shows the monthly chart of the British pound against the US dollar, onto which a series of cycles have been drawn. Observe the profound effect the second largest cycle has on price action, with major price lows coinciding with all the troughs of this cycle. In addition, the second trough of this cycle is accompanied by the troughs of all the other cycles, coinciding with the very strong downward influence that pushed price down to 1.037 in February 1985. Since that low we have seen a good recovery, but this failed twice around the 2.00 level, and soon after the largest cycle began to decline.

Note that because cycle troughs are synchronized while cycle peaks are not, the effect of their combined cyclic pressure on price action will not be even. This "uneven" effect of summation can sometimes produce confusion when although a cycle trough is seen, there is some upward price movement. In this case, the cyclic pressure of the next larger cycle must be studied to give clues as to why price has not behaved as expected. For instance, in Figure 7.3 we see the obvious combined effect of the cycle troughs on the British pound and the price recovery thereafter.

One question that arises is: Where is the next larger cycle positioned? Did it find a low at the same time as the others in February 1985 or was it at a high? In this instance, it is likely that the largest cycle found a low at the same time. If this had not been the case, then it would be pointing downwards after

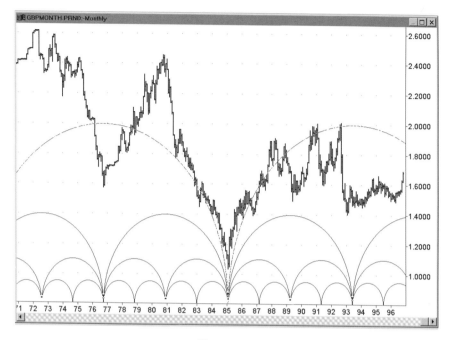

Figure 7.3
Cycles drawn onto the monthly chart of the British pound against
the US dollar.

February 1985 but we have seen little evidence of corresponding price weakness. If this is correct, then the largest cycle will not find a high until the turn of the century and we can expect the British pound to continue consolidating in a broad 1.2–1.80 range for several more years.

TRANSLATION

According to the principle of synchronicity, cycles will reach troughs at about the same time. Many practitioners of cycle analysis often talk about a time band around these exact cycle troughs, a band within which price action tends to find lows rather than find a price low precisely on the cycle trough. We have also seen that cycle peaks do not occur at the same time, thus giving an uneven effect on price action. It follows, therefore, that cycles should be measured from trough to trough. This is clearly the situation in Figure 7.3 of the British pound.

There have been attempts to measure price peak to peak, peak to low, and low to peak. But this is quite complex and goes beyond the coverage of cycles in this book. What we will look at is the effect of translation, which is a simple concept.

Translation is the concept where, when price is in a broad uptrend dictated by the larger cycles, periods of upward movement last longer than the corrective downswings, and as the larger cycles turn down, periods of downward pressure last longer than the corrective upswings.

Figure 7.4 illustrates this concept. Four cycles are shown and as price action starts from the left, it can be seen that the first correction is approximately equal to the initial upward move. However, the low of the correction is above the start of the initial move. This shows that the next larger cycle is pulling price higher and the combined effect of summation is dictating that cyclic values are increasing. The next upward move is stronger and the rally lasts much longer than the correction. This is *right translation* and is the effect of the larger cycles, 3 and 4, moving higher, giving price a stronger

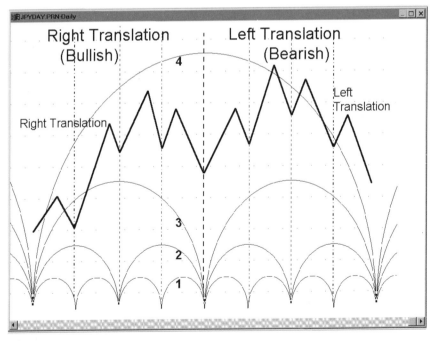

Figure 7.4
Cycles plotted onto price action (bold line) to show the effect of translation.

lift. As cycle 3 dips, the time span of the upward price move reduces slightly and into the cycle 3 trough, price falls back more sharply. This is *left translation*. Then as the second cycle 3 takes off again and as cycle 4 is still high, price rallies longer than the corrective downward movement. Eventually, at the peak of the second cycle 3, while cycle 4 is declining, we see a stronger price correction during which left translation is witnessed and price movement down continues longer than the corrective upswing.

Finally, at the combined troughs of all the cycles, we see that the move to the absolute price high took much longer than the correction and this itself is right translation. Together with this, since the corrective low on the right of the chart is above the low at the start of the rally, we see that the next upward movement should be stronger, taking us to new highs. From this we can surmise that a cycle 5 also found a low at the left of the chart and it is at its highest point at the extreme right of the chart.

Figure 7.5 displays translation in the US dollar–Japanese yen currency market. It highlights two factors when assessing bullish and bearish markets—translation and the degree of upward or downward correction during periods of downward or upward movements, respectively. On the left side of the chart, in the 44-week cycles A and B, we see distinct left translation where the correction periods are shorter than the periods of downtrend. Similarly, the downward moves see new lows being recorded, thereby maintaining the overall bearish trend. At the end of cycle B, we see a stronger recovery as the next larger cycle (88 weeks) reaches its trough, allowing for stronger subsequent upward movement. Price peaks about halfway through the the third 44-week cycle and then declines to a new low but not as low as before.

In the cycle D, we see an interesting combination of events. Although there is a group of cycles pulling lower into a trough, there is right translation. However, the degree of correction is very small and the resultant effect, despite the right translation, is a strong downward move as all four cycles exert influence. In cycle E, we see an equally strong recovery as all cycles begin to turn higher and there is very strong right translation. The correction downwards at the end of this is very brief and shallow. Thus we can reasonably expect to see price

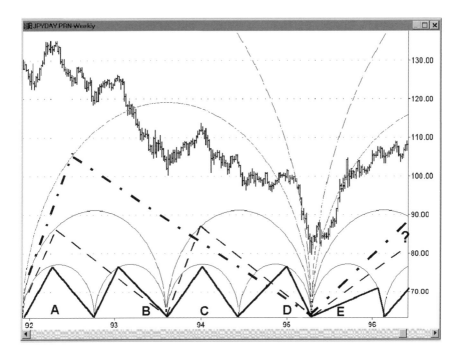

Figure 7.5
Weekly USDJPY currency market chart with cycles and
translation plotted in.

strengthening further. This indeed occurs and it looks to have
right translation again. Thus, if we imagine an additional cycle
drawn at the 79.75 price low, a cycle that is twice as large as
the cycles drawn, we can begin to expect price strengthening
further even though the second larger cycle is beginning to
point lower. This gives quite a bullish picture. Of course, we
must look for other technical factors to support this view, and
one would be the break of the previous major high at 113.65.

This is further confirmed if we look at the translation of
the larger cycles. The 88-week cycle starts with strong left
translation that is repeated in the move down to 79.75.
Similarly, the 176-week cycle has distinct left translation.
Subsequent to the cycles reaching their trough at 79.75, we see
that the 88-week cycle is showing very strong right translation.
This appears to be repeated in the 176-week cycle, thus
confirming that the cyclic expectations are for further price
strengthening.

DETRENDING

While the previous examples have been fairly obvious, there are many times where this is not the case. Where there is a clear trend, it can often be difficult to establish where the cycle lows should appear, especially in shorter-term charts. So, in order to remove the effect of a trend, we can "detrend" the market. Detrending is a process of measuring market fluctuations after the effects of trends have been removed. How do we remove the effect of trends? We discussed in Chapter 3 that the moving average is an indicator of trending markets. If we measure the fluctuation of price movement away from a moving average, we can obtain a more accurate reflection of relative strength.

But what period length of moving average should we use? At the beginning of this chapter, we examined the basic principles of cycles and saw that cycles have a tendency to be related to each other by a multiple of two in both duration and amplitude (principles of harmonicity and proportionality). Using these principles, choose a moving average of the length of the cycle and *move it back by half its length*. This is a *centered* moving average. So, in the case of the US dollar—Japanese yen weekly market we saw in Figure 7.5, we should detrend around a 44-week centered moving average. Figure 7.6 shows how the cycle detrend is calculated; the left chart shows price with a 44-week centered moving average. For each bar, the distance between the high of each bar to the moving average is measured (e.g. A) and the distance between the low of each bar to the moving average is also measured (e.g. B). The centered average from which the measurements of A and B are made is taken as a constant value of zero to create a detrended chart. The outcome is shown in the right chart of Figure 7.6.

Figure 7.7 shows the detrended chart of the US dollar—Japanese yen weekly market. The interesting point to note here is the consistent peak of price around the 8.0 level on the detrended chart, which means that for six years, any corrective price rally was stalled ¥8.0 from the 44-week centered moving average. Note also how at every cycle trough detrended price occurred *below* the moving average although a support level of −8.0 is not quite as consistent due to the dominant downtrend.

Figure 7.8 is another example of a detrended chart added to a price chart. In this case, the WTI Crude Oil market also

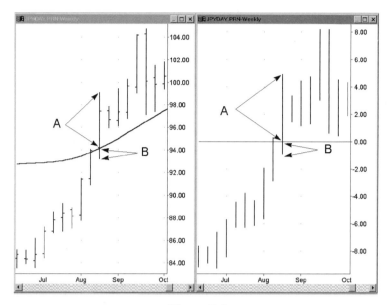

Figure 7.6
The left chart shows a normal bar chart with moving average applied.
The right chart shows the detrended chart with the moving average
rescaled to zero with price bars plotted as a value above and below
the moving average.

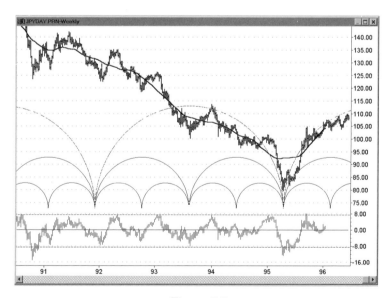

Figure 7.7
Weekly USDJPY market with cycles and a detrended chart (below)
calculated as a distance from a moving average.

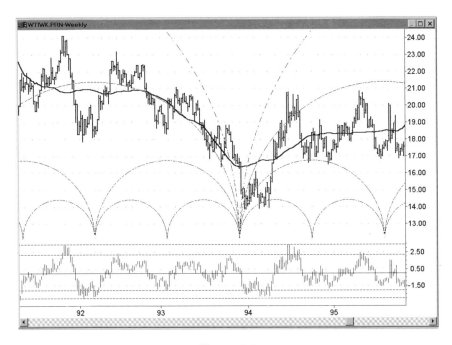

Figure 7.8
Weekly WTI Crude Oil market with cycles, moving average,
and detrended chart (below).

has a 44-week cycle. Note the extremes of the detrended chart around the zero line and how there are two predominant levels that provide support and resistance around the centered moving average. It is interesting to note that often, price managed to penetrate the inner bands when there was either a peak or trough of the next larger 88-week cycle. Note also the left translation in the first part of the chart. After the low is seen at $13.90, note how this translation changes to right translation—a sign of bullishness.

Finally, to confirm the choice of the length of the centered moving average as the period length of the predominant underlying cycle, look at Figure 7.9 which shows the same WTI crude oil chart as in Figure 7.8, but with 44-week and 20-week centered moving averages. The 44-week detrended chart is the higher of the two detrended charts. Since price hugs a shorter-term moving average more closely, note how if a shorter-term moving average is used, price crosses through the moving average more frequently, causing the detrended chart to look

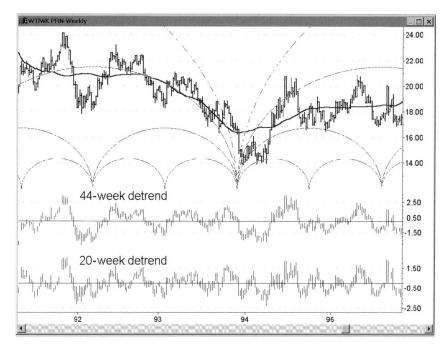

Figure 7.9
*Weekly WTI crude oil with detrended charts calculated with 44-week and
20-week moving averages. Note how the 20-week detrend causes a messy
plot with cycles less easy to identify.*

confusing. This often prevents the identification of the
underlying cycle peak or trough.

RECOGNIZING CYCLE PEAKS

While cycle troughs can be measured as being equidistant, the
measurement of cycle peaks is not so straightforward.
Measurements for trough to peak, peak to trough, and trough
to trough can be made but the process is quite complex and
subject to greater fluctuation than for measurements between
troughs. In some ways, the identification of cycle peaks is really
a matter of integrating all forms of analysis, but I shall
introduce here one further concept that has assisted in many
cases. It is another use of Relative Spread Strength (RSS), the
indicator introduced in Chapter 4.

Although RSS was developed for a completely different
purpose, I find RSS is an excellent tool in the longer-term

charts for identifying broad timing of cycle peaks. To recap, RSS is calculated by running the spread between two moving averages through the RSI formula before smoothing it to give a broad upward and downward sweep. From this section we know that moving averages are intrinsic to detrending price charts. A centered moving average cannot be used because it is a simple moving average moved back by half its period length and therefore no value exists for the most recent periods. However, by using the cycle length for one moving average and one-quarter of this for the second moving average, we have made RSS reflect the underlying cyclic flow of the market. This is a reflection of the fact that a simple moving average of half the cycle length can be used for detrending (though it produces less accurate indications), and if we then take a further half of that value, we have noted the harmonic principle of cycles.

Figure 7.10 shows the US dollar–Japanese yen currency market with RSS (at the bottom of the figure) using lengths of 44 and 11 weeks for moving averages. In general, cycle peaks and troughs are matched with peaks and troughs in RSS, respectively. As a guideline, when RSS falls below 20 a cycle

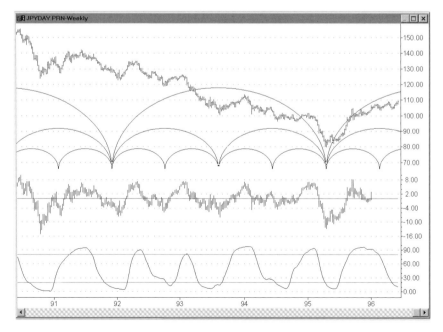

Figure 7.10
Weekly USDJPY currency market with detrended chart and RSS (below).

trough is expected, look at other forms of analysis to confirm a price low; when RSS rallies above 80, look at other forms of analysis to confirm a price high. It is important to understand that RSS crossing above 80 or below 20 is not the sell or buy signal—it is part of a group of supporting factors. I shall cover this in greater depth in Chapter 9 on integrating different forms of analysis. For now, I shall show a few more examples of RSS together with cycle charts.

Figure 7.11 is a chart of WTI crude oil with RSS clearly displaying broad indications of price highs and lows. Figure 7.12 is a chart of US 30-Year Bond Yield which displays a 49-week cycle (predominantly 98 weeks) with RSS giving good supporting indications of cycle peaks and troughs. Note also how the guideline resistance areas on the detrended chart can be used to identify cycle highs. Figure 7.13 shows Japanese Government Bond Futures which has a predominant 54-week cycle. RSS matched this market quite well with only one or two exceptions and could be used with approximate support and resistance in the detrended chart.

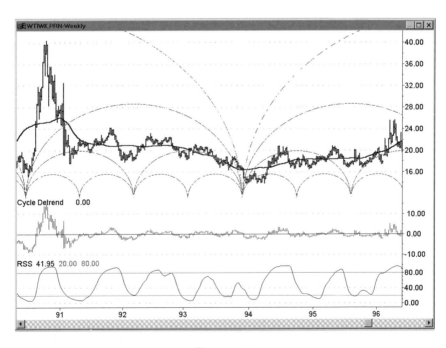

Figure 7.11
Weekly WTI Crude Oil market with detrended chart and RSS (below).

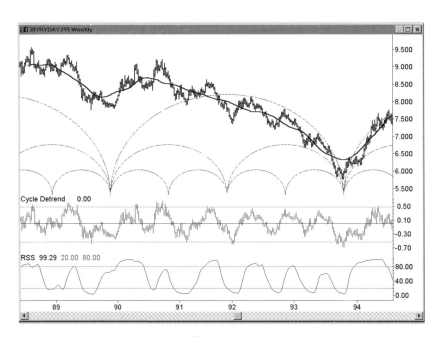

Figure 7.12
Weekly US 30-Year Bond Yield with detrended chart and RSS (below).

Figure 7.13
Weekly Japanese Government Bond Futures market with cycles, detrended
chart and RSS (below).

CHAPTER 8

Cycles: Hints and Tips

One of the problems I initially faced when attempting to apply cycle analysis was the abstract nature of the theory of the "forces" behind cycles. It is a difficult subject to measure with any accuracy, and without the ability to apply mathematical formulae to the different price reactions at various points along the entire spectrum of cycles, the concept can appear confusing at the outset. This chapter attempts to provide some insight to some of the patterns and how to control expectations drawn from cycle analysis.

APPLYING THE WRONG CYCLE LENGTH

First, let us look at the effect of using the wrong cycle length. Figure 8.1 shows the weekly chart of WTI Crude Oil market with 45-, 90-, and 180-week cycles applied. The cycle troughs look reasonably accurate with price lows coinciding with them. In addition, where more than one cycle reaches a trough simultaneously, price action appears to see more upward and downward movement, as would be expected from the principle of summation. At the extreme right of the chart where all three cycles reach their trough simultaneouoly, we would expect price to find a low and subsequently accelerate upwards. Indeed, the initial upward reaction at this point supports the fact that all three cycles should be exerting upward pressure. However, soon after we find price moving to new lows. Why is this the case?

Figure 8.2 shows the same chart but with 48-, 96-, and 192-week cycles and the 12-period Cutler's RSI applied. The change of the shortest cycle length by three weeks seems innocuous initially. But this type of change can make a large difference to the point we are analysing. Looking at Figures 8.1 and 8.2, there are eight each of the 45- and 48-week cycles, and the cumulative effect of the 3-week change creates a cumulative effect over the entire period of 24 weeks. This makes a substantial difference in timing.

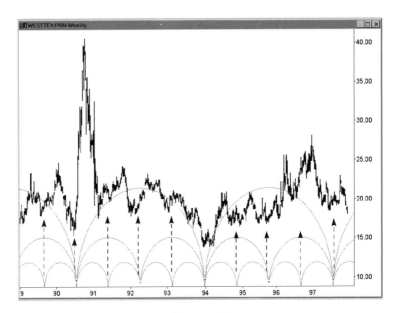

Figure 8.1
Weekly WTI Crude Oil market with 45-, 90-, and 180-week cycles. Note how price lows tend to coincide with cycle troughs.

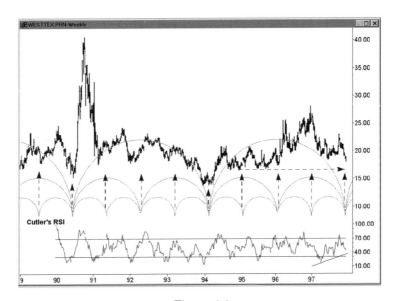

Figure 8.2
Weekly WTI Crude Oil market with 48-, 96-, and 192-week cycles. Note how, compared to Figure 8.1, the cycle as troughs still match price lows. Cutler's RSI is also shown to highlight momentum analysis with cycle troughs.

Thus, it is important to understand that cycle analysis provides only *approximate* timing of cycle peaks and troughs, and we should be aware at all times of the possibility of even a minor change to our cycle length having a much larger effect on the current analysis. It is therefore of vital importance that cycles play just one part of the analysis and that assumptions of price highs and lows at cycle extremes are matched by important breaks of supports or resistances in price action. In Figure 8.2 we note that there is crucial support just below current price and there is potential for a bullish divergence in Cutler's RSI.

If we take this one step further by looking at the daily chart, we can establish the levels that, if broken, would contribute to our underlying analysis of a price reversal. Figure 8.3 shows the daily price chart with the original cycles suggesting a cycle/price low at point A. How soon could we have known that our cycles were drawn incorrectly and when we could have changed our analysis to match the new (longer) cyclic picture?

After point A we would have been satisfied with the upward move although it was not very high and did not test the previous high. Soon after the cycle trough at point B, price moved up to break the previous high and this would have added a great deal of encouragement to our scenario. After this price high, there was no acceleration as would have been implied by a wave count that would have signaled price rising quite sharply in a series of wave 3s. The decline from that high, once it had breached 50% of the upward move, would have been a concern, and at the cycle trough at point C, we would have looked for price strengthening since the two shorter cycles were finding a low while the longer cycle was at a high. Given that our weekly cyclic picture in Figure 8.1 implied that the longer-term cycles had found a low and were subsequently rising, any weakness at this point would have triggered the final acceptance that we had been premature in our expectations of a price low and a check of cycles would have been made.

Figure 8.4 shows a new daily cyclic picture that matches the weekly cyclic chart in Figure 8.2. The rally after point A in Figure 8.4 is confirmed by the two shorter cycles turning higher. However, as we reach the peak of the shortest cycle, the longest cycle dips and the decline in price seems to match well. With the longer weekly cycles coming down, the recovery at

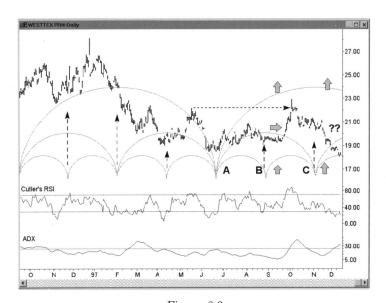

Figure 8.3
Daily WTI Crude Oil market with cycles, Cutler's RSI and ADX plotted.
Cycle troughs appear to match price lows except for the price decline after
point C that appears to be contradictory.

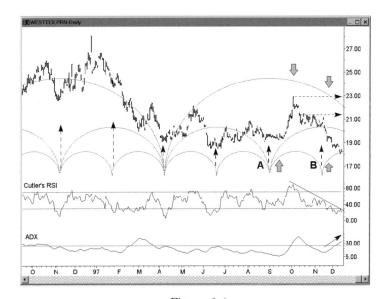

Figure 8.4
Daily WTI Crude Oil market with cycles drawn to match the weekly
cycles in Figure 8.2, and with Cutler's RSI and ADX applied. The shift
of weekly cycles gives a more logical feel to the daily cycles and
momentum indicators.

point B is short-lived and price action continues lower. Looking at price action and the momentum indicators, there is no reason to currently alter the short-term bearish stance. ADX is rising, suggesting a trend is still in place. There is a downtrend line on Cutler's RSI and with the steep gradient of this downtrend line, it should be expected to break quite soon and a correction in price should accompany this. This should provide a corrective peak before a further decline into new lows around the time of the combined cycles trough. Any subsequent reaction from this second low must first break that corrective peak and then the resistance line indicated on the chart. From there we could reasonably anticipate further medium- to long-term price strength. Any failure to overcome these resistance levels could change our entire analysis.

CYCLE LOWS AND CORRECTIONS

One of the most confusing elements of the Elliott Wave Principal is whether price action will see a simple or complex correction. A complex correction often signals the first wave A developing as a three-wave move. At this point we do not know whether this will complete the correction (in an ABC pattern) or whether a complex correction is likely. Cycles can very often solve this problem or at least provide a warning that an alternative structure should be considered.

Figure 8.5 shows the British pound–US dollar chart used in Figure 6.1. Here, price rallied in a five-wave pattern followed by a decline of between 50% and 61.8% of the rally. The wave count shows the choice of two alternatives. How could cycles have given us more indications? Figure 8.6 shows a longer history of the same market and with cycles applied. Here, price has kept to an approximate 50-week cycle (and therefore 100-, 200-, and 400-week cycles). Although price has occasionally found lows slightly ahead and slightly after cycle troughs, this has been a good broad indicator. Note that the 50-week cycle came to a trough when price (at (b) or -a-) eventually made a low. This is obviously a longer-term view of cycles. We can also break this down on the daily chart to see the effect.

Figure 8.7 shows the daily chart for a period before the point of analysis to display the approximate 96-day cycle, and Figure 8.8 shows how this cycle has progressed to the point of

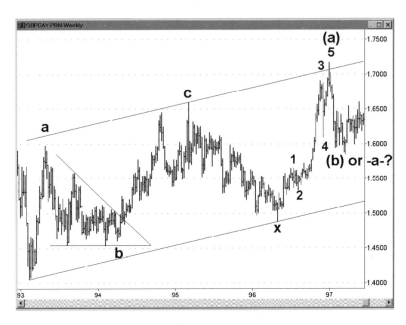

Figure 8.5
Weekly GBPUSD market as seen in Figure 6.1.

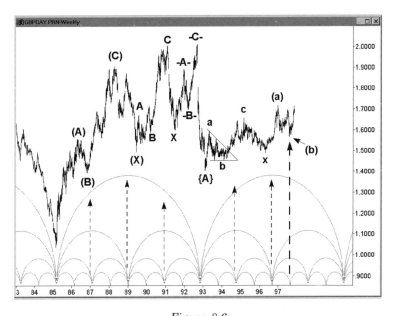

Figure 8.6
Weekly GBPUSD chart showing a longer price history and with underlying cycles of 50, 100, and 200 weeks. Note how a logical sequence of rallies and declines matches the cycles.

analysis and also price action after this period. Three cycles reached a trough at point B and the shaded arrows display the forces generated. In fact, as price declined to the low marked a, we see that even the three shorter cycles were dipping. This suggests that price should not recover very strongly. This, however, is where the principle of summation should be considered. Refer back Figure 8.6. The three shorter weekly cycles found a low at (X), and as these three cycles subsequently move up, the largest cycle neared its peak. The combined effect of all the cycles suggests a period of strength and so, when considering the shorter cycles on the daily chart in Figure 8.8, it is important to remember that the larger cycles are giving positive readings and allow for stronger rallies than the daily cycles might suggest. However, as the larger daily cycle also declines more sharply, the price decline from b becomes sharper. Note also that by the time we reach the cycle trough at c, price is still above the wave (X) low at 1.4893, which is logical given the strong weekly cycles. With this knowledge, the fact that we found a major daily cycle trough

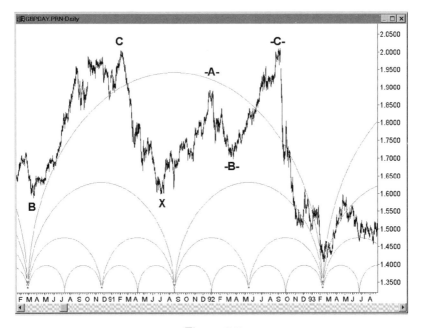

Figure 8.7
Daily GBPUSD chart chart showing an underlying 96-day cycle to the low at around 1.40 in early 1993.

while weekly cycles were positive and that wave c is equal in length to wave a, we can reasonably forecast that prices should rally from the wave (b) low.

Another example of this type of cycle behavior within corrections is seen in Figure 8.9 which shows the same chart as in Figure 6.16. Figure 6.16 addressed the question of wave counts of 535 representing both ABC structures as well as 121 structures but with the implications of each count being different. To recap, an ABC count would imply that the correction is potentially complete, or at least would generate an X wave before a further ABC structure. A count of 121 would imply the build-up before a series of strong wave 3s that would take price action strongly in the direction of the wave 1s. Figure 8.9 actually has an incorrect wave count—showing a triangular structure developing—but how could we control that with cycles?

Figure 8.10 shows the weekly cyclic picture of the US dollar against the Japanese yen and from this it can be seen

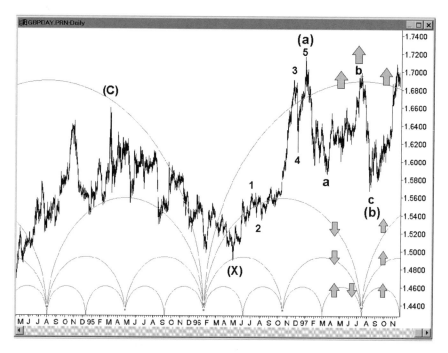

Figure 8.8
Daily GBPUSD chart from early 1994 showing the same cycles as in Figure 8.7. Note the position of the cycles at the wave (b) peak.

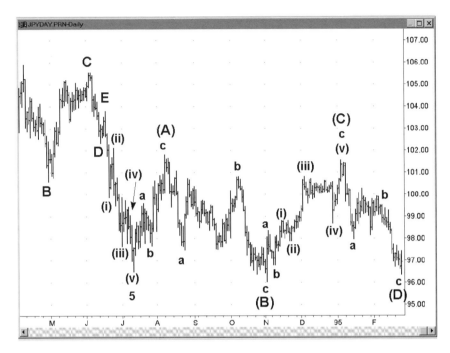

Figure 8.9
Daily USDJPY chart showing the same (incorrect) wave count
as in Figure 6.16.

that the overall cyclic picture was particularly bearish. All four cycles are declining strongly and as such, we can hardly expect any correction at this point to be particularly strong or long. We can see that the original low at 96.50 occurred at the 43-week cycle low and this smaller cycle has reached a peak as price reached the 101.55 peak, labeled as wave (C). Figure 8.11 shows the same price action but in the daily chart and with the 27-day cycle shown together with 54-, 108-, and 216-day cycles. We can see that the 216-day cycle (equivalent to 43 weeks) has found a peak and has begun to decline. The 108-day cycle is rising towards its peak while the 54-day cycle has topped out and the 27-day cycle is moving lower. If we also take into consideration the longer-term weekly cycles being obviously bearish, we cannot expect much of a rally from price at all. Thus any breach of the low around 98.0 would precipitate very aggressive weakness into the major weekly cycle lows. This is shown in Figure 8.12 and shows how the price low came at the

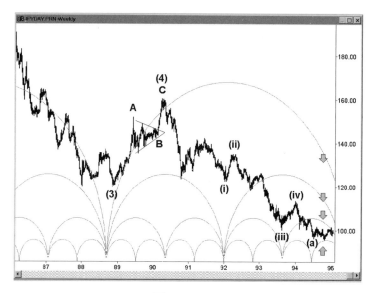

Figure 8.10
Weekly USDJPY market with 43-, 86-, 172-, and 344-week cycles drawn.
Note how the three longer cycles are pointing lower at the 96.50 low while
only the 43-week cycle suggested a rally.

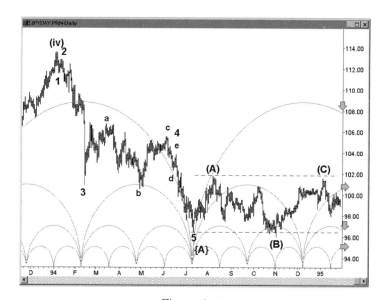

Figure 8.11
Daily USDJPY chart with cycles. {A} indicates the 43-week
cycle trough. Note how the larger cycle has reached a high and is
declining while the shorter cycles are mixed. Also remember how the
weekly cycles are bearish.

point where all daily and weekly cycles simultaneously found a low. Also note that since all these cycles subsequently began to rally after the low, price also rallied sharply.

A final example combining Elliott Wave counts with cycles to judge potential reversal points is seen in Figure 8.13 which shows the daily chart of the US dollar against the German Deutschmark during a rally from the low of 1.3445 in March 1995 through to the 1.8915 peak in August 1997. I have given the rally a potential wave count, although I have very strong convictions about the rally from the low in October 1995 labeled as -2- to the high in August 1997 labeled as -3- being a five-wave move. In support of this, note the following Fibonacci relationships:

Wave II = 0.50 of wave I.
Wave III = 1.618 of wave I.
Wave IV = 0.236 of wave III.
Wave V = 0.618 of distance between waves I and III.

The subsequent correction (which I have not labeled) is also equal to:

Wave -1- = 0.382 of wave III.

In this rally also note the following:

• Wave 2 corrected 50% of wave 1 at the combined cycle low of four cycles.

• The waves IV and 4 lows corrected 23.6% of wave 3 at the combined low of three of the cycles. It should also be remembered also how the larger cycles were pushing higher at this point, providing continuing upward momentum and reducing the extent of the corrections.

Wave 5 (wave -3- completion) occurred towards the high of the largest cycle and the subsequent correction (not labeled) corrected 38.2% of wave 3 and occurred at the combined cycle troughs of five cycles. This correction also declined to the span of the previous wave 4 and close to the base of a small area of congestion that looks to have provided a wave (ii) of wave 5.

Thus, approximate identification of corrective lows in both time and price can be obtained by a combination of Elliott wave count, Fibonacci relationships together with cycle peaks and

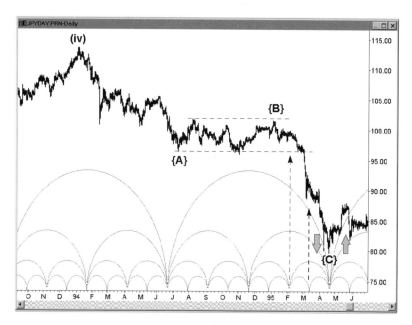

Figure 8.12
Daily USDJPY chart showing how price developed from Figure 8.11. Note how after {B}, progressively all cycles turned lower.

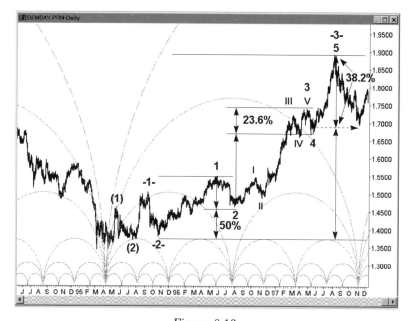

Figure 8.13
Daily USDDEM chart with cycles, Elliott wave count, and Fibonacci relationships.

troughs. As a cautionary note, when assessing cycle troughs and peaks, it is beneficial to ensure that important support and resistance levels are broken before strongly indicating that a particular trending move has completed. Always look for break of the extreme of the previous wave 4 or the B wave in a corrective three-wave structure. There are occasions where cycles are not entirely precise and at these times the danger of premature forecasts of reversals become more apparent. It is preferable to identify signs of momentum shifts at these points, perhaps in the form of a bullish or bearish divergence.

EXERCISE CAUTION DURING PERIODS WHERE LONGER-TERM CYCLES ARE REVERSING STRONGLY

If the principle of summation is considered, it will be realized that occasions when longer-term cycles are reversing, the emergence of strong trending moves are common and the corrections within these trending moves often tend to be shallow and brief. It is at these times that detrended charts are particularly useful.

Figure 8.14 shows the chart of the weekly Hang Seng Futures contract with five cycles applied. Note that price has been in a long-term uptrend with the 12,785 peak towards the center of the chart occurring just ahead of the peak in cycle 5, and the subsequent corrective trough occurring at the peak of cycle 5 and at the combined troughs of cycles 1 to 4. If we look specifically at the points marked A and B, we see that while cycles 1 to 3 are pointing lower, price actually rises. During this period, cycle 4 is at its peak while cycle 5 is still rising, giving a positive influence. If we then consider the position of a cycle 6 (not shown), we must also deduce that it is also at very high levels and thus the combined negative effect of cycles 1 to 3 have little impact upon price. However, note how in this instance the detrended chart rarely moves above the central zero line and how the shallow correction in price between the areas marked A and B also displays a distinct cycle low in the detrended chart. As the cycles 1 to 3 begin to rise again, price rallies and then corrects sharply into the next cycle 1 trough just after B. From this, we see that cycle 4, while high and thus providing continued positive influence, is actually beginning to decline.

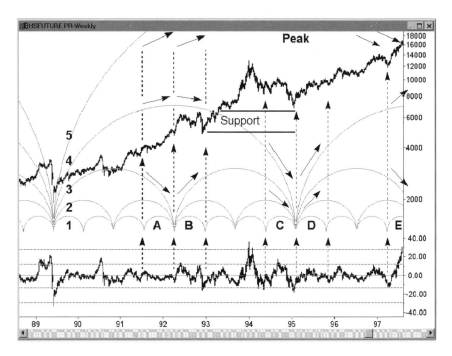

Figure 8.14
Weekly Hang Seng Futures and detrended chart. Note the relationship of
support and resistance to cycle peaks and troughs on the detrended chart.

Then as cycle 3 rises with cycles 5 and 6, price is carried to the 12,785 peak before correcting sharply into the combined troughs of cycles 1 to 4 between the points marked C and D. At this point, while cycle 5 has found a peak, the other smaller cycles are all negative and their combined effect is to cause a sharp correction. However, note that the corrective low at 6,850 is above the price trough between A and B at 4,745 and thus further price strength to new highs is probable. Note that at this point the detrended chart becomes more volatile around the central zero line. However, it shows that while the peak at 12,785 causes a stronger move up higher than normal, the subsequent decline failed to move below even the higher of the two support lines drawn.

As cycles 1 to 4 rise, we see that although cycle 5 is now declining, it is still at high levels and the continuing price strength may be attributed to a high cycle 6. Finally, at point E, we can see that cycle 4 is once again finding a peak while cycles 1 to 3 are declining, suggesting that a correction is likely. If we take into account that cycle 5 is declining at this point and to a level equal to the area around point A, we may suggest that this should be a slightly deeper correction than has been seen until now. If we take into account cycle 6, we know this is still at a high level, and as price is higher than at any other time, it is likely to be rising and reaching a peak. Thus, the combined effect of cycle 6 rising only slightly while cycle 5 is declining and cycle 4 is finding a peak, is for a price to find a peak and then a stronger decline to take hold. We can also see that the detrended chart is approaching the same extreme levels as seen at the 12,785 peak, and this therefore cannot continue for much longer.

Figure 8.15 shows the US dollar against the Japanese yen and an example of an extreme reversal in cyclic pressure as the yen strengthened dramatically against the dollar into the combined cycle troughs of the six cycles shown (and other longer cycles which cannot be drawn), followed by an equally dramatic change to yen weakness as the cycles reversed higher. During this period notice how the detrended chart finds a strong support line which is never penetrated. While the price lows are quite visible, the combination with the detrended chart brings more information to judge the cycle lows at all points labeled below the bar chart. The problem that we face is the fact that even the eventual trough of cycle 4 (to the right of the chart) has almost no effect on price and can cause doubts about the occurrence of a cycle low.

Here we must look at both the principle of summation and the pattern on the detrended chart. Remember that the detrended chart displays the movement of price against a centered moving average. (This can be substituted by a simple moving average of half the length of the underlying cycle.) Thus, by the first trough of cycle 1 we can see that the larger cycles have not yet had sufficient time to rise much. The first trough at point A marks the beginning of a series of detrend lows that fail to move below this level, thus providing a significant support level. Point B sees a slightly sharper reaction at the cycle 2 trough while cycle 3 is at its peak. Remember that the other larger cycles are still rising. Thus the correction is shallow and is followed by a minor trough at point C where cycle 1 is at a trough, cycle 2 is at a peak and cycle 3

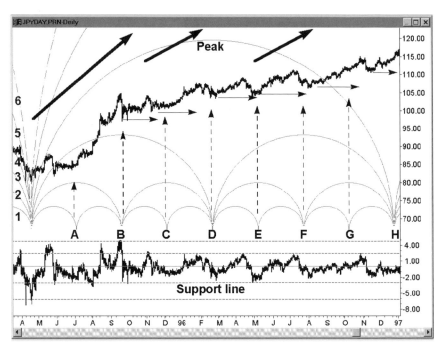

Figure 8.15
Daily USDJPY chart displaying the number of cycle troughs seen at
the 79.75 low in April 1995. These longer-term cycles generated
positive pressure, and price action never penetrated below the series
of corrective lows shown.

is declining. The detrended chart found a low at the same level as at point A while the detrended low at point C fails to reach even this low.

The subsequent price action provides important information. At point D we see the combined troughs of cycles 1 to 3, and the detrended chart also declined to meet the support line. However, price action records only a minor low when the assumption would have been that such a cycle low would cause a downward stronger reaction lower. This reflects the influence that the longer cycles are having on price. Point D also marks the peak of cycle 4 and therefore it may have been expected that after a while, we would witness a general period of weakness. However, this never occurs and all subsequent price lows continue to move higher. This is a clear sign that the longer cycles are pushing strongly higher, that we are seeing right translation and that higher price levels will occur.

At point E, we once again see the detrended chart failing at the same support line, and at point F (the peak of cycle 3) fails to move as low as this support line, though it does mark a low below the zero line. This is followed by the decline into the cycle 4 low which actually appears to occur earlier than expected. Soon, price begins to rally after point G. This gives us a further sign that price will rise to new highs.

The Elliott wave count during this period is very complex and subject to different interpretations. However, the most important factor to note is that price never broke below the previous significant lows, marked on the chart by horizontal arrows. At all times a forecast of reversal would only be qualified by a break of these lows, and until this point any strong predictions of price reversal lower would not have been supported by Elliott guidelines.

CYCLE POSITIONS DURING TRIANGLES

I have noticed a common combination of cycle positions when triangles develop. Triangles that subsequently break lower will occur during periods when the major long-term cycle is moving lower and the intermediate cycles are in a final period of an upward move before combining to move lower. Triangles that break lower occur during periods when the underlying long-term cycle is moving higher and the intermediate cycles are forming a low before rising again.

Figure 8.16 shows the Japanese Government Bond Futures contract during an underlying decline in the late 1980s, before a combined reversal of cycles took price higher in the 1990s. I have marked 4 cycles although an additional cycle has also been drawn in as it descends into the eventual low in 1990. The underlying cyclic pressure is therefore lower, and as we see the combination of cycles 1 to 3 forming a trough around the end of 1987, we see a move lower in what appears to be a wave (A) of a zigzag lower. Wave (B) develops as a triangle and here note the pattern of cycle influences. At the bottom of wave (A) we have cycle 4 at its peak while cycle 5 (not labeled) is already declining and having an increased negative effect on price action.

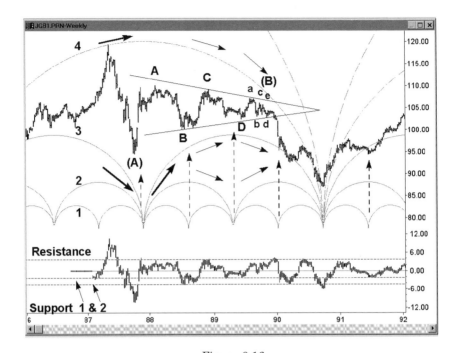

Figure 8.16
Weekly Japanese Government Bond Futures chart showing a large triangle
structure that developed in the late 1980s. Note the combination of cycles
and conflicting pressures that result in a sideways triangle.

As cycles 1 to 3 rise, we see that price rallies, But by the time cycle 1 has moved to its next trough, we see quite a deep correction. This forms waves A and B of the triangle. Then, as cycles 1 and 3 rise and cycle 2 finds a peak, price responds by rallying to a wave C peak. The effects of the declining cycles 4 and 5 cause this peak to fall short of the wave A peak and from here, price declines into the wave D trough. This is higher than the wave B trough since cycle 3 has found a peak while only cycles 1 and 2 form a trough. From this wave D low, we see cycles 1 and 2 rise, but the combined influence of the three declining larger cycles prevent price from rallying above the wave C peak. Eventually after a complex triangular wave E, price breaks lower into the combined cycle troughs of all five cycles. Note how the detrended chart was contained by one resistance line above zero while two support lines formed below the zero line.

The point to note here is that we know from the Elliott guidelines that triangles occur only in waves B or 4 positions, that is, just before the completion of a directional move. It is, thus, logical to expect these patterns to occur just ahead of intermediate cycle troughs or peaks. Let us look at a second example in Figure 8.17, again of the Japanese Government Bond Futures contract. The figure shows all four cycles finding a combined trough, and cycle 5 finding its peak. The same support and resistance lines on the detrended chart are also marked.

Here we see that the major cyclic direction is higher, with cycle 5 at a peak and cycle 6 at high levels, probably still rising. Thus we expect a correction into the combined trough of cycles 1 to 4. After we have seen a wave 3 peak, a correction ensues. The wave 3 high occurred towards the peak of cycle 2 and as cycle 3 was beginning to decline. We see a decline into the cycle 1 trough to form wave A, followed by a move higher in price that records new highs towards the peak of cycle 1. The new highs are possible as cycles 5 and 6 are still moving higher and creating a positive effect on price. As cycles 5 and 6 continue to rise, we have a general decline into the combined cycle trough of cycles 1 to 4. This forms the wave C of the triangle and as all cycles begin to rise, price forms the last two legs—waves D and E before the combined effect of all cycles forces price higher.

As a final example, Figure 8.18 shows the weekly US T-Bond Futures contract in the large volatile rally since 1980. It shows how a large triangle developed at the end of the 1980s through to the early 1990s and broke higher as influenced by cycle 5 and possibly cycle 6 (not shown). The large rally eventually reached the peak labeled as wave (A) as all cycles began climbing higher. Then just after the peak of cycle 3, we see a sharp decline into the combined troughs of cycles 1 to 3 to form wave A. Cycle 4 was finding its peak at this time. With all three shorter cycles turning higher, price rallied once again, but failed to surpass the wave (A) peak since cycle 4 had begun to decline and cycle 5 was beginning to flatten out towards its peak (eventually seen at the wave (C) peak). This formed wave B. With cycle 3 rising and cycles 1 and 2 declining we see completion of waves D and E before the break higher.

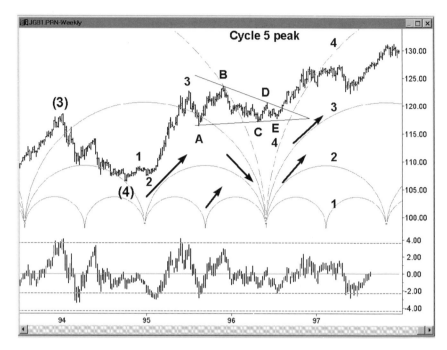

Figure 8.17
Weekly Japanese Government Bond Futures chart shows how an
intermediate cycle trough often provides the final wave extreme of the
triangle. Note that cycle 5 is at its peak and cycle 6 (not shown) would
still be climbing.

The break higher is interesting since it created strong right hand translation in cycle 4 and also implied further strength after completion of the move to wave (C) and the correction lower into the combined troughs of cycles 1 to 4. Although I have not marked this corrective low, the fact that it has failed to breach the wave (B) low, while cycle 5 is at its peak and cycle 6 probably rising, suggests that the correction should be labeled as a wave (X) to be followed by a further ABC pattern.

In summary, the most important factors to assimilate with cycles are the effects of translation and summation. Some of the examples shown have displayed strong translation— situations when price continues to rally until near the end of the entire cycle, or rallies for a only a short while after a major cycle low. With the principle of summation and the observation

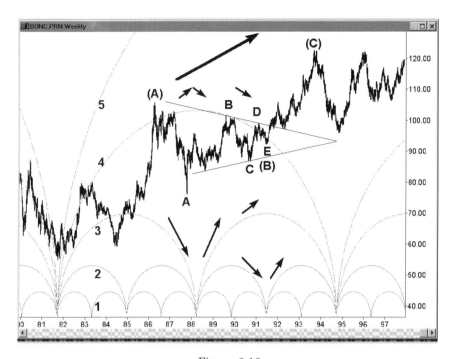

Figure 8.18
Weekly US T-Bond Futures chart showing the large triangle that developed between the late 1980s and the early 1990s. Here, the cycles are in slightly different positions but the largest cycle shown (cycle 5) is in a strong rising move, keeping prices stable.

of Elliott guidelines, greater understanding can be achieved with the result that stronger anticipation of future direction and degrees of trends or corrections can be forecast. It is not a simple concept to assimilate nor apply but with study and practice, the structure of cycles can become an invaluable asset.

CHAPTER 9

Integrating Analysis Techniques

Although this book covers a variety of analysis techniques, it is by no means comprehensive as it is a selection of techniques that I use. Each technique is discussed individually. Hints and tips on using the Elliott Wave Principle and cycles are included in two chapters. The previous sections in this book have also introduced the process of integrating different analytical methods.

I have found that many traders tend to look at indicators in isolation, and while each indicator gives excellent trading signals at times, the problem of consistency plagues each indicator. Often the question "How do you use this indicator?" is raised, prompted by an indicator that initially produces profitable trades and gains traders' confidence in using it, only to have this confidence reduced by a series of bad trades. The temptation then is to discard the indicator and search for another. In truth, no single indicator can provide the "Holy Grail" we seek. But, in my experience, a *combination* of analytical techniques is able to guide us through what to expect from price and which indicator has greater predictive potential at a particular time.

This chapter presents a series of situations that should help traders piece together the several different elements I have described and refine an approach of analyzing the market. I feel strongly about these concepts but I also understand that each trader will probably feel more comfortable with a slightly different combination of techniques. It is for the trader to decide, by experimentation, the combination that works for him/her—the underlying method of integrating analysis will remain the same.

Another vital ingredient to technical analysis is keeping an open mind to other techniques. Frequently analysts become attached to the first combination of techniques they adopt and give scant regard to others. I admit my own guilt towards this attitude in the past. But I have now discovered the advantage of listening to other analysts and on some occasions I have picked up useful ideas that make sense to me and fits in with my view of how the market develops. Indeed, the basic concept of combining techniques is necessary and these combinations can give such powerful signals that the effort will be rewarded.

I have chosen a combination of the Elliott Wave Principle, cycles, and momentum analysis as my preferred techniques. I have often been asked the reason for choosing this combination. I feel these techniques provide non-overlapping information about the market while complementing each other in terms of expectations. The Elliott Wave Principle provides me with a structure—signaling both direction in every time frame and an expectation of how the move should develop—in five or three waves. Together with Fibonacci analysis, the Elliott Wave Principle identifies waves that are related to each other, and therefore potential retracements or target projections. This identifies price levels that signal potential alternatives or tell me when I am wrong. With the addition of cycles, I can develop preferences of wave counts, identify with greater accuracy approximate times for reversal as well as when a trend is more likely to continue (or accelerate) or stop. The inclusion of momentum indicators confirms when momentum is accelerating or decelerating, and links this confirnation with the timing implied by cycles and levels shown by Elliott Wave and Fibonacci.

Before integrating all three analyses methods, let us put together a structure that will allow us to formalize as much as possible an approach to our analysis. The most important element is time. I believe very strongly that even if the analysis is short-term, we must first look at the longest possible time frame, assess the implications drawn from this, move on to the next lower time frame to make similar analysis before working our way through each shorter time frame. This way we can gauge the characteristics to be expected from the market. This enables us to draw an informal list of possible analysis conclusions from each method for each time frame. A potential list of possible conclusions for each time frame follows:

Monthly Charts

Cycles	Up / down / sideways?
	Are the longer-term cycles pointing higher or lower?

How strong is the influence of these longer-term cycles?

Are we at a reversal point? If so, at which cycle(s)?

Elliott Wave	What is the favored wave count?

What does this wave count imply?

Which wave count would the favored wave count signal? Five- or three-wave structure?

What are the potential targets or support and resistance levels?

Momentum	Is there evidence of a trend?

Considering the cyclic and Elliott expectations, what would we expect to see from momentum analysis at this point?

Weekly Charts   Assess the same information as for the monthly charts.

If the monthly charts suggest a five-wave move, do we see this?

Are there any alternative wave counts or break levels?

Daily Charts   Assess the information as for the previous two time frames.

Does the daily wave count support the monthly and weekly projections?

Are there any break levels?

Although it is difficult to formalize such an approach to analyzing a market, for each time frame we can suggest that we look for as much information to complete the following:

Time frame   (Monthly / Weekly / Daily / Intraday)

CYCLES	ELLIOTT WAVE	TARGETS	SUPPORT/RESISTANCE
Up, Strong	Up five waves	0.618	Fibonacci levels
Up	Up three waves	1.00	Wave B extremes
Neutral	Alternation	1.382	Wave 2 of wave 5
Down	Down three waves	1.618	Wave 4
Down, Strong	Down five waves	2.618	

Bearing the above in mind, let us now look at examples of actual situations and how they may be analyzed.

WEST TEXAS INTERMEDIATE CRUDE OIL

Let us examine the West Texas Intermediate (WTI) Crude Oil market of May 1993. Prior to this, the Gulf War had driven prices up dramatically to $40.45 in October 1990. This was followed by a choppy but equally dramatic decline to a low of $17.62 in March 1991,and subsequently a period of relatively low volatility as price action converged into a tighter range until our time of analysis in May 1993.

Figure 9.1 shows the above price movements in the weekly chart of WTI crude oil. Using the Elliott Wave Principle, the first thing that strikes me about any chart is the balance of impulsive and corrective wave structures. I usually start my wave count with the corrective wave patterns since three-wave structures tend to be easier to identify. Occasionally it can be difficult to know whether these corrective three-wave structures are going to break in the direction of the underlying trend or develop in a more complex pattern. In Figure 9.1, I immediately see a triangle. The question then is whether this triangle forms part of a continuation pattern within a downtrend, or whether it forms part of a more complex correction before a downtrend could resume.

Each of the wave counts shown could have been made at that time. When price reached the first low marked {C} or {A}, we had to decide whether the decline completed an ABC pattern following which we would see further rallies, or whether we would see an {X} wave followed by a further (A)(B)(C) pattern downwards. We could also suggest that the first decline from $40.45 completed an ABCX{A} pattern, implying an -A--B--C- pattern to complete wave {B}, which would then decline. Or perhaps the triangle marked (a)(b)(c)(d)(e) was indeed the wave {B} and from the wave (e) a

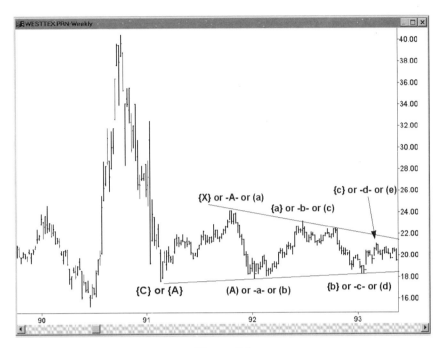

Figure 9.1
Weekly WTI Crude Oil market and potential wave counts.

wave {C} would emerge lower. These are the potential wave counts that can be derived from weekly chart.

To identify the structure of the decline from the $40.45 high to the $17.62 low, we should consult the daily structure, which may make the almost haphazard weekly structure more understandable. The daily chart is shown in Figure 9.2. Although another wave count could have been used for the chart, I have favored the one shown due to Fibonacci relationships. In wave {A}, wave 5 is approximately 61.8% of the drop from waves 1 to 3. Wave {B} falls just short of a 50% retracement of wave {A} and rises to the apex of the triangle of wave 4. The decline from the wave {B} peak is very sharp thus making it difficult to identify the waves -1- and -2-. However, given the velocity of the drop, we can judge the subsequent wave -3-, which was followed by a wave -4-, and a wave -5- that fell slightly short of 61.8% of the distance from the top of wave {B} to the end of wave -3-. Wave {C} is also about equal to wave {A}.

Having identified this structure, we would then be looking at the counts that would have the triangle develop in one of

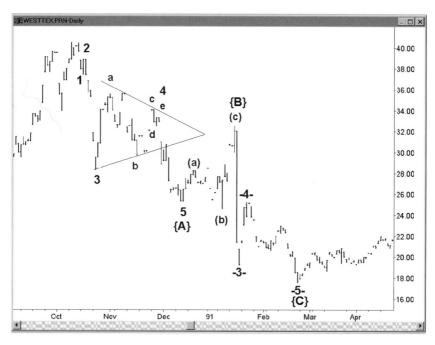

Figure 9.2
Daily WTI Crude Oil chart showing the wave count from the $40.45 high,
down to the $17.62 low of late February 1991.

three ways. Figure 9.3 shows the first of these. The rally from
the $17.62 low formed wave {X}, and this was followed by a
decline with wave (A) and wave (B) developing as a triangle in
which we have seen waves [a],[b],[c], and is now forming a
wave [d] to be followed by a wave [e] to complete wave (B)
ahead of the next decline in wave (C).

Figure 9.4 shows the second wave count alternative with
the rally from $17.62 as wave -A- of a more complex correction,
and wave -B- as completed at the time of analysis. Wave -B- is
followed by a wave -C- rally to form a larger wave {X} before a
further (A)(B)(C) decline.

Figure 9.5 shows the final potential wave structure where
the rally from the $17.62 low formed wave (a) of a triangle
(a)(b)(c)(d). At the time of analysis, we had just completed the
wave (e) peak to complete triangular wave {X} and this would
be followed by an (A)(B)(C) pattern.

The most frequent dilemma we face as analysts is choosing
from among different possibilities. This is where using other

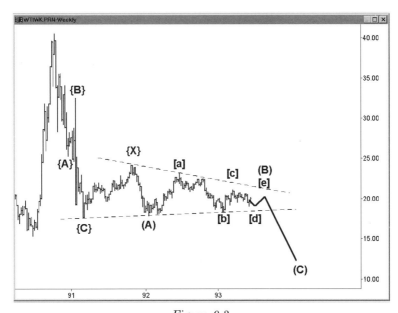

Figure 9.3
Weekly WTI Crude Oil market and the first wave count alternative that would anticipate a minor corrective rally followed by a wave (c) decline.

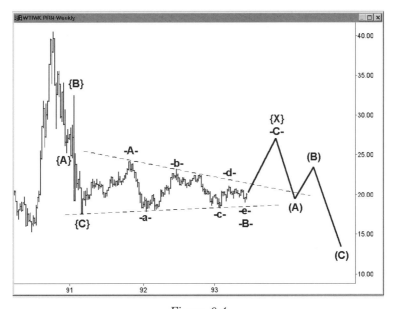

Figure 9.4
Weekly WTI Crude Oil market and the second wave count alternative that would anticipate a corrective wave {X} followed by a subsequent (A)(B)(C) decline.

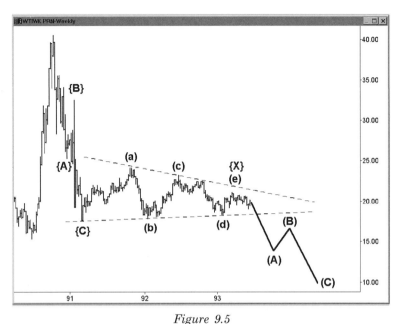

Figure 9.5
Weekly WTI Crude Oil market and the third wave count alternative that
would anticipate a direct decline in an (A)(B)(C) pattern.

forms of analysis becomes necessary. Figure 9.6 adds to the
cyclic pattern, Cutler's RSI and my RSS to the WTI chart. The
basic cycle is 44 weeks long, and the cycle troughs match the
price low. In May 1993, all major cycles (44-, 88-, 176-, and 352-
week) were declining. This gives a bearish impression. Cutler's
RSI (20 periods being approximately half the 44-week cycle)
sees peaks and troughs roughly matching price highs and lows.
At the point of analysis, Cutler's RSI is in neutral territory but
has turned lower. RSS is also a good indicator, giving broad
indications of when to expect price highs and lows. At the point
of analysis, RSS has broken above the 80 level, suggesting that
we should look for signs of price finding a peak.
   To summarize the weekly picture:

Cycles	Elliott Wave	Targets
4 major cycles pointing lower	Approaching triangle completion in wave B	Triangle target approx $14.00

Momentum	Support/Resistance
RSI neutral/down RSS at highs	Previous triangle low at $18.32 Most recent triangle low at $19.07

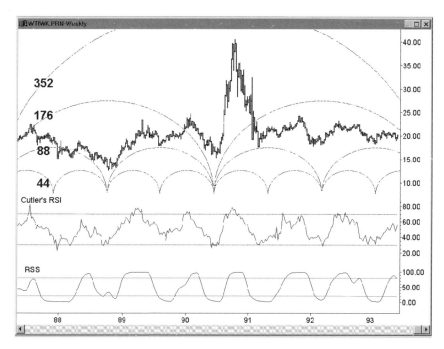

Figure 9.6
Weekly WTI Crude Oil market with cycles, Cutler's RSI, and RSS. The
period of analysis in May 1993 is on the extreme right of the chart.

Thus we can now discard the wave count shown in Figure 9.4 as this would require cycles to be positive. Instead we will favor the Elliott wave counts in Figures 9.3 or 9.5, both of which would look for immediate price weakness. To confirm this move, we should look at the daily chart and this is shown in Figure 9.7. Figure 9.7 displays the daily and weekly Bollinger Bands in the WTI chart. Note how the daily bands tend to contain shorter-term price action. After breach, the weekly bands contain the larger wave structure. We have seen rejection of price by the weekly bands at the minor peak just after wave (a), and at waves (c) and (d). Notice that I have favored the wave count in Figure 9.3 due to the structure of the waves from wave (c) onwards. Had this been the structure shown in Figure 9.5, the triangle would have completed towards the right of the chart labeled wave (c) in Figure 9.7. Subsequent to this minor peak at wave (c), a further -a--b--c- pattern developed. Although this could form wave (i) of a diagonal triangle lower in wave (C), I feel the degree of

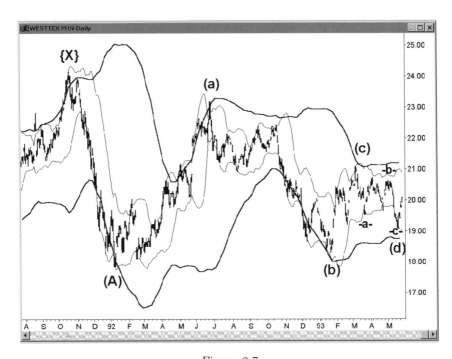

Figure 9.7
Daily WTI Crude Oil market with daily Bollinger Bands in thin lines and weekly Bollinger Bands in bold lines.

recovery after the next low tends to favor the chosen wave count. It is also supported by a few Fibonacci relationships:

Wave (c) = 50% of wave (a)
Wave (d) = 38.2% of wave (c)

Within wave (d),

Wave -a- = Wave -c-

Therefore we are probably looking at a final wave (e) to complete triangle wave (B) and thus the beginning of wave (C). Where is wave (e) likely to stop? Figure 9.8 shows the same section of price action along with daily cycles and Cutler's RSI. The two shorter cycles are now pressing lower with the next larger soon to find a peak. This fits in nicely with our wave count. We must remember also that the weekly cycles had shown a negative picture, thus we cannot expect the shorter cycles to show much strength. Cutler's RSI has not risen to a classic overbought level, but has risen to meet a downtrend line that has developed. In terms of price action, it is unlikely that price would rise above the wave -b- peak of wave (d). Thus far, the rally from wave (d) has risen almost 50% of wave (c). If we took the classic Fibonacci projection of wave (e) as 61.8% of wave (c), we would reach a target above the resistance shown in Figure 9.8.

The daily summary:

Cycles	Elliott Wave	Targets
Two shorter cycles dipping	Looking for wave (e) of triangle	$20.62 maximum
Larger cycle peaking		$19.02 – 50% of wave (c)
Momentum		**Support/Resistance**
Declining RSI peaks		Sppt: $19.07 – wave (d)
RSI quite high		Res: $20.62 – wave (b) of (d)

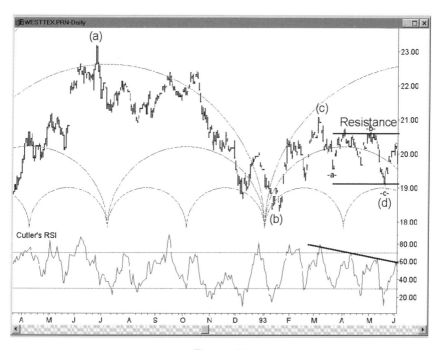

Figure 9.8
Daily WTI Crude Oil market and cycles along with Cutler's RSI. Note the resistance level at wave -b-.

Therefore, we can make a reasoned judgment that we have found, or are very close to finding, the peak of the wave (e), and a decline should be forthcoming soon. If we are incorrect in this analysis, we can have a tight stop above the wave -b- and above the daily/weekly Bollinger resistance. A break of the trough of wave (d) would confirm the resumption of the downtrend. Once this break occurs we can establish targets for wave (C), which can be either wave equality of (A) or 61.8% of wave (A). The targets implied by these would be $14.00 (wave equality) or $16.40 (61.8% of wave (A)).

Figure 9.9 shows subsequent price action. As can be seen from Figure 9.9, the above analysis proved accurate and the wave (e) peak stalled below the resistance level shown previously. This was followed by a further decline that first stalled at $16.40 to form wave (i) of a diagonal triangle. Subsequent to the completion of wave (ii), which retraced almost 61.8% of wave (i), price once again declined into the major weekly cycle low at $13.87 with wave (iii) measuring

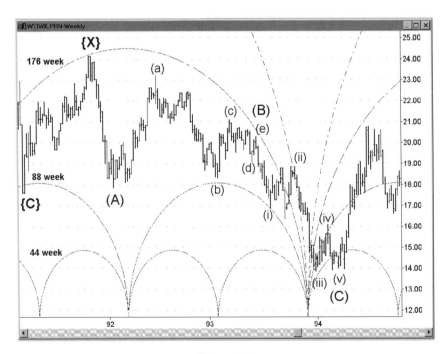

Figure 9.9
Weekly WTI Crude Oil with 44-, 88-, and 176-week cycles and price action after May 1993.

approximately 138.2% of wave (i). After a further correction in wave (iv), the final thrust lower failed to penetrate the wave (iii) low of $13.87 and formed a failed fifth wave. Note also that we had earlier arrived at a target of $14.00 (wave equality of wave (A)).

December 1993 – December 1995

Let us look briefly at how WTI crude oil performed from Figure 9.9's wave (C) low onwards. The weekly chart of Figure 9.9 continues in Figure 9.10, showing the subsequent price action in the following two and a half years. The most noticeable feature of the chart is the accuracy of the cyclic structure based on the 44- to 45-week cycle. After the completion of wave (C) at the failed fifth $13.87 low, price rallied sharply (a common feature after a failed fifth) and quickly retraced to the triangle end of wave (B), (once again a common occurrence after completion of an ABC pattern). It can be seen that all three cycles shown have reversed and are collectively influencing

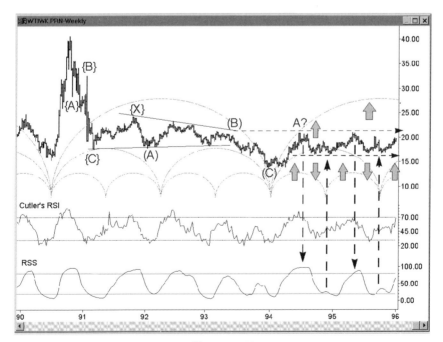

Figure 9.10
Weekly WTI Crude Oil market with Cutler's RSI, RSS, and cycles for the period following Figure 9.9.

price action. At the peak marked A? (we cannot be certain at
this point whether we will see further moves higher or whether
this rally is just part of a correction in a larger downtrend), we
can see that Cutler's RSI has reached a peak when RSS has
moved above the 80 level. With the shorter 45-week cycle then
dipping, the subsequent retracement moved back 61.8% into
the cycle trough. At this corrective low, RSI displayed minor
bullish divergences while RSS was at a low. With both the 45-
and 180-week cycles turning higher, price once again moved
higher. At this point, we could have considered that the
combination of the upward cyclic pressure would take price to
higher level of wave A. Indeed price strength was seen, as
should have been expected, but the effect of the dipping 90-
week cycle provided a drag on price as it found a peak just
below the wave A high. Note how Cutler's RSI just reached
overbought and RSS moved above 80 once again.

The subsequent decline once again retraced approximately
the same support level. However, here we see a different
picture emerging. Cutler's RSI displayed a minor bullish
divergence while RSS bounced along at low levels, also showing
minor bullish divergence. This time both the 45- and 90- week
cycles reach their troughs, and as such we could expect the
forthcoming price action to combine with the high 180-week
cycle to take prices to above the wave A level. Again, this
looked to me to be a triangle and I therefore counted this final
low as a wave -e- of wave B. This is shown in Figure 9.11. Final
confirmation of a larger rally would be a move above first, the
wave -d- peak, then the resistance level at waves A and -b-.

JAPANESE 10-YEAR GOVERNMENT BOND FUTURE

The next example shows the chart of the Japanese Government
Bond Future (JGBF) market in October 1990. The first chart,
Figure 9.12 shows the weekly bar chart with cycles and Elliott
Wave count.

The most dominant feature of the chart is the large
triangle that developed from the end of 1987 to the end of 1989.
The final wave e appears to have developed in a complex
triangular formation, a fairly rare event, but one which I have
seen on a few occasions. Price then broke below the triangle to
the period of analysis. According to the Elliott guidelines,
triangles occur in wave 4 or wave B positions. Both positions

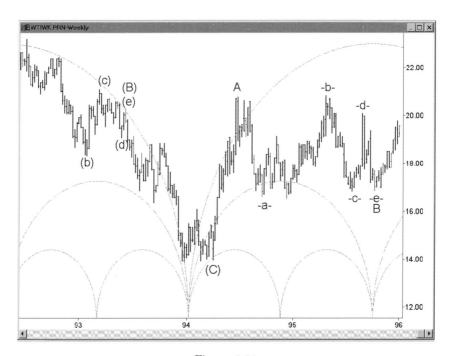

Figure 9.11
Weekly WTI Crude Oil chart showing decline to wave (C) low and the
subsequent sideways price action.

imply that the moves after completion of the triangle are
terminal. If we consider the cyclic aspect, the major cycles
shown are matched in general by price lows at waves (A), B,
just before wave D, and on the way down to the low of wave 3.
We can see that price continued lower and so there would
appear to be a cycle trough at the period of analysis. The
bounce at the wave 3 low also approximately matched the
triangle target taken from measuring the base and projecting
this from the point of breakout. However, after a brief
correction, price declined further to the period of analysis,
where the triangle formed an apex, a common timing for the
end of a trending move. This fits in nicely with the cycle
trough. Note that RSS also has found levels below 20, which
suggests we should look for signs of price reversal.

If we now look at Figure 9.13 we see the cyclic picture
again, but this time with slow stochastics and ADX. The weekly
JGBF chart followed quite well a form of slow stochastics,
giving a timely sell signal at point A just as price broke below

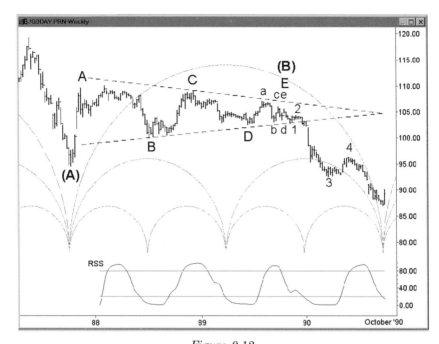

Figure 9.12
Weekly Japanese Government Bond Futures market with cycles and RSS
applied. The dominant feature of the chart is the large triangle that broke
lower to the period of analysis.

the triangle base. While this occurred close to a cycle low, we
must take into account that the longer-term cycles were clearly
bearish at this point. This type of movement occurs quite
frequently at such a stage in the cyclic structure. Price
continued lower for a while after this, and ADX began to rise
above 25, indicating that price was in a downtrend. This
avoided the traditional buy signals from slow stochastics and
finally signaled an end to the trend at point B when ADX began
to decline and this formed the end of wave 3.

As ADX declined, a fresh opportunity to sell arose as
stochastics declined at point C. Stochastics continued to decline
and then turned higher, but only after ADX had started to rise
once again, indicating the renewal of the downtrend.

At the period of analysis, ADX just dipped and stochastics
turned higher. I notice in many situations where ADX has been
rising, but gradually, a weak trending move is implied and
reversals can tend to be quite strong. This, therefore, gives a
bullish bias.

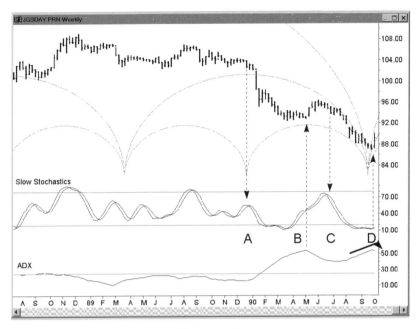

Figure 9.13
*Weekly Japanese Government Bond Futures market with slow stochastics
and ADX applied. Note how the cycles indicate a low at the same time as
ADX dipped, suggesting an end to the trend.*

Our weekly summary looks like this:

Cycles	Elliott Wave	Targets
Down but reversal soon?	Down – 5 waves Looking for fifth of fifth wave	(Triangle) 92.50 – Breached Wave (C) = Wave (A) at 80.87 Wave (C) = 0.764 of wave (A) at 86.68

Momentum	Resistance	Breaks
ADX peak? Stochastics cross higher	Wave 4 at 96.28 Wave (B) between 104.50 and 105.50	Wave 4 at 96.28

We have weekly ADX suggesting potential weak momentum. Stochastics have turned higher and we are looking for a fifth wave of wave 5. Confirmation of a weekly break does not occur until wave 4 has broken at 96.28. Once this breaks, we can look for a recovery towards the wave (B) completion at 104.50/105.50 at a minimum.

To fine-tune this event, we should look at the daily bar chart. This is shown in Figure 9.14 from the low of wave 3. Wave 4 develops as a zigzag within which wave b has been counted as a double zigzag – although an alternative count treating this as a triangle would also be valid. After completion of wave 4, price decline continued once again. It is interesting to note that wave (iii) is equal to 2.618 of wave (i), wave (iv) is 0.382 of wave (iii), and wave (v) is just under 0.618 of the entire move from wave (i) to the end of wave (iii). Wave (4) is 0.236 of wave (3). If we then take 0.382 of the distance from the beginning of wave (1) to the end of wave (3), we can project a target of 86.85, and taking 0.618 of the same distance would give a target of 84.97. At the period of analysis, we reached a low of 87.08, just above the first target of 86.85 (and close to the weekly target of 86.68 which is wave (C) = 0.764 wave (A).

Figure 9.15 enlarges the decline of wave (5) and adds the momentum picture, using stochastics and ADX. ADX shows a broad trend until the end of wave (3) and begins to show a mild trend in wave (5), though there is little strength behind this.

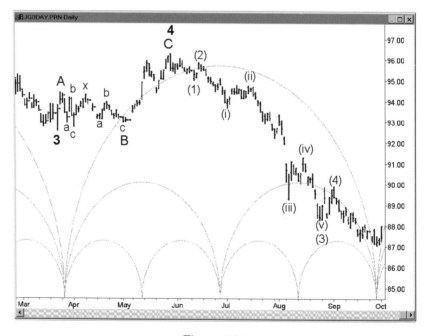

Figure 9.14
Daily Japanese Government Bond Futures market displaying the wave count down from wave 4 and anticipating a wave 5.

Meanwhile, the stochastics matched price highs and lows quite well, and at the 87.08 low, stochastics turned up as ADX dipped once again. This gave a buy signal. Figure 9.15 also showed that wave (5) declined as a diagonal triangle and there is a clear wedge shape that began with the peak of wave (iv). The day after the buy signal, we see that the top of this wedge was broken.

Our daily summary will look like this:

Cycles	**Elliott Wave**	**Targets**
Down but reversal due?	Down – 5 waves Fifth wave complete?	Wave (5) = 0.382 of waves (1) to (3) at 86.85 Wave (5) = 0.618 of waves (1) to (3) at 84.97
Momentum	**Resistance**	**Breaks**
ADX peak	88.07 diagonal triangle	88.07 diagonal triangle
Stochastics turning higher	Wave {iv}	Wave {iv} Wedge top broken

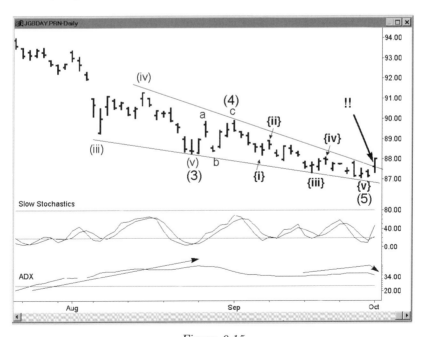

Figure 9.15
Daily Japanese Government Bond Futures chart showing the final diagonal triangle decline and break of the downtrend line. Also shown are slow stochastics and ADX.

If we combine the weekly and daily charts, we have a potential end to the downtrend at the cycle trough and triangle apex, and a weekly buy signal from stochastics. On the daily chart, we have another buy signal from stochastics, together with a break of downward wedge. The picture is clearly bullish and we can expect a rally to at least 91.28, the wave (iv) peak. From the weekly chart, we can expect a move back close to the previous wave 4 at 96.28.

In fact, this higher level was achieved and even broken, with the first major peak in price action at 97.81, before a correction and multi-year gains.

HANG SENG INDEX

The next example we look at is the Hang Seng Index (HSI), arguably one of the most actively traded markets, with speculation being a favorite pastime of the Chinese! The period of analysis is just after the February 1995 low of 6,890. The market had made a dramatic rally in the early 1990s, moving higher on a wave of speculation driven by strong confidence in the former Territory's future, until the index reached a peak in January 1994 at 12,599. From that peak, the index lost much of its shine and progressively moved lower to 6,890 in February 1995. Our analysis centers on whether technical analysis could have predicted that time as a critical low for the index.

As usual, I begin with the longest data I have and this is shown in Figure 9.16, the weekly bar chart showing data from late 1986, the associated cycles, Cutler's RSI and the Elliott wave count. Note that I have used a semi-log scaling, a method commonly used to measure indices that move over a long period of time from relatively low to high values. In this case, the HSI moved from approximately 1,600 in late 1986 to the peak of 12,599 in 1994. It is generally more relevant to show this price change as a percentage rather than absolute price.

The wave count I have shown is tentative, based on the fact that the initial price action looks very much like a triangle, although the peak at wave (D) is slightly higher than at wave (B). As long as the triangle follows the Elliott guidelines of having three-wave internal structures, the count remains valid. We can deduce that if this is a triangle, then it must either be a B wave or wave 4. Since the index has been in a long-term

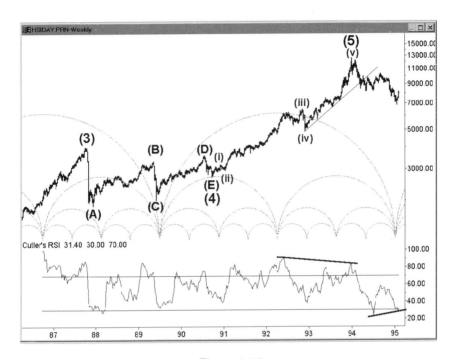

Figure 9.16
Hang Seng Index with cycles, Elliott wave count, and Cutler's RSI.
A semi-log scale has been applied.

uptrend, this is more likely to be wave (4). Therefore, the
subsequent rally to 12,599 must be wave (5). The internal wave
structure fits well, with wave (iv) retracing 38.2% of wave (iii)
and wave (v) extending 161.8% of wave (i) through wave (iii).
However, at this juncture, we do not have sufficient data to
decide whether this wave (5) is the fifth of a larger wave 5 (and
thus we shall see a more dramatic decline) or merely the end
of a larger wave 3 (after which a further wave 4 should be seen,
followed by another wave 5, and then the decline). It is also
interesting to note that the 6,890 low of February 1995 marked
an approximate 38.2% retracement of the wave (5) rally.

The cycles shown in Figure 9.16 are approximate only.
While I have drawn them to coincide with the low of 6,890, we
must be cautious in case we "curve fit" cycles to find this low
conveniently. For now, the cycles should be treated as showing
a *potential* for a major low only and we should look at other
indications to determine whether they are accurate. Note that

I have placed the trough of the largest cycle at the wave (C) low of the triangle, a common occurrence during longer-term rallies. Cutler's RSI contributed to a forecast of a high, finding strong divergence at the 12,599 high. Notice also that Cutler's RSI displays a good bullish divergence at 6,890, suggesting that the cycle troughs may be accuratly positioned.

Figure 9.17 shows an alternative momentum picture with my own Momentum Bands together with ADX. Momentum Bands are a fairly good guide that indicate support and resistance levels and, at times, have shown where key breaks have occurred. Points A and B provided good resistance, and the bands then gave support at point C, where price tested both trend and corrective supports. From this support, price reversed higher to test corrective resistance, then broke through, thus confirming a new weekly uptrend. This trend held above the trend support for some time, saw a brief spike down around January 1994, but closed above. After a correction upwards as price attempted to move through the 12,599 peak, price action clearly broke below trend support at point E, after which we saw a swift test of the corrective support. Two corrective rallies failed to break previous corrective highs, and price continued to mark two further lows, the last being at point F, where it failed to cleanly penetrate corrective support. From here, the HSI attempted to recover more strongly, breaching the two previous corrective peaks and indeed corrective resistance. However, with this correction failing, price began to drop again towards a rising corrective support band—the breach at point G displayed signs of a clear break downwards. At the period of analysis, we see price decline to the 6,890 low and retest trend resistance at point H.

Finally, from Figure 9.17, we see that ADX has risen to around 25, not really displaying a trend, and turned flat. This would guide us into following momentum indicators, though caution is advised since any further weakness would cause ADX to move higher once again.

The weekly summary is:

Cycles	Elliott Wave	Targets
Finding major low?	Looking for wave 4 low	0.382 retracement of wave (5) at 7,000

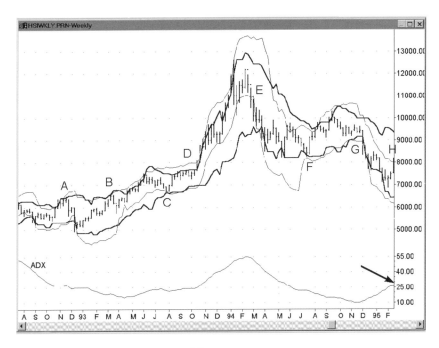

Figure 9.17
Weekly Hang Seng Index with Momentum Bands and ADX applied. The
thin bands are the trend support and resistance while the bold bands are
corrective support and resistance.

Momentum	Support	Resistance
ADX flat	7,000 – Fibonacci	8,460 – previous
Potential bullish	retracement	minor peak
divergence in RSI	6,810 – 2.618 of	7,955 – 0.382 of
	wave -a-	wave -b- decline

To get further clues, we must look at the daily picture and
Figure 9.18 shows the daily Momentum Bands with ADX. Once
again, the Momentum Bands gives some very good indications,
initially showing break of trend resistance and then
consolidation resistance at point A. The bands then provided
support at point B and again at C, with slight slippage
thereafter. The corrective resistance band held well at points D
and E before price broke through corrective support at point F
(and weekly crrective support at point G as seen in Figure
9.17), thus confirming a downtrend. Price then moved lower
towards 7,600 where a sharp correction reversed to break trend
resistance. Price subsequently rallied to almost test corrective

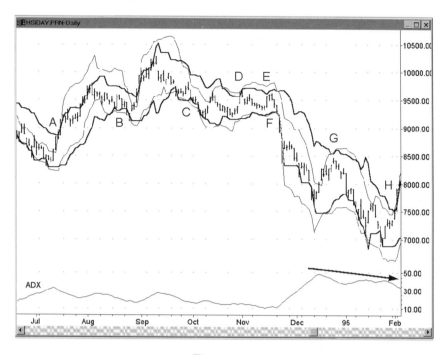

Figure 9.18
Daily Hang Seng Index with ADX and Momentum Bands applied. The thin bands are the trend support and resistance while the bold bands are corrective support and resistance.

resistance at point G, before continuing lower to the 6,890 low. After the 6,890 low, the HSI rallied to test and broke both trend and corrective resistance bands. This suggests that a larger upward move can occur. Indeed the ADX had been showing that momentum was slowing, and at the period of analysis, ADX was declining, suggesting that the overall downward move was slowing at the very least and had potentially reversed.

Let us now look at Figure 9.19 which shows the daily cyclic picture together with Cutler's RSI and Elliott Wave count.

In support of the wave count, wave (C) equals 1.618 of wave (A) and finds a low at the intermediate cycle trough. Wave (X) retraces almost 50% of the first ABC pattern, finding a high at the peak of the second largest cycle. From there, a further -a--b--c- pattern down develops with wave -c- being nearly 2.618 of wave -a-. This finds a low at the combined cycle

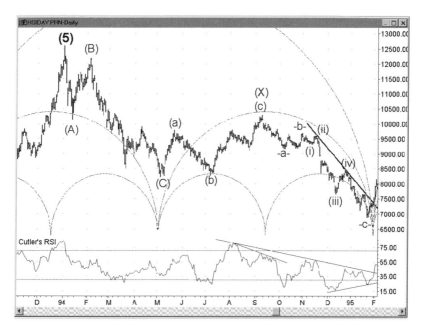

Figure 9.19
Daily Hang Seng Index with Elliott wave count, cycles, and Cutler's RSI.

trough. (Referring back to Figure 9.18, we see that the decline from the wave -b- high broke corrective support in the daily chart. This coincided with the break of the corrective support on the weekly chart in Figure 9.17.) The decline to the 6,890 low was accompanied by a bullish divergence on the daily Cutler's RSI (to support and confirm the weekly bullish divergence). Price has risen to break a clear downtrend line from a point just after the wave -b- peak. In addition, we see a break of a downtrend line on Cutler's RSI.

The daily summary follows:

Cycles	Elliott Wave	Target
Finding a low	Potential completion of wave (v) of wave -c-	6,810 – 2.618% of wave -a-

Momentum	Support	Resistance
ADX declining	6,810 – 2.618 of	7,645 – minor peak
RSI – bullish-divergence	wave -a-	in wave (v)
Break of down-trend line		8,460 – wave (iv) peak

Thus, our bias from the weekly and daily pictures of momentum is that the decline has slowed and potentially reversed. With weekly RSI diverging, ADX no longer indicating a trending market, and corrective resistance having been broken, we could also favor a reversal of the downtrend.

Thus, with a Fibonacci target being met, a break of downtrend line, RSI resistance line, Momentum Band resistance, lack of daily or weekly trend, and cycle lows in both daily and weekly charts, the analysis supports an argument for further gains which should at least reach the wave -b- high, and potentially much further. This would also imply that the weekly cycles drawn in Figure 9.16 are accurate. As such, we could expect a much stronger recovery and even the potential for a new high in the index.

Subsequent weekly price action of the HSI can be seen in Figure 9.20. As all cycles turned up, price rallied in tandem. Wave (1) reached a minor corrective high (in the final decline to the 6,890 low). Wave 1 then rallied to just below the wave X high. At that time, we may have been looking for a longer correction to coincide with the 37-week cycle trough. However, although price declined, it rallied to a new high before making a second decline coinciding with the 37-week cycle trough. It is from here that we saw a stronger move upwards to complete wave 3.

Note how the triangular wave 4 coinciding with the 74-week cycle trough gave us a strong indication of further price strength. I have found this a common occurrence when longer-term cycles are moving higher. The normal reaction is to expect to see a deeper correction with a cycle trough, treating the climb from the 6,890 low as a diagonal triangle. However, frequently the longer-term positive cycles keep price action moving higher, and the cycle trough actually meets the end of a triangle. When the triangle ended, we would be more certain of a new high in price, certainly above the previous 12,599 peak of January 1994. Unfortunately, due to lack of sufficient price history, we cannot project a target for the expected peak. Instead, we would have to project it from the internal wave structure of this wave {5}.

Following the completion of wave (3), we saw a further decline coinciding with the 37-week cycle to complete wave (4). Price then rallied to the eventual wave (5) peak. This also completed wave {5} of one larger degree.

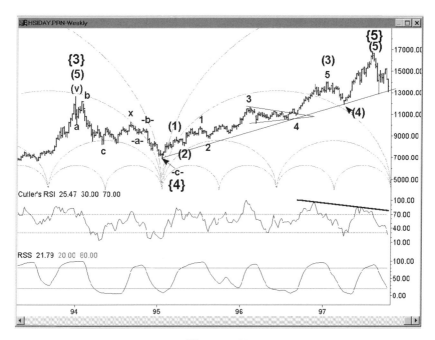

Figure 9.20
Weekly Hang Seng Index with cycles, Cutler's RSI, and ADX showing
development of price from the wave {4} low.

Note how waves 1, 3, (3), and (5) occurred at points where RSS was at overbought extremes. Conversely, waves 4 and (4) occurred at points where RSS was at oversold extremes. Also, the peak at wave 1 was accompanied by a bearish divergence, as was the peak just after wave (3) (an expanded flat wave (4)) and at wave (5)—again matching the RSS extremes. We also saw oversold levels in RSI at wave 2, just after wave 4, and at wave (4). Note the Fibonacci relationships:

Wave (2) = 38.2% of wave (1)
Wave 2   = 61.8% of wave 1
Wave 3   = 161.8% of wave 1
Wave 4   = 50% of wave 3
Wave 5   = Length of wave 1 through wave 3
Wave (4) = About 38.2% of wave (3)
Wave (5) = 61.8% of length of wave (1) to wave (3)

At this juncture, we have seen price decline to a support line, with RSI having dropped to oversold levels and RSS at a low. However, while there is a chance that a move sideways may be seen, with larger cycles now being bearish, and should this support line be broken, the risk is for a stronger move down. Indeed in line with the Elliott guidelines, we should expect a decline to the second wave of the fifth, that is at 8,100. We are close to this major cycle trough and thus it is possible that we shall see further weakness.

US DOLLAR–JAPANESE YEN MARKET

Our next example covers the US dollar–Japanese yen currency market in its decline from the corrective high of 160.20 in 1990. I have, as usual, started with the monthly chart and this is shown in Figure 9.21 with an Elliott wave count and underlying cyclic picture. The following are the prices at each major price reversal:

Start	362.25	Wave A	261.50	Wave 1	223.00
Wave (1)	315.00	Wave B	199.25	Wave 2	264.50
Wave (2)	357.75	Wave C	277.25	Wave 3	120.00
Wave (3)	254.25			Wave 4	160.25
Wave (4)	307.00				
Wave (5)	176.50				

At this juncture, I shall comment on the Fibonacci relationships of the waves. There are a few that fit the usual relationships though not many in the wave structures of -A- and -B-. I am always cautious when considering monthly cycles as the monthly data history is relatively short and it is quite possible that I fit the cycles into the structure, a process I call "curve fitting". However, what I look for is much as I have shown—major cycle troughs matching price lows together with smaller cycle troughs coinciding with the same structure. I am not totally contented with wave -A- not coinciding with the convergence of all four cycles shown, but the fact that the cycle troughs coincided with the wave B low gives more comfort especially since the three cycle troughs met price low at waves (3) and 3. In addition, the troughs of cycle 1 coincided with a number of major price lows. The major point to note about the cycles is how all four cycles shown are pointing down heavily, thus suggesting little respite to a strong downward trend. We are also looking for a fifth wave to develop lower.

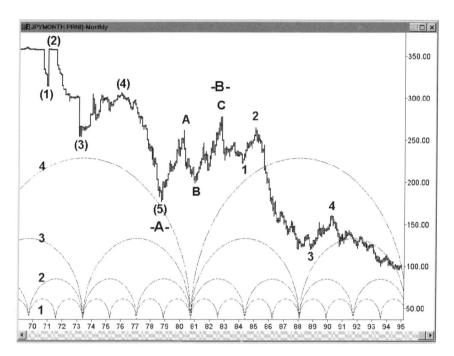

Figure 9.21
Monthly USDJPY currency market with Elliot wave count and cycles.

Let us generate a few targets from this monthly structure. Subtracting the length of wave -A- from the peak of wave -B-, we obtain a target for wave -C- at 91.50. Wave 3 is 261.8% of wave 1. Taking a projection for wave 5 of 61.8% of the movement from the start of wave 1 to the end of wave 3, we obtain a target of 63.00. Taking 50% of the distance of wave 1 through wave 3, we obtain a target of 81.62.

Figure 9.22 shows the Figure 9.21 chart with Cutler's RSI and ADX but without cycles. As cycle 1 in Figure 9.21 has a period length of 22 months, I have used an 11-month RSI. There are a few divergences in the RSI that look as if they would have confirmed other supporting analyses for reversals. At the period of analysis, there is potential for a bullish divergence to form, but we would require a break above 113.60 (the previous corrective peak) to suggest that this divergence could be sustained. ADX has just dipped by one point. This could be significant but given the cyclic picture in Figure 9.21, we must treat this with caution.

The monthly summary follows:

Cycles	Elliott Wave	Target
Strongly lower	Looking for wave 5 of wave -C-	81.62 – 50% of the length of wave 1 through wave 3 63.00 – 61.8% of the length of wave 1 through wave 3

Momentum	Support	Resistance
ADX just turned lower RSI – bullish-divergence?	96.00 – recent low	113.65 – previous corrective peak

Figure 9.23 shows the same monthly chart but this time with an alternative wave count. This alternative wave count has the October 1978 decline of 176.50 as the end of wave -1-. Thus, we are expecting wave -3- to move lower. We should also be looking for wave 5 to complete this wave -3-. This would then be followed by a wave -4- and wave -5-. However, since the implications for both situations are the same, this is merely academic.

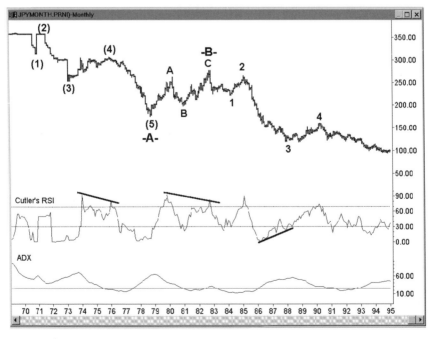

Figure 9.22
Monthly USDJPY currency market with Cutler's RSI & ADX.

Figure 9.24 shows the weekly chart of the same market. Here, I have confirmed the wave count but I will look at wave 5 more closely in a moment. The four cycles shown in the monthly chart (in Figures 9.21 and 9.23) are reproduced in this weekly chart. Notice how closely the cycle troughs coincide with most of price lows. At the extremes of cycle 1, we see price or momentum divergences, or oversold or overbought extremes in Cutler's RSI. Cycle 1 has period length of about 42 weeks and I have therefore used a 21-week RSI. ADX has been fairly choppy, especially in the wave 3 decline to 120. But it should be remembered that at this point in the monthly chart, ADX was rising. At the period of analysis, we have seen ADX decline to below 30 while RSI shows indications of a bullish divergence. However, we must be cautious about calling a reversal until a significant peak has been penetrated—in this case at the previous high labeled wave (iv), at 113.60.

We should now look at the decline from 160.20 labeled as a wave 4. Figure 9.25 shows the diagonal triangle wave count together with cycles, Elliott wave count, Cutler's RSI, and

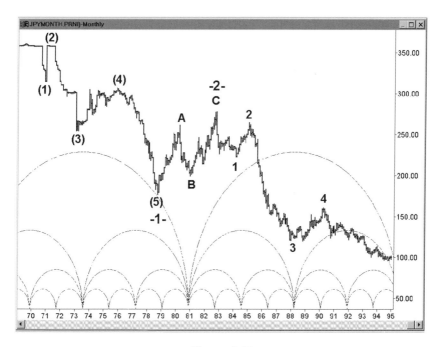

Figure 9.23
Monthly USDJPY currency market with alternative wave count and cycles.

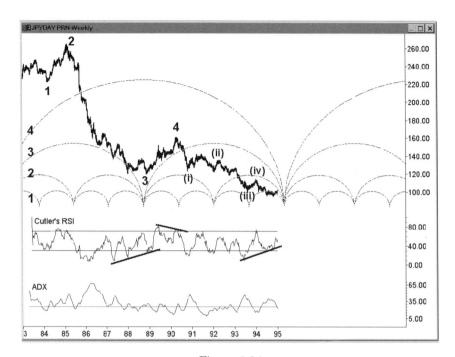

Figure 9.24
*Weekly USDJPY currency market with Cutler's RSI, ADX, cycles, and
Elliott wave count from the wave 2 peak.*

ADX. (Figure 9.26 shows the same chart with Cutler's RSI and
my RSS). In the decline from the wave 4 peak at 160.20, we see
that waves (i) and wave (iii) are of approximately the same
length. Within wave (iii), the wave c is 1.618 of wave a. At the
period of analysis, there has been an initial decline to 96.50,
followed by a sideways consolidation. This can be labeled waves
a and b of the final wave (v). By taking the length of wave (iii)
and multiplying this by 0.618, we arrive at a target of 93.00,
while a move of the same length as wave (iii)—and therefore
also of wave (i)—we arrive at a target of 80.

I have used an 11-week Cutler's RSI. This is only one-
quarter of the underlying 44-week cycle. I have found that
sometimes the 22-week period can be too long. The 11-week
RSI tends to find peaks and troughs around the same time as
price highs and lows, occasionally showing bullish or bearish
divergences. The 11-week RSI also matches the cycle peaks and
troughs while price highs and lows also coincide nicely with the
peaks and troughs of RSS.

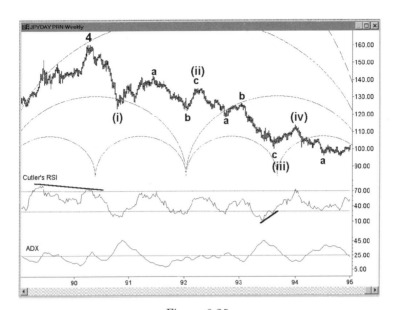

Figure 9.25
Weekly USDJPY currency market with cycles, Cutler's RSI, and ADX. The
Elliott wave count suggests a declining diagonal triangle that is looking for
completion of waves b and c to complete (v).

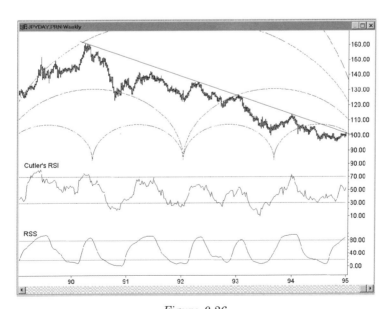

Figure 9.26
Weekly USDJPY currency market with cycles, Cutler's RSI, and RSS.
Note the test of the downtrend line from the 160.20 peak at the far
left of the chart.

At the period of analysis, we have RSS above 80 and Cutler's RSI at high levels. We have a potential cycle high and we are just reaching the trendline resistance. If we briefly refer back to Figure 9.21, we see that at this point the monthly cycles were coming down hard, giving negative pressure. We can also suggest that since we have not met the targets at 80 and 63 referred to earlier there is still a potential for price to move towards these lower target level. Let us now look at the daily chart to assess if the bearish bias suggested by the weekly chart is correct and whether we can finetune the peak.

The weekly summary follows:

Cycles	Elliott Wave	Target
Strongly lower	Looking for	93.00 – 0.618 of
44 week – peaking	wave c of wave (v)	wave (iii)
	to complete wave 5	80.00 – wave (i)
		equality of wave (iii)

Momentum	Support	Resistance
Moving lower	96.00 – recent low	113.65 – previous
RSI – bullish-		corrective peak
divergence?		101.80 – previous
		minor peak.

Figure 9.27 shows the daily chart of the same market with cycles, Elliott wave count, and Cutler's RSI. The first decline to 96.50 was counted as wave {A} of a decline from 113.65 and completed at 96.50. This also marked a 44-week cycle trough and provoked a sharp rally up to 101.80, where minor bearish divergence formed. This is labeled wave (A). Subsequently, a long complex correction developed. Attempts to analyze price action during the correction were very difficult. In retrospect, we can see that the entire correction developed as a flat. The wave (B) was a zigzag in which the intermediate wave B developed as a flat (marked abc). The end of wave (B) occurred just below the end of wave {A} at 96.10 with Cutler's RSI at very low levels. However, the wave (B) occurred at a minor cycle trough (not shown since a $27\frac{1}{2}$-day cycle cannot be plotted). The Japanese yen has a prominent $27\frac{1}{2}$-day cycle and it was at one of these cycle troughs that the reversal occurred. At this point, we could not have been sure that we would move back to the 101.80 high since price lows and cycle troughs were slightly out of synchronization, although we see the longest

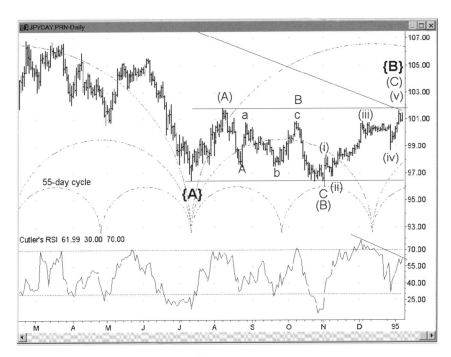

Figure 9.27
Daily USDJPY currency market with basic 55-day cycle. Note how wave
(B) occurred around 27½ days – half the length of the 55-day cycle.

cycle shown was still finding a peak. Thus, as price rallied up to 101.80, we could anticipate that with all cycles reaching their peaks, a price peak was due. In addition, we see a distinct five-wave rally from the 96.10 low. If we measure wave (A) and add this to the 96.10 wave (B) low, we obtain 101.40. At the peirod of analysis, we had reached 101.55 and Cutler's RSI shows very strong potential bearish divergences.

The daily summary follows:

Cycles	Elliott Wave	Target
Longer cycle peaking	Looking for wave (c) of wave {B}	101.80 – wave {A} peak
Shorter cycles rising	Looking for wave 5 decline	101.40 – wave (C) = wave (A)

Momentum	Support	Resistance
Bearish divergence on Cutler's RSI	96.00 – recent low	101.80 – wave {A} peak
	98.70 – wave (iv) low	

Thus with the weekly chart clearly indicating a cyclic high, a high RSS and Cutler's RSI meeting a very long-term downtrend line, and the daily chart showing a clear flat correction with target level between 101.40 and 101.80, bearish divergences and daily cycle peaks, we must come to the conclusion that further price weakness can be seen.

The April 19, 1995 Low At 79.75.

Figure 9.28 shows the subsequent price action from the 101.50 peak to the 79.75 low. This shows how price broke below the previous 96.10 low, then accelerated downwards strongly as the long-term cyclic chart made a significant trough while Cutler's RSI formed a bullish divergence at the lower target of 79.00/ 80.00.

Figure 9.29 shows the rally from the 79.75 low. This is actually a difficult period during which to analyze the market as several wave counts were possible. While the strong rally could be anticipated because of the strongly reversing cycles and the break in the five-year downtrend line from the 160.25 peak, the wave structure after wave (3) was particularly complex. Weekly Cutler's RSI over much of this period formed strong bearish divergences but price action never fulfilled these divergences. This is an example of the analysis requirement when identifying divergences i.e. after development, divergences must be confirmed by price reversing through important Elliott support levels. In this case, price never really dipped low enough to break through, first, the wave (4) support, and then, waves a, c, and e. When seen in conjunction with Figure 9.27, we see a wave (iv) high at 113.65 with price action forcing its way higher to test this important level. Wave 1 of {C} (in Figure 9.29) briefly penetrated this point, rising to 115.00 but then fell back. But on the wave 2 retracement, price coincides with an 83-week cycle low and prices rallied strongly thereafter.

I do not pretend to suggest that I labeled the wave structure in this manner as price rose. Often, I look for the bearish divergences to succeed for a brief time before the longer-term cycles take price higher. The cyclic chart was difficult as longer-term cycles suggested a period of weakness, but these never materialized. This forces me to be always cautious when waiting for the break but also quick to reverse

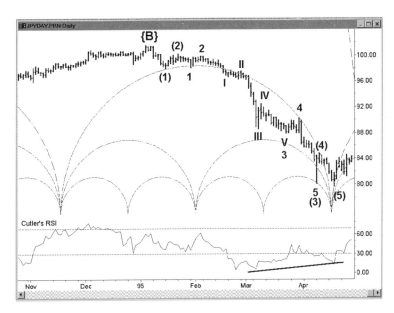

Figure 9.28
Daily USDJPY currency market with Cutler's RSI showing subsequent price action and decline to 79.75.

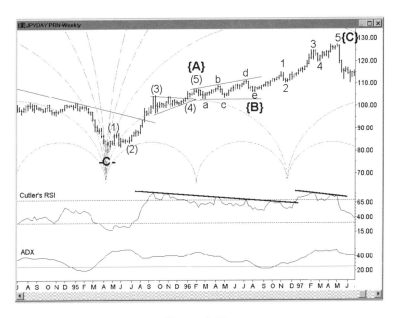

Figure 9.29
Weekly USDJPY currency market with cycles, Cutler's RSI, and ADX showing price action after the 79.75 low. Note the strong influence of the longer cycles pulling price higher.

my initial judgments to allow for further price rallies. The wave structure was labeled in retrospect, but through constant measurements I noticed several wave relationships that, at that time, assisted in identifying support and resistance levels. For instance:

- Wave (3) is 261.8% of wave (1).
- The first wave a of wave (4) is exactly 38.2% of wave (3).
- Wave (5) stalled at the apex of the triangle wave (4).
- Wave b is 138.2% of wave a.
- Wave c retraces almost to the base of wave a.
- Wave d is 138.2% of wave c.
- Wave e is equal to wave c.

From this point, wave 1 rallied to the previous wave (iv) peak at 113.65 (and just above), wave 2 retraced 50% to coincide with the 83-week cycle trough, and wave 3 then rallied to 161.8% of wave 1. Wave 4 marginally failed to retrace 38.2% of wave 3, and then wave 5 rallied 38.2% of the distance from the beginning of wave 1 to the end of wave 3. Unfortunately, the entire five-wave structure did not have wave equality with wave {A}.

Figure 9.30 shows the weekly chart as price continued from the wave {A} peak, along with cycles, ADX, and Cutler's RSI super-imposed on RSS. Note how wave (A) declined to the trough of the second wave of {C} before price moved higher though price did not exactly match the cycle trough. However, at this low, Cutler's RSI reached low levels while RSS also reached levels below 20, and both at a time when ADX had ceased rising and subsequently declining. Price then proceeded to move higher until the point marked at (B).

It is interesting to note that as we approached this peak at (B) many of the market participants were exceptionally bullish about the dollar and were looking for price to move higher over the 140 level. To many, the decline from the wave {C} peak to the 110.56 low—marked wave (A)—was considered to be a complete correction. However, with the assistance of Fibonacci relationships, Elliott Wave, and cycles, we could have avoided this trap. If we had measured the distance from the wave {A} peak to the wave (A) low and multiplied by 1.382, we would have arrived at a value of 133.96.

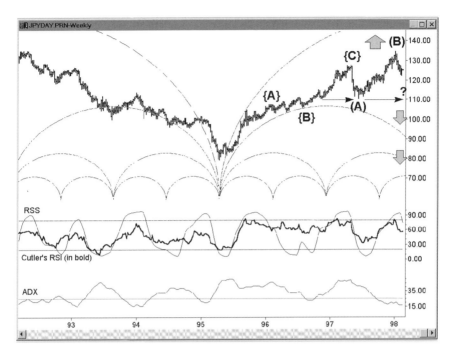

Figure 9.30
Weekly USDJPY currency market with Cutler's RSI, RSS, and ADX
showing potential cyclic pressures.

Of course, it is possible to consider the decline to 110.56 as a complete correction. But if we consider the cyclic picture, we would see that there was a major cyclic low due in the middle of 1998, and we should at least see a downward correction in this time frame. This would have guarded us against an extreme bullish picture and suggested that the decline to 110.56 was wave (A) of a correction. We would then have considered the alternatives of a three-wave decline in wave (A)—this being a triangle, flat, or expanded flat. At the time of the low, any of the three alternatives was possible—but at least we could suggest that the dollar would move higher close to the peak of wave {C} at 127.50.

If we look at Figure 9.31, we see the daily chart with cycles, Elliott wave count, Cutler's RSI, and ADX. The rally proceeded in a choppy manner, much as would be expected with a wave (B). By the time the cycle trough occurred around the wave (b) low, we could be certain that further strength would come and favored either a flat or expanded flat. In my own analysis, I warned of a rally towards 127.50 again and if this level was breached, then further strength could be anticipated to 134.00. This indeed happened, with price reaching a peak of 134.43 on January 7, 1998. From the weekly chart in Figure 9.30, we see the largest cycle still moving up, and this caused the development of an expanded flat. However, the three shorter-term cycles were now moving down strongly, implying that we would see very little chance of further move higher. RSS peaked above 80 while Cutler's RSI also reached a level of 80 and ADX was low. This supported the view of a peak.

The daily chart in Figure 9.31 also confirmed a high daily Cutler's RSI, even evidence of a minor bearish divergence while ADX was low. Thus, with the largest cycle having peaked at the time of wave (b) and now declining, the 216-day cycle soon to find a peak, the 108-day cycle having peaked and now beginning a decline, and the 54-day cycle having less effect against the stronger declining weekly cycles, it supported the evidence for a peak at 134.43.

The implication from this would be a textbook decline down to the wave (A) low at 110.56, though we would also have to watch the 117.49 level which marks the point where wave (C) would be equal to wave (A). At this juncture, the dollar had declined to 122.63, not far above the wave (b) low at 118.70, with some time to go before the larger cycle low.

This highlights the strength of integrating all forms of complementary analysis techniques to provide a stronger and more informed view of how price action is developing.

US DOLLAR–GERMAN DEUTSCHMARK MARKET

The currency market of US dollar–German Deutschmark during the rally from the 1.3445 low in March 1995 as it approached 1.90 in August 1997, provides the setting for the next example of integrating technical analysis in a foreign exchange market. This rally marks the longest stretch in 10 years of a continuing strong dollar.

Again, I have started with the monthly chart (in Figure 9.32) showing price action from the late 1960s through to the period of analysis, detailing the cyclic structure along with an Elliott wave count. Due to the relatively short data history for

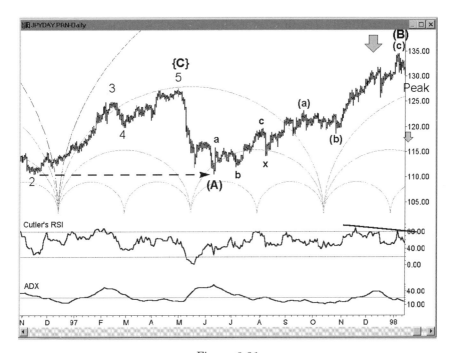

Figure 9.31
The peak of the second cycle occurs along with a bearish divergence
in Cutler's RSI and ADX at low levels.

this time frame, it is difficult label the large decline on the left of Figure 9.32. In retrospect, given the equally strong recovery that rallied above the level of the previous fourth wave, I have favored this initial decline as being wave -A- with the subsequent rally being wave -B-. This would imply that the decline from the 3.4770 high in February 1995 is wave -C-. We are, therefore, looking for a five-wave move down.

This wave count would appear to match the cyclic structure. I have shown four major cycles—48-, 96-, 182-, and 384-month cycles. Wave -A- occurred at the confluence of all these cycles while the low at 1.3445 occurred at the confluence of the first three cycles and at the peak of the 384-month cycle. There is always the question, when applying cycles, of where the cycle troughs should meet. As a comparison, Figure 9.33 shows the 384-month cycle coinciding with price low at 1.3445. However, this may suggest that we have seen a long-term major low at 1.3445 and the cyclic pressure would be suggesting that the dollar will be strong for many years to come. It is always tempting, when making an initial analysis of the cycles, to place the largest cycle trough at the most recent major price low. However, looking at the performance of price in Figure 9.33, we see that the major influences of the cycles do not match. For instance, when the dollar was declining to the 1.6470 low in December 1978, the 384-month cycle was moving higher while the shorter-term cycles were moving lower. But, as the 384-month cycle turned lower together with the three shorter-term cycles, we should have expected to see price decline more strongly than what actually occurred after the 2.0480 high in June 1989, after which all cycles converged.

There is just one other possibility: the 1.3445 low did in fact complete a wave -C- and that price would break through 2.0480 by some degree but this would develop into a wave -X- before a further ABC decline. At the current point, this is academic and we shall look instead at the current analysis.

Thus, the cyclic structure in Figure 9.32 looks to be more logical, and the wave structure implied from this suggests that the current rally is part of a correction in a five-wave decline

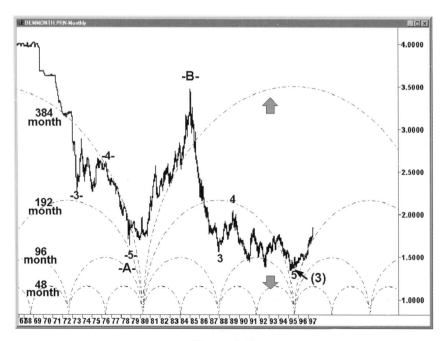

Figure 9.32
Monthly USDDEM currency market with cycles and Elliott wave count.

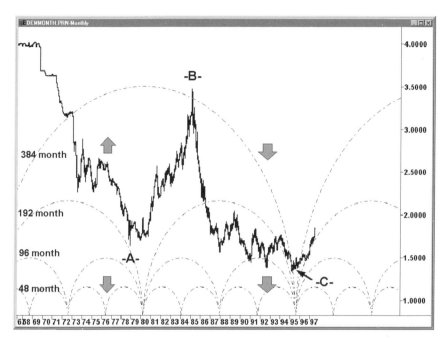

Figure 9.33
Monthly USDDEM currency market with an alternative wave count.
However, note how all cycles converged at wave -C- suggesting a stronger
decline, when in fact the decline had been less than convincing.

in wave -C-. If we now move to Figure 9.34, the cycles are removed, and Cutler's RSI and ADX added. The 2.0480 level marked is critical. If we follow the Elliott guidelines on corrections, we would expect price to remain below the previous wave 4 peak at 2.0480. Cutler's RSI is at very high levels that have historically provoked a correction at the very least—this occurs during the mid-point of the rally up to 3.4770 and also at the 3.4770 peak. A very distinct support line can be drawn under Cutler's RSI rally to this point. A break of this line would indicate that some correction is possible. However, at the same time ADX has begun to rise and is around the 30 level suggesting that a monthly trend may be in place.

Finally, the levels of the major reversal points in the decline from 3.4770 are shown in Figure 9.35 and these are:

| Wave (1) | 2.9580 | Wave 1 | 2.7420 | Wave (i) | 1.4430 |
| Wave(2) | 3.2630 | Wave 2 | 2.9650 | Wave (ii) | 1.8470 |

Wave (3)	1.3445	Wave 3	1.5620	Wave (iii)	1.3865
		Wave 4	2.0480	Wave (iv)	1.7684
		Wave 5	1.3445	Wave (v)	1.3445

Note the following relationships:

Wave 2   = 0.382 of wave 1.
Wave 3   = 2.618 of wave 1.
Wave 4   = 0.28 of wave 3.
Wave 5   = 0.40 of the length of wave 1 to wave 3.
Wave (ii) = 0.66 of wave (i).
Wave (iii) = 0.764 of wave (i).
Wave (iv) = Wave (ii).
Wave (v) = 0.92 of wave (iii).

Note that there are several good Fibonacci relationships, with others being quite close. This gives some confidence that the wave count shown is correct.

We should now look at any potential support and resistance levels together with target levels. The easiest to identify are the resistance level of 2.0480 being the wave 4 of the decline in wave -C-, and the first corrective peak after the decline from 2.0480. This was at 2.0045. From Elliott's point of view, there are no nearby major lows. In fact, the most recently identifiable trough was the actual wave (3) low at 1.3445. This is too far away to be of any immediate consequence. Perhaps we could take a Fibonacci retracement level. But until we have identified a critical high, this process would be futile. Thus, no support can be identified from the monthly chart and we must look at the weekly chart to receive a better idea.

The monthly summary is:

Cycles	Elliott Wave	Target
Major cycles higher 48-month cycle at a high	Looking for wave (4)	Peak below 2.0480

Momentum	Support	Resistance
ADX beginning to trend?	None immediately available	2.0045 – previous peak
Cutler's RSI extremely high		2.0480 – wave 4 peak

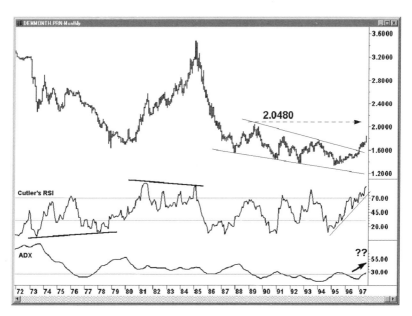

Figure 9.34
Monthly USDDEM currency market with Cutler's RSI and ADX. Note how at the period of analysis on the extreme right, ADX begins to move higher. Also note the support line below Cutler's RSI.

Figure 9.35
Monthly USDDEM currency market with Elliott wave count and reversal levels.

Figure 9.36 shows the weekly chart from the end of 1991 to the period of analysis, together with Elliott wave count and cyclic structure. There is a basic 34-week cycle and this multiplies into 68-, 136-, and 272-week cycles. Although there is some degree of lateral movement, the cycle troughs broadly match price lows and we see a confluence of all the cycles at the 1.3445 low. The wave count shows in more detail the end of the diagonal triangle decline from the 2.0480 wave 4 high seen in Figure 9.32. This pattern comprises definite three-wave moves. I have not yet labeled the rally from the 1.3445 and will do so later. For now, note the following:

In the wave (iv) rally,
Wave 3 = 1.618 of wave 1.
Wave 4 = 0.382 of wave 3.
Wave 5 = 0.618 of the length of wave 1 through wave 3.
Wave B declined to the level of the second wave of wave 5.
Wave C = 0.50 of wave A.

In the wave (v) decline,
Wave c was broadly equal to wave a with an expanded flat wave b.

Finally in Figure 9.36, consider the cyclic conditions at the period of analysis. A long rally from the 1.3445 low reached a level of 1.8915. As mentioned earlier, this rally lasted 29 months, 11 months longer than any rally since the 1.5620 low in 1985. This suggests that the longer-term cycles are positive and we are seeing right translation. By the time we reach 1.8915, the 272-week cycle is still pointing higher, almost at its peak, while the shorter 34-, 68-, and 136-week cycles are pointing lower. Due to this, we should soon be seeing a period of correction. But, given the right translation and that the 272-week cycle is still high, we can deduce that this correction should not be very deep, and that probably further strength will subsequently be seen. Also, this correction should find a price low close to the combined troughs of the three shorter-term cycle, and this occurs about 13–15 weeks later.

Figure 9.37 displays the same period of price action with Cutler's RSI and ADX applied. There is not a great deal of information to be gathered from this chart. Cutler's RSI shows

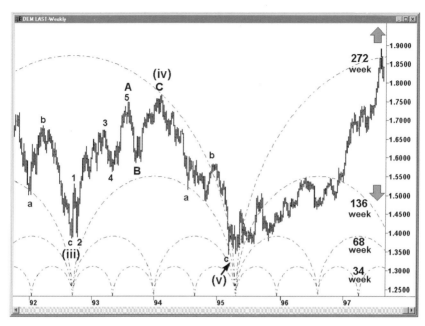

Figure 9.36
Weekly USDDEM currency market with cycles and Elliott wave count.

some propensity to diverge in the past, but not to a great extent. ADX, on the other hand, broadly identifies sustained movements in trends. At the period of analysis, a large bearish divergence has developed while ADX is faltering. Looking at the ADX, we will see that it indicated a trending move as the dollar rallied to the minor peak just above 1.70, then declined as price moved in a sideways consolidation. Then, as price rallied to the 1.8915 peak, ADX once again turned higher. However, this second "peak" in ADX (though not quite confirmed yet) was lower than the first. This is often seen at price peaks as the final rally is not as strong as the prior rally—reflective of the strength of a wave 3 followed by the lesser power of wave 5. We, therefore, suspect that we are seeing a sizable peak at this point.

Finally, to complete the weekly analysis, let us look at the rally from the 1.3445 low through to the 1.8915 peak as shown in Figure 9.38. Referring back to Figure 9.32, we know that we are looking for a wave (4) to develop and this should be in three waves. The first area (circled in Figure 9.38) is very confusing.

Even at this juncture, we do not know how to count this. I suspect that, given the speed of the decline into the 1.3445 low, there may be a failed fifth—the initial rally to around 1.4628 is merely a fourth wave to be followed by the failed fifth. From the potential failed fifth low, we saw a rally above 1.50 followed by a decline to 1.3805. This is still a slight mystery but I suspect that given the strength of the long-term cycles, it is either a wave A of an ABC structure upwards, or it is still part of the failed fifth, in which case the rally from 1.3805 is wave (A) of a wave (4) correction.

However, what is particularly clear is the rally from 1.3805. Note the following:

Wave 2 = 0.50 of wave 1.
Wave 3 = 1.618 of wave 1.
Wave 4 = 0.236 of wave 3.
Wave 5 = 0.618 of the length of wave 1 through wave 3.

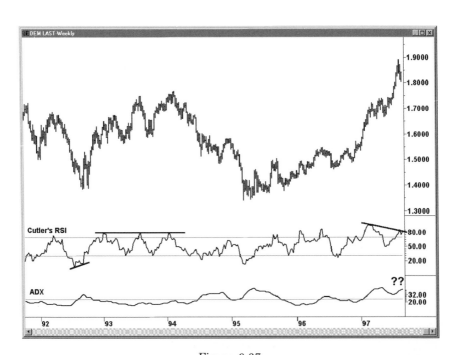

Figure 9.37
Weekly USDDEM currency market with Cutler's RSI and ADX. Note the potential bearish divergence while ADX is still rising.

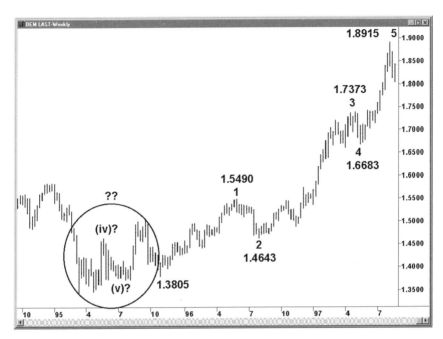

Figure 9.38
Weekly USDDEM currency market showing a confused area (circled)
with a tentative count of a failed fifth. The subsequent rally is a clear
five-wave rally.

In fact, the last measurement provided a target for the dollar at precisely 1.8888—thus the peak at 1.8915 is only 27 points away from being perfect. This gives a high probability that we have seen a major peak at 1.8915 to complete wave 5 and (probably) wave (A) of wave (4). Or possibly we have seen a complete ABC structure and this has completed wave (4) or we will see a double zigzag or even a triangle developing. Given that the weekly cyclic structure in Figure 9.36, as suggested we should be witnessing a peak with an approximate 13- to 15-week decline, and the momentum picture displayed a bearish divergence, we can be very confident that we should see a corrective wave (B) that should move to the span of the wave 4. This was between 1.6683 and 1.7373. If this is a wave (B), we can also look at a 0.382 retracement of the entire move from 1.3805 to 1.8915. This should gives us a target of 1.6962 which lies perfectly in the span of the Wave 4.

The weekly summary follows:

Cycles	Elliott Wave	Target
Cycle high due 34-, 68-, and 136-week cycles bearish	Looking for wave (4) or wave (A)	38.2% correction at 1.6962
Momentum	**Support**	**Resistance**
ADX peaking Bearish divergence on Cutler's RSI	1.6962 wave (4) target	1.8915 – wave 5 peak Wave (iv) of wave 5 cannot be seen

Next, as usual, we move to the daily chart to see whether we can confirm our analysis of the weekly chart and finetune reversal signals. This is shown in Figure 9.39 which shows daily cycles and momentum analysis. The wave structure from wave -2- of wave 3 until wave 5 is shown. This appears quite straightforward with wave 4 retracing 23.6% to the same level as the base of wave -4- from where the rally to the peak of wave 5 is seen. Note how the 32-day cycle matches price lows, most noticeably at the troughs of wave -2-, wave -4-, and wave 4 with all three 32-, 64-, and 128-day cycles converging into a trough at the base of wave 4.

Cutler's RSI has worked well with retracements to the oversold level at wave -4- and wave 4 with ADX indicating a trending move during the wave 3. (Thus, no strong reversal of Cutler's RSI). After the move to 1.8915, we see ADX turn lower, suggesting that the immediate trend has ended. At the point of analysis, we see the 32- and 64-day cycles converge and rise. While this is normally a bullish signal, given the strong downward pressure of weekly cycles, this rally should be stunted. Cutler's RSI did not show any bearish divergence, but declined from a very high level, and with ADX at low levels, we would be advised to look for shorter-term trading signals from extremes of this indicator.

Figure 9.40 displays the final rally to the end of wave 5. This appears to have developed as a diagonal triangle. It does not fit into converging trendlines in a wedge pattern. But looking closely at the initial wave (i), we see that this came in three waves, followed by a wave (ii) that was definitely a triangle. In fact after this, wave (iii) was exactly 1.618 times wave (i), and in accordance with the guideline of alternation,

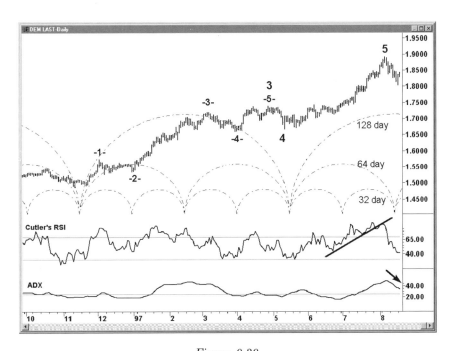

Figure 9.39
*Daily USDDEM currency market with 32-, 64-, and 128-day cycles along
with Cutler's RSI and ADX. Note the broken uptrend line on Cutler's RSI
and how ADX declined.*

we see a short sharp wave (iv) followed by a wave (v) that was
0.382 of the distance from wave (i) through to the end of wave
(iii). Subsequently, we saw break of trend support and also,
perhaps more importantly, the breach of the wave (iv)
retracement level. This was a sign that the five waves were
complete and that further downside would be seen.

The daily summary follows:

Cycles	Elliott Wave	Target
Short-term cycle low	Wave (iv) breached	1.6962 in wave (4)
Weekly cycles bearish	Probably wave 1 of A complete	or wave (A)

Momentum	Support	Resistance
ADX declining	1.8050 (recent low)	1.8915 – wave 5 peak
Cutler's RSI near low		1.8584 – (0.618 retracement)

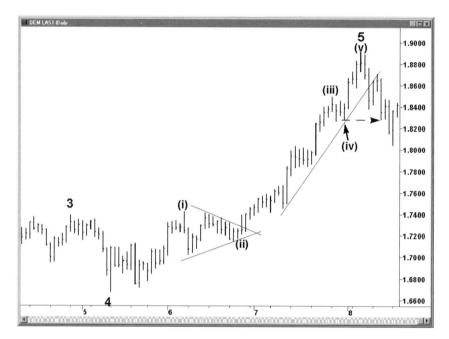

Figure 9.40
Daily USDDEM currency market displaying the wave 5 rally that
developed as a diagonal triangle. Note break of the uptrend line.

Finally, just to see how we can break the picture down
even further, Figure 9.41 displays the four-hour bar chart of
the wave 5 rally. Notice how the daily cycles can broadly be
superimposed upon an intraday chart. While some cycle lows
are as accurate in timing (due to the influence of the larger
cycles), the basic concept remains intact. Also note the bearish
divergence of Cutler's RSI at the 1.8915 peak with the same
pattern in ADX—ADX had risen in a trending move, then
declined with a correction, rose again but to a lower peak at the
price high. The wave count of this is shown in Figure 9.42
where I have labeled the diagonal triangle. The wave (iii)
appears to have come in a double zigzag with the second abc
having waves a and c of equal length.

If we look at a complete picture of all three summaries, we
see a picture of a long-term wave (4) in a large correction from
the 1.3445 low within which we are looking for an intermediate
wave 5 to be completed. Monthly cycles still appear to point
higher, although weekly cycles suggest potential for a brief

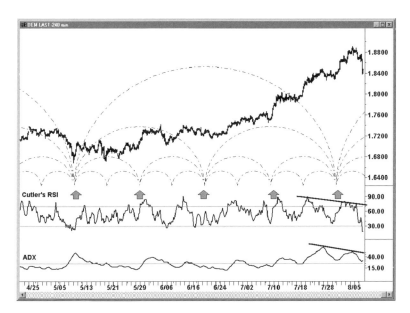

Figure 9.41
Four-hourly USDDEM bar chart with cycles, Cutler's RSI, and ADX. Note
the clear bearish divergence on the right with a similar pattern in ADX,
thus giving an early signal to the end of the uptrend.

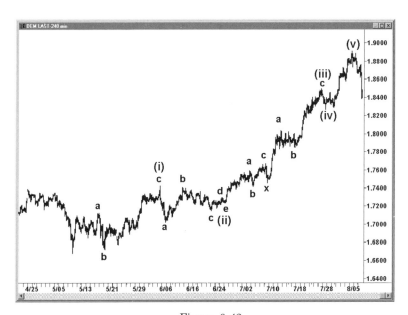

Figure 9.42
Four-hourly USDDEM bar chart showing the Elliott wave count to the
1.8915 peak.

pullback of some 12–15 weeks towards the level of the previous wave 4 between 1.6683 and 1.7373. The daily picture confirms a reversal with the previous wave (iv) broken, and thus we feel confident of a picture of a medium-term wave (B) developing at least to the 0.382 retracement level at 1.6962 (and possibly further).

Figure 9.43 shows subsequent trading which confirmed this analysis with a 14-week decline to 1.6950—to hit the initial target perfectly. This occurred at the major weekly cycle low. I have labeled this decline as wave A and currently, with waves appearing to be developing in threes, it would favor the development of a wave B that has the risk of being a triangle. After completion of this wave B, it would be likely that a decline should occur. The 1.6950 low will act as a signal for a different wave count should it be breached. Further support will be found at the 50% retracement level at 1.6360 and the 61.8% retracement at 1.5760.

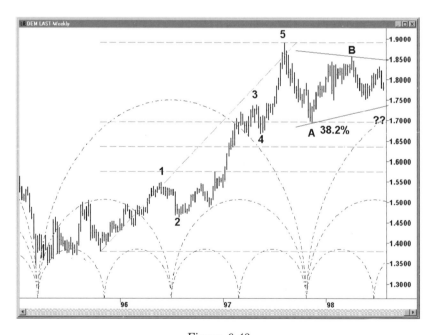

Figure 9.43
Weekly USDDEM currency market showing price action subsequent to the 1.8915 peak. The cycles as shown earlier are also plotted along with Fibonacci retracement levels. Note how the decline to wave A retraced 38.2% of the entire five-wave rally.

GOLD MARKET

To give a different approach, I shall show an analysis of gold that I held for quite a period but which turned out to be incorrect. I would love to be able to say that my analysis was always correct, but this is not true. The objective of presenting this incorrect analysis is: first, to show how even an incorrect analysis can provide some good signals, second, to show where the analysis is proven to be incorrect, and finally, to show why collecting a long data history could provide clues that are not held in shorter data history.

Figure 9.44 shows the monthly chart I possessed at the time, dating from 1986 through to the period of analysis in February 1996. It is difficult to be sure of the cyclic structure from such a relatively short monthly chart. I had placed the cycles as shown, but was not particularly happy with them. However I could see no better alternative. It was also difficult to be certain of the Elliott wave count, but it was fairly clear that the decline from the high at the left of the figure at the

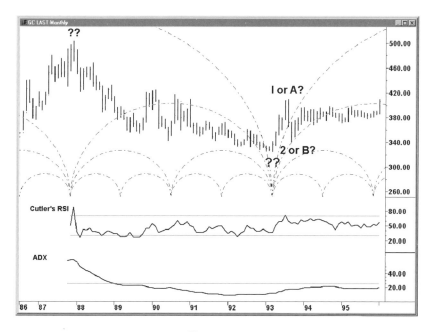

Figure 9.44
*Monthly gold market dating from 1986 with cycles and potential
Elliott wave count. Cutler's RSI and ADX are also plotted and indicate
absence of trend.*

end of 1987 to the 325.75 low in March 1993 was a volatile, choppy move that was more reflective of a series of three-wave moves rather than trending five-wave moves. The rally from there up to 409.50 in August 1993 looked (from the monthly chart) to be impulsive and thus, would require a further high. The momentum indicators shown were neutral. Cutler's RSI was flat while ADX had not shown signs of any trend for eight years.

In summary, there is very little of which we can be certain. The impression is of a recent cycle low with a trending wave from 325.75 to 409.50 I was biased in favor of further highs being seen.

Figure 9.45 displays the weekly chart from the 325.75 low to the point of analysis. Since the initial 409.50 high (the strong recovery of gold having drawn requests for analysis from clients) I had been correct in calling a low at 340.80, which I labeled B or (2) . I had been suggesting that since the first wave to 409.50 appeared to come in five waves, we should see a

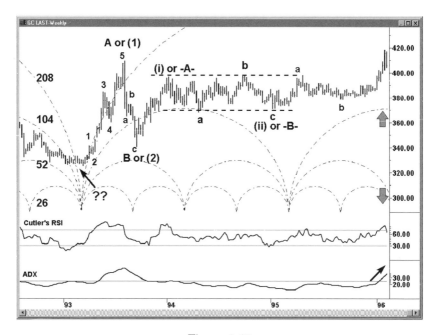

Figure 9.45
Weekly gold market with 26-, 52-, 104-, and 208-week cycles and Elliott wave count with Cutler's RSI and ADX. Cutler's RSI shows overbought but ADX is also climbing.

further five waves upwards that would attain a level above 409.50. The subsequent rally to 396.65, labeled (i) or -A-, looked positive. However, we then saw a long sideways consolidation that lasted for the entire 1994. This is when I began to have doubts about any immediately strongly bullish view. I called a rebound from the 371.25 low which is labeled (ii) or -B- since we saw the three shorter-term cycles converge into a trough around the same time while Cutler's RSI dipped into oversold while ADX was low.

Subsequently gold price rallied to test the channel resistance, corrected and then rallied once again into the period of analysis to reach 418.15. Since the rally had been quite strong, ADX had been rising to confirm the trend while Cutler's RSI had also moved to classic overbought levels and a dip had begun to bring it down once again. The cycles drawn were giving conflicting signals—the 26- and 52- week cycles converging to find a trough, while the 104-week cycle was finding a peak and the 208-week cycle was still high, but past its peak and beginning to decline.

Let us look at the Elliott Wave structure a little more closely. In Figure 9.46, the labeling shown in Figure 9.45 is repeated with price levels of what I believed were the key wave reversals added. Within this, I could generate several potential Fibonacci targets.

Assuming a 1-2- with the current rally as wave 3:

```
Wave (1)    = 409.50
Wave (2)    = 340.80 – 0.746 of wave (1)
Wave 1      = 396.65
Wave 2      = 371.25 – 0.50 of wave 1
If wave 3   = 1.618 of wave 1, then target is 455.00
If wave (3) = 1.618 of wave (1), then target is 476.30
```

Assuming an ABC pattern, we have the same targets but can add to them:

```
If wave (iii) = Wave (i), then target is 427.10
If wave (iii) = 0.618 of wave (i), then target is 405.76
If wave c     = Wave a, then target is 410.25
If wave c     = 1.618 of wave a, then target is 426.80
```

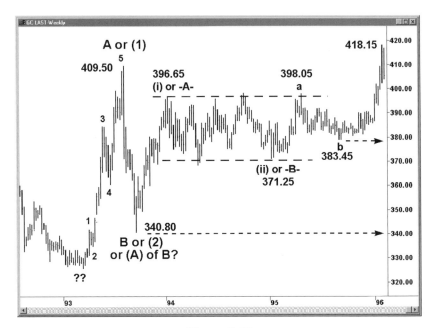

Figure 9.46
Weekly gold market with Elliott wave counts and key reversals marked.

I have also added a further possibility. By this point, I had noticed the conflicting signals given by the four cycles shown. The two longer-term cycles pointed higher, while the two shorter-term cycles were reaching a trough. This suggests a more bullish structure. However, given the long sideways ranging that has been labeled as wave (ii), I also considered the possibility of an expanded flat correction in which the decline to 340.80 was wave (A) of B. This rally we were seeing was wave (B) of B and the result would be a subsequent decline back to the 340.80 level before a rally. If we take classic Fibonacci measurements for an expanded flat we arrive at:

If wave (B) = 1.382 of wave (A), then target is 435.75
If wave (B) = 1.236 of wave (A), then target is 425.70

From the above targets, the most frequently recurring target level is around 425–427. While it has not been shown, the previous highest retracement level was 425.00. Thus I favored a move to retest the 425.00 level. It would be normal in a trending move to retest a previous level of resistance. I had also considered that given the cyclic structure, an expanded flat correction was also more probable. With longer-term cycles still high and ADX rising, this looked a reasonable forecast.

Figure 9.47 shows daily price action until just after the 418.15 peak. In accordance with my bullish scenario, I had labeled a bullish wave count. However, by February 12, 1996, just seven days after the 418.15 peak, price declined dramatically back to 405.75, and in the process broke a support trendline that had been drawn from the wave -2- low. The steepness of this decline was a concern as the underlying wave structure suggested that we should be seeing a series of fourth/ fifth waves in a wave c that should reach the 425 level. Break of the trendline and also a bearish divergence in Cutler's RSI confirmed a bearish market, while ADX had also turned down from a high level. In addition, the intermediate daily cycle had also dipped, and I had to begin looking for a more bearish wave count. Further signs of reversal would come on a break of the

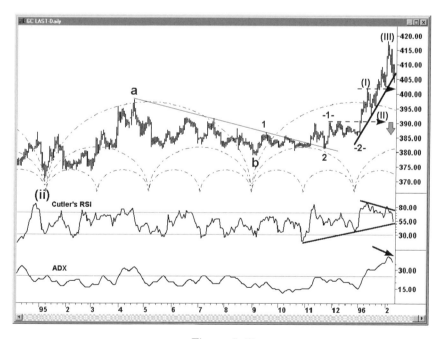

Figure 9.47
Daily gold market with cycles, Cutler's RSI, and ADX. The Elliott wave count is a bullish count, still looking for wave (v) of wave -3-. However, the break of the support line, the bearish divergence in Cutler's RSI, and ADX declining while cycles were topping, give opposing evidence.

wave (I) peak (that would break Elliott's rules) and also the
wave 1 peak. Subsequent to this, any move below wave b at
383.45 would reverse the wave structure.

Within two weeks, all of the above breaches of key support
had occurred and I reversed my forecast to the wave count
shown in Figure 9.48. It can be seen that I had decided that the
wave (B) of larger wave B had fallen short of the target level
around 425–427. I was then looking at an intermediate bearish
market that had an implied target at approximately the 340.80
wave (A) low. Note also the weekly cycles were by then pushing
lower and therefore I felt comfortable with this revised forecast
since this had been one of the original possible counts I had
held.

The next question was how wave (C) of larger wave B
would develop. Looking at the cyclic structure, it seemed logical
that this next major low should occur at the confluence of the
four major cycles shown. This implied a decline lasting
approximately 36 to 40 weeks. Clearly, as a wave C, it must

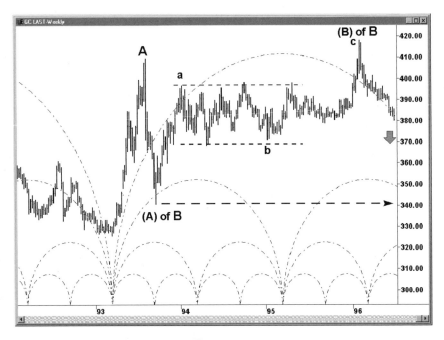

Figure 9.48
Weekly gold market displaying the peak at (B) of B and bearish cycle
influence.

develop in five waves. Potentially, since there was still nine months of this decline to come, a diagonal triangle may be favored.

Figure 9.49 shows the development of this predicted decline that found a low just below 340.80 and within two weeks of the cycle trough. I was quite obviously delighted with the results of this analysis and tentatively forecast for gold to now begin rallying. All four cycle troughs were converging, with ADX just beginning to show signs of flattening and perhaps declining, and Cutler's RSI having found classic oversold levels. However, no divergence was seen. I normally prefer to see divergences form at strategic reversals, but it is by no means universal. However, the collection of signals appeared to suggest that a period of strength in gold should now be seen. To confirm my analysis, I required a break back above 367.60, which represented a Fibonacci 38.2% retracement of the entire decline from 418.15. If I was wrong in my analysis, then a

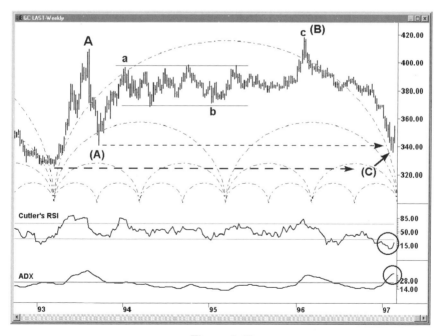

Figure 9.49
Weekly gold market displaying the decline from wave (B) to the 340 target,
and now marked as wave (C). Cutler's RSI was at oversold, though there
was no divergence, and ADX beginning to show signs of flattening.

break below the 336.40 low would be seen and final confirmation would be a decline below the 325.75 low on the far left of the chart, which had been the beginning of the entire rally to 418.15.

Figure 9.50 shows the subsequent price action. It can be seen that my original forecast of a rally was proven correct but this was shortlived. A further decline occurred but remained briefly above the 336.40 low. By the first week in July 1997, a sharp decline that breached both the 336.40 low and the 325.75 low was seen. This suggested a much stronger bearish pattern. I had to abandon the cyclic structure and look at a more bearish picture.

It was then that I came into possession of longer monthly data. This is shown in Figure 9.51, which also shows the development of gold price from the late 1960s through to July 1998. A logarithmic scale is applied to the data. The major feature is the large sideways triangle that developed and was

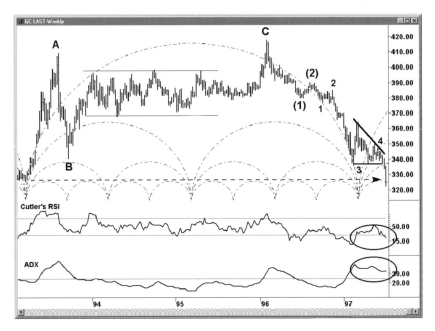

Figure 9.50
Weekly gold market showing the corrective rally following the 336.40 low. Note how Cutler's RSI moved back higher while ADX dipped. Break of the 336.40 low indicated a more bearish wave count and the 336.40 low now marked as a wave 3.

indeed broken as price breached the 325.75 low in 1997. Also note the major cyclic structure that suggests an additional 33 to 36 months of bearish price development for gold in the direction of the triangle break. A target generated by the triangle is at about 150, and this falls nicely in the range shown between the 103.50 low in August 1976 and the previous high at 195.30 in December 1974. The wave structure applied suggests that after a wave (X) we should see a further three-wave decline. It is difficult to suggest how this will occur at the current time, but given the time frame of three years to the major 392-month cycle trough, we cannot expect a deep correction, but more a sideways correction.

The point of this analysis is to demonstrate that the techniques practiced and described in this book are not foolproof. However, while my overall analysis for some three years was incorrect, I had been able to forecast the basic direction correctly during this period, and due to the observance of the Elliott guidelines together with cycles and

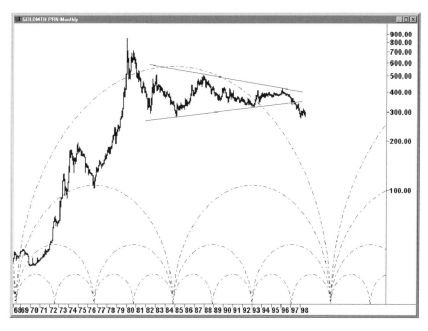

Figure 9.51
Monthly gold market dating from the late 1960s displaying a large
triangle with break of the triangle low providing a bearish outlook.
Cycles also look bearish for the next three years.

momentum analysis, I had recognized the reversal signals quite early, subsequent to actual reversal points. Finally, the necessity to find the longest period of data possible and incorporate this into our analysis will make valuable contributions to the success of our predictions.

NIKKEI-225 INDEX

The fact that the Japanese Nikkei-225 Index saw an astounding rally in the 1980s, only to be followed by a dramatic decline, is now well-known. However, let us look at the chart at the time just after the initial crash to see how much we may have been able to forecast.

Figure 9.52 shows the monthly chart from the mid-1950s to the period of analysis in August 1992. A logarithmic scale has been applied to show the percentage rise during the long rally from the beginning of the chart through to the 38,957 peak in December 1989. I have placed on this chart a series of cycles that give a strong picture with a confluence of these

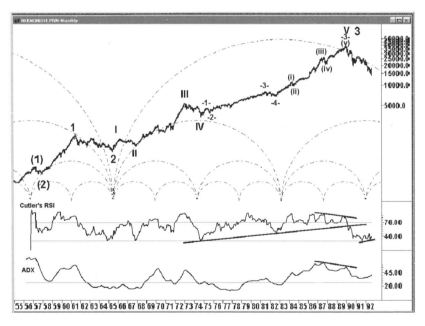

Figure 9.52
*Monthly Japanese Nikkei Index chart dating from the mid-1950s with
cycles, Elliott wave count, Cutler's RSI, and ADX.*

cycles coinciding with the wave 2 low during the mid-1960s after which all four cycles drove price higher in the subsequent 15 years. At the period of analysis, the largest cycle began to decline, the next lower cycle reached a peak while the two shorter-term cycles appear to be reaching their troughs. Due to the corrective declines being quite shallow during this wave (3) rally, I suspect that if a larger cycle was drawn, it would have found a trough coinciding with the wave 2 low, which is still rising. However, the result of this cyclic structure would lead to the analysis that the cycle troughs of the two shorter-term cycles would imply that a temporary price low should occur followed by a period of correction.

The Elliott wave count labeled has not only interesting Fibonacci relationships but also interesting implications. Let us first look at the Fibonacci relationships (based on a percentage change and not linear):

Wave III = 4.236 of wave I.
Wave IV = 0.382 of wave III (slightly less).
Wave V = 2.618 of length of wave I through wave III (slightly more).

In wave V:
Wave -2- = 0.618 of wave -1-
Wave -3- = 2.618 of wave -1-
Wave -4- = 0.236 of wave -3-
Wave (v) = Length of wave (i) through wave (iii)

In wave -5-
Wave (ii) = 0.33 of wave (i)
Wave (iii) = 2.618 of wave (i)
Wave (iv) = 0.236 of wave (iii)

and overall, Wave 3 = 4.236 of wave 1

Of course, this wave count is tentative. However, the implication is quite interesting. First of all, we are still in a wave (3) rally where we have seen only the first three waves. After a correction, we can expect the Nikkei to rally above the 38,957 peak. At the period of analysis, we have to assess whether we have seen the completion of wave 4. The cycles certainly suggest a rally. However with the two larger cycles declining and at a peak respectively, this seems less likely.

Looking at the momentum picture, we see that a bearish divergence occurred at the 38,957 high while ADX had mapped out a pattern often seen at major peaks. It had risen into the wave (iii) peak, declined during the wave (iv) correction, and then risen again in the rally into wave (v) but to a level lower than before. A stronger decline was also confirmed after the support line on RSI had broken during the initial drop from the peak. At the period of analysis, there are suggestions of a minor bullish divergence. However, ADX has begun to rise again during the sharp drop in price from 38.957, suggesting that a potential downtrend is beginning to develop. It is best to be cautious at this point. While spiky tops or bottoms can cause this situation, since ADX did not decline below the 25 to 30 levels, there is also the risk that the steep gradient of the decline will cause a period of choppy price action while the market settles down after the roller coaster ride seen since the 38,957 peak. At this point, we can only acknowledge the bullish divergence that has occurred close to a moderate cycle low. In terms of support level, price has breached the wave (iv) low, implying that a decline to the span of wave (ii) may well be possible. This also matches with a 0.382 correction of wave 3.

The monthly summary follows:

Cycles	Elliott Wave	Target
Major cycles high	Looking for wave 4	Wave (ii)?
Minor cycles at a low?		

Momentum	Support	Resistance
ADX beginning to trend?	None immediately available	27,270 previous peak
Bullish divergence in Cutler's RSI?		

Figure 9.53 displays the weekly picture with cycles and momentum analysis during the final rally to 38,957 and the subsequent decline to the period of analysis. Looking first at the cyclic picture, we see that the four cycles drawn have a high correlation to price action with lows at wave IV, just after wave (iv), wave A and wave -A-. Finally, we can see that all four cycles converge to a trough at the time of analysis. As mentioned before, caution should always be exercised with

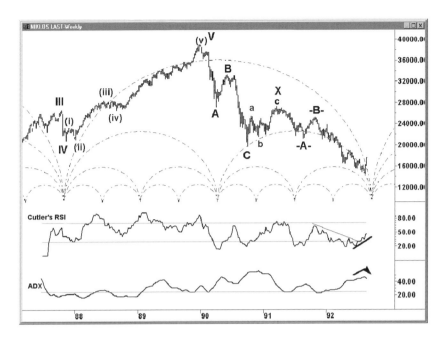

Figure 9.53
Weekly Japanese Nikkei Index chart with cycles, Elliott wave count,
Cutler's RSI, and ADX. Note how we are looking for a wave -c- low while
cycles are turning. There is a bullish divergence in Cutler's RSI, and ADX
has dipped.

cycles in case a degree of curve-fitting has been made.
However, with the monthly cycles finding a low, it follows that
the weekly cycles should also be finding a low at the same time.
We must also be aware that they need not be specifically
accurate, and ensure that we have sufficient additional
supporting analysis. Having made this cautionary note, the
entire price structure of rallies and declines seem to match the
cycles drawn and this gives a good degree of comfort.

The Elliott wave count shown looks straightforward. It is
interesting to note that after the Fibonacci relationships
described in the monthly analysis, during the wave (v) shown
on the weekly chart, wave (iii) was equal to wave (i) multiplied
by 2.618 and wave (v) was equal to wave (i) through wave (iii)
multiplied by 1.618.

Before looking at the wave count from the wave V peak, let
us first look at the momentum picture. There was a good, clear
bearish divergence at the peak while ADX had been declining.

After the uptrend is completed, we see that Cutler's RSI has broadly been accurate in measuring overbought levels at the peak and wave X, while at waves B and -B-, Cutler's RSI fell short of reaching overbought levels, and oversold levels were clearly seen at A, C and -A-. At the period of analysis, we begin to see a "local" bullish divergence. By this, I mean that the divergence has not developed over wave -A- till now, but over the last part of the decline from wave -B-. This normally indicates, at the very least, a brief pullback before further weakness, although it can indicate a stronger reversal.

ADX has seen quite a choppy ride, spending much of the time above the 25 to 30 levels. But interestingly, we see that the recent rise has been much slower than previously seen and has barely risen at all. This can also be a sign of weak momentum and can often herald quite sharp reversals. At the period of analysis, we see that price has indeed risen sharply over two weeks, the first being an outside reversal week and ADX has just dipped lower indicating a potential end to the trend. This, together with the bullish divergence, gives us a stronger hint of an end to the trend.

Due to the extremely volatile behavior of price during the decline, it would have made the analysis with just Cutler's RSI and ADX quite difficult. I have, as an alternative measurement of momentum, applied Momentum Bands to the chart as shown in Figure 9.54. Starting at the rally towards the peak, we see that this final move came with price remaining above trend support (TS) that finally broke at A. This would have implied that we should see a period of correction at the very least and a test at corrective support (CS). This occurred at point B, and direct breach would have given us a stronger feel that the bearish divergence seen on both monthly and weekly charts would herald a bigger correction.

Price then declined sharply, remaining below trend resistance (TR), until a sharp reversal that broke above TR at point C. We must also remember that we had just seen Cutler's RSI at an oversold level, and thus a break of TR would imply a correction at least and probably a retracement to reach corrective resistance (CR). Though not very strong, this occurred at point D at a time when Cutler's RSI was close to overbought. With this in mind, we would suspect that a reversal back to CS would be possible, but we would have been

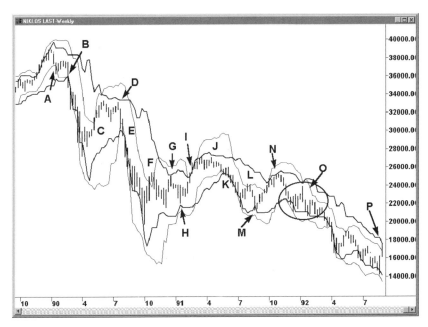

Figure 9.54
Weekly Japanese Nikkei Index with Momentum Bands applied. The thin bands are the trend support and resistance and the bold bands indicate corrective support and resistance.

cautious about expecting the downtrend to resume since Cutler's RSI had fallen short. Retest of CS and also breach occurred at point E, implying that we should see further losses. It is possible that we would have treated this breach with caution, watching the previous low in case price reacted from this point. But once breached, this prompted further losses with price once again remaining below TR.

At the next trough, Cutler's RSI was once again at oversold levels. Subsequent breach of TR would have implied a further correction and a test of CR. Although weekly Momentum Bands failed to give levels during the following sideways move, we did finally see price contained by CR at point G and by CS at point H before breach of CR at point I. This would normally imply further strength, but remember that Cutler's RSI was at overbought levels at this time while ADX was declining. Failure at point J to penetrate CR and then decline through CS at point K would have supplied us with signs that further losses were possible.

The next decline was not as strong or robust as the earlier declines from the 38,957 peak. After a brief test and marginal breach of TR at point L, the decline to CS at point M while Cutler's RSI was at oversold levels would have implied a further rally. This occurred with breach of TR and a move to test CR. At point N, we saw price attempting to penetrate CR. With Cutler's RSI failing to reach overbought levels, we may have decided that further strength could be seen. We should also be consulting the daily Momentum Bands but we shall look at this a little later.

However, price declined and, within the circled area, tested and marginally broke CR. This was followed by a correction to CR, and then price reversed once again, this time breaking below CS to indicate a downtrend. This downtrend remained below TR and at one point was even rebuffed at TR until the period of analysis. We must remember that Cutler's RSI is showing a local bullish divergence and ADX had just dipped lower. Price had also rallied strongly over the past two weeks, the low bar being an outside reversal and has now breached TR and reached CR.

Figure 9.55 shows the Elliott Wave count from the peak. We appear to have seen a decline made up of ABCX-A--B--C-. In other words, we have seen a double zigzag. Within this, the Fibonacci relationships are not as strong as in the uptrend.

In wave A (approximately):
Wave (ii) = Wave (i) x 0.50
Wave (iii) = Wave (i) x 2.618
Wave (iv) = Wave (iii) x 0.382
Wave (v) = Length wave (i) through wave (iii) x 0.50

Wave B = Wave A x 0.50

In wave C (approximately):
Wave (ii) = Wave (i) x 0.96
Wave (iii) = Wave (i) x 4.236
Wave (iv) = Wave (iii) x 0.236
Wave (v) = Length of wave (i) through wave (iii) x 0.50

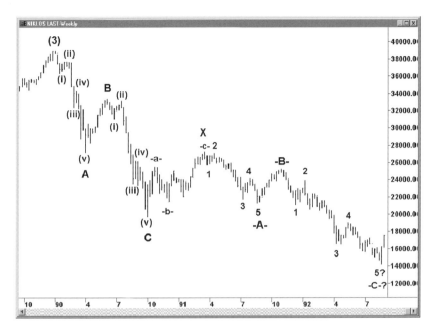

Figure 9.55
Weekly Japanese Nikkei Index with Elliott wave count suggesting the completion of a five-wave decline in wave -C-.

In wave X:
Wave -c- = Wave -a-
Wave X = Length of wave A through wave C x 0.50

Wave -A- has very few identifiable Fibonacci relationships.
Wave -B- = Wave -A- x 0.618

In wave -C-:
Wave 2 = Wave 1 x 0.618
Wave 3 = Wave 1 x 1.618
Wave 4 = Wave 3 x 0.382
Wave 5 = Length of wave 1 through wave 3 x 0.50

If we are to suggest potential targets for this decline, then:

Wave -A- x 1.618 = 14,256
Wave -A- x 2.618 = 9,648
Length of wave 1 through wave 3 x 0.50 = 14,675
Length of wave 1 through wave 3 x 0.618 = 13,653

Resistance levels are at the previous wave 4 at 19,003, at 50%, and 61.8% corrections at 19,725 and 21,030, respectively. Price has declined and reversed from 14,194.

The weekly summary follows:

Cycles	Elliott Wave	Target
All four cycles at a major low?	Looking for wave 5 of wave -C-	14,675 – wave 5 target 13,653 – wave 5 target 14,256 – wave -C- target

Momentum	Support	Resistance
ADX dipping	14,256	19,003 – previous peak
Bullish divergence in Cutler's RSI?	14,675	19,725 – 50% correction
Test of CR in momentum bands	13,653	21,030 – 61.8% correction

From the monthly and weekly summaries we have cyclic indications of a major low along with supporting momentum analysis. We should now move to the daily charts to ensure that we have supporting daily indications of our suspicions of a reversal.

Figure 9.56 shows the daily chart from the completion of wave -A- through to the low that we suspect to be the end of wave -C-, along with cycles and momentum analysis. I have drawn three cycles. But always consider the longer-term cycles also at this point. It would also be possible to draw a fourth cycle on this chart that would start just to the left of the first point of data shown through to the completion on the right side of the chart where cycles 1 to 3 converge. Thus we have an overall picture of declining longer-term cycles, but all converging at the same point.

If we look at the cycles shown, it can be seen that the shortest cycle provided a number of price troughs. The degree of strength shown subsequent to these cycle lows varies, though in general, it can be seen that the length of the declines are significantly longer than the corrective rallies, thus suggesting that price is demonstrating right translation, a sign of a bearish market. At the center of the chart, at the convergence of all three cycles shown, we may have suspected that a stronger correction may take place. The fact that it was shortlived and that price continued to edge lower is an additional sign that the longer weekly cycles were pushing

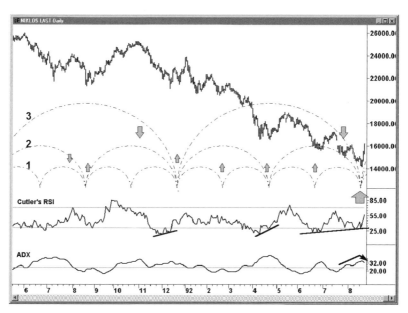

Figure 9.56
Daily Japanese Nikkei Index with cycles, Cutler's RSI, and ADX.
A cycle reversal is due with mild bullish divergence in Cutler's RSI
and a dip in ADX.

down on price and that the rallies were corrections only.

Cutler's RSI found few occasions to rise to overbought levels and this may have caught us looking for stronger rallies than were actually seen. However, we must always bear in mind the effect of the longer cycles, and if these are in a heavy down phase, we must be prepared for price and Cutler's RSI to demonstrate this problem. In addition, there have been several occasions where a bullish divergence has brought an upward reaction when a cycle trough has been identified. At the point of analysis, we can see that a longer-term bullish divergence has developed and, once again, at the convergence of all three cycles.

ADX has seen a long period of choppy behavior as the stop-start downtrend developed. It is noticeable that many of the occasions that ADX has risen above 25–30 levels, it managed only a half-hearted rise, suggesting that the downtrends have not been strong. At the period of analysis, it is rising but the recent rally caused it to dip along with the bullish divergence in Cutler's RSI.

Again, as price action is choppy, I have applied Momentum
Bands to the chart and this is shown in Figure 9.57. Starting
from the left of the chart, we see price in a downtrend having
penetrated CS at point A. There is a minor correction at point
B where price penetrates the TR. This would have caused us to
look for a move to CR. However, this did not occur and the
penetration of CS at point C prompted further losses. After this
decline, we see at point D that price has reversed and risen
above TR. This stronger reaction again suggests that price
should witness a stronger upward reaction. If we refer back to
Figure 9.56, we see that at this point we have a cycle trough
with a bullish divergence. Therefore, the test back at the CS at
point E would have provided a strong signal of a temporary low
and we could anticipate a rally to CR at the very least.

By point F, this had occurred and, in fact, CR is briefly
broken. If we refer back to Figure 9.54, this point occurred
during the downtrend from point O where price rallies for four

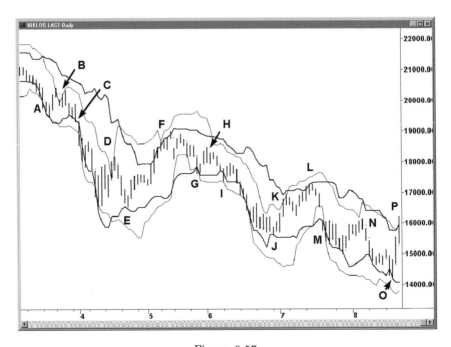

Figure 9.57
*Daily Japanese Nikkei Index with momentum bands. The thin bands are
the trend support and resistance while the bold bands are corrective
support and resistance.*

weeks to test the TR, but, does not penetrate TR. By referring to the next longer time frame, we can control our expectations at these times. While we may have wondered whether there was potential for further gains, our view would have been tempered by the weekly TR and thus we would have waited until this level was broken. Instead price reverses to the TS that has risen sharply and then penetrates to imply a test at CS. This occurs at point G and after a brief pullback that did not quite test CR at point , we saw the downtrend resume, confirmed by a breach of CS at point I after which the trend turned more aggressive. By point J, the decline in price had slowed and we see the classic reversal pattern where, after a small pullback, price re-tests CS after it has declined and has risen again. Referring to Figure 9.56 we see that this occurs at a cycle trough and while Cutler's RSI is at oversold levels confirming the potential for reversal.

Break of TR is seen at point K and test of CR at point L. By this point, Cutler's RSI had almost reached overbought levels. Price then broke lower to test TS that had risen sharply and then gapped lower to penetrate CS at point M. After a short consolidation, price continued lower, attempted to rise higher as it almost tested TR at point N, before declining one last time to point O, where our cycles are converging and Cutler's RSI is displaying bullish divergences on both weekly and daily charts. Price then penetrated both CR and TR at point P, and thus confirmed the bullish divergences have potential to cause a stronger correction.

Let us finally look at the Elliott Wave picture. This is shown in Figure 9.58. There are approximate Fibonacci relationships although there are some more accurate:

Wave II = Wave I x 0.618
Wave III = Wave I x 1.618
Wave IV = Wave III x 0.382
Wave V = Length of wave I to wave III x 0.50

In wave V:
Wave (ii) = Wave (i) x 0.618
Wave (iii) – Cannot find a specific relationship
Wave (iv) = Wave (iii) x 0.618
Wave (iv) = Wave (ii) x 1.618
Wave V = Wave (iii)

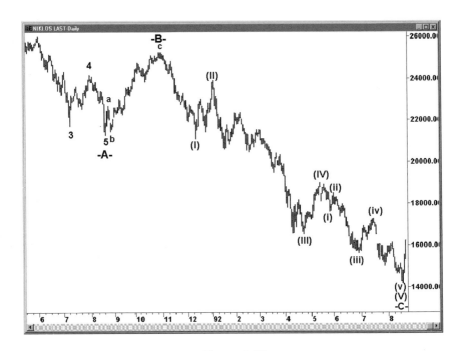

Figure 9.58
Daily Japanese Nikkei Index with Elliott wave count confirming a
diagonal triangle wave (v) to complete wave -C-.

We could also go through an exercise of matching Fibonacci targets for waves with Momentum Bands as these would also give additional clues along with momentum indicators as to potential reversal points along the way.

The daily summary follows:

Cycles	Elliott Wave	Target
Short-term cycle low	Completion of wave (v)?	14,250 Wave V target
Long-term cycle low	Completion of wave -C-?	13,640 (0.618 of Wave I to III)

Momentum	Support	Resistance
ADX just dipping	14,194 low	16,140 – wave (iv)
Bullish divergence in Cutler's RSI	13,640	17,275 – wave IV

Collating the information from the three summaries, we see the minor monthly cycles and major weekly and cycles looking to find a low at around this time. While monthly cycles suggest there is still a further low to be seen at a later time, the initial impetus should be higher or sideways for some years. This is supported by the fact that weekly and daily cycles are finding major lows, thus implying a few years free of the downtrend.

From the Elliott wave counts, we are looking for a wave 4 to develop and it would appear that a double zigzag has been mapped out from the 38,957 peak. If we combine this with the cyclic picture, we can expect a second wave X to be followed by one last ABC decline into the combined monthly cycle lows. Again, this supports the view of a period of upward or sideways correction that should remain below the last wave -B- at 25,250.

The Elliott wave count on the weekly chart supports the view that the second ABC structure appears complete, as does the wave count on the daily structure. While some of the Fibonacci relationships are approximate only, there appears to be a high correlation in wave relationships, and this extends down to the convergence of Fibonacci targets around the 14,250 level. The low at the time of analysis was 14,194 and thus very close to the 0.50 targets generated from both Wave -C- and also within the daily five-wave count in Wave -C-.

Finally, from the momentum picture, we see that weekly downward momentum has waned considerably as indicated by the meager rise in weekly ADX followed by the dip. This picture is repeated in the daily chart while the monthly Cutler's RSI shows signs of a bullish divergence. With this overall picture of slowing momentum and Fibonacci targets having been met, we wish to see evidence of price reversal. This is confirmed in both the weekly and daily Momentum Bands by appropriate breaches of corrective resistance together with a break above the minor wave (iv) in the daily chart.

Now that we have established a major reversal, we can look at potential resistance levels. The maximum of these has been mentioned at 25,254—the previous wave -B- high. Others can be established by measuring 0.382, 0.50, and 0.618 retracements of the second ABC decline. This provides resistances of:

0.382 – 19,190
0.50 – 20,730
0.618 – 22,275

Figure 9.59 shows the subsequent price action since that low and it can be seen that a long and volatile sideways move has developed until this juncture. The final high was found at 22,750—only 500 above the 0.618 retracement level. It is interesting to note that the monthly cycles are now pointing down and are due to find a low around the middle of year 2001. I have also put onto this chart a Fibonacci retracement tool that shows that we have already breached the 23.6% retracement of the wave 3 with the 38.2% retracement coinciding with the wave (ii) low at around 9,750. This is quite a dramatic forecast but we can judge whether it will be accurate by closely watching price action. We can also see

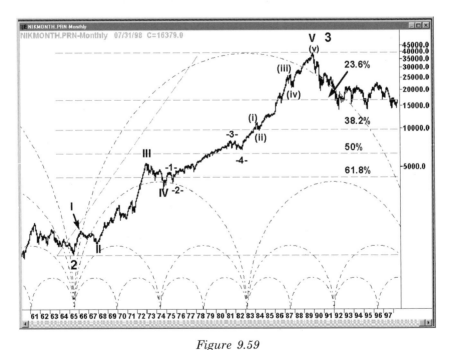

Figure 9.59
Monthly Japanese Nikkei Index displaying price action subsequent to the first decline from 38,957. Note the sideways price action and also the position of all cycles suggesting downward pressure for a further three years. A Fibonacci retracement has been applied to show that a 38.2% retracement is due at 9,750.

whether it follows the weekly cyclic picture and ensure that our momentum picture matches these indications. Whether it is correct or not, at this juncture we cannot be certain. However, it has given us a framework within which we can plan our forecasts and also, if it proves incorrect, the breaks that will confirm that we should be looking for a different forecast.

CONCLUSION

This last chapter has highlighted methods of integrating various techniques of technical analysis to provide a combination of signals that ultimately provide a more powerful forecast. I have demonstrated how I have found a combination of Elliott Wave, cycles, and momentum analysis has given me more accurate signals. However, the reader may find another group of techniques to appear more logical. It is important that the underlying techniques used actually bring to mind a logical concept that has meaning and describes the market behavior in a way that describes the underlying psychology of price movement. It is also important that complementary techniques form the combination of tools to be used.

The collection that I have described has just that. Elliott Wave provides structure—an expectation of how price should develop recognizing trends, consolidation, and levels that should be attained to provide support or resistance. Cycles provide direction, strength of movement, and potential reversal points. Momentum adds to these two techniques an idea of the underlying strength price movement, slowing down of trends or lack of trend. In this way, each technique overlaps a little with each other and avoids too many opposing signals. Instead they tend to confirm and add to the overall picture rather than duplicate each other. If signals contradict, it indicates that one indicator is wrong. More attention can then be paid to the evidence shown by each technique in order to identify the correct signal earlier.

It is also important to understand that technical analysis, much as with any other form of analysis, is not fully accurate though the frequency of accurate calls is probably more to do with the skill of the analyst. With experience, readers will begin to recognize situations where more weight should be placed to say, Elliott Wave instead of cycles, or vice-versa. If a forecast has proven to be incorrect, then flexibility should be adopted in changing emphasis among the techniques used.

One of the most important lessons I have learned is to be open-minded about analytical techniques. Where once I was dismissive of certain methods, now I tend to listen and adopting small parts of ideas that blend with my view on what drives price behavior. If in 10 years' time I choose to write a book on this subject again, I am sure (and hope) that I will have added other techniques to these that I have described here.

Finally, as mentioned at the start of the book, technical analysis is not a skill that can be learned overnight but one that requires constant attention. From the fact that the reader has taken time to read this book, I assume that he or she has an interest in the subject and I sincerely hope that the methodology I have described has instilled some of the enthusiasm that I hold for technical analysis. I wish all the very best in their endeavors.

INDEX